IMAGES *of America*

SPRINGFIELD

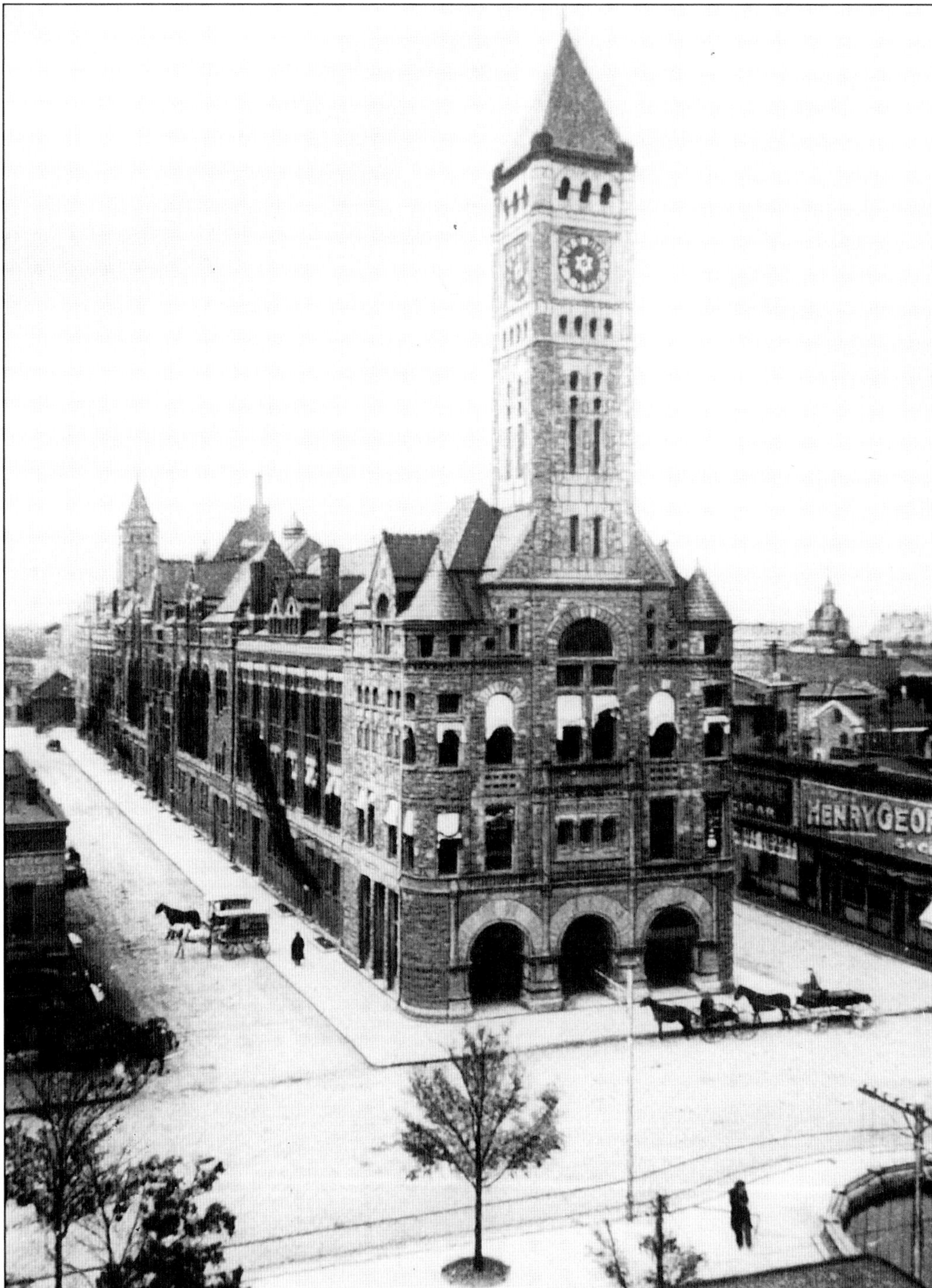

Old City Hall Building, Future Site of the Clark County Historical Society, c. 1900. This building, built in 1890, will become the home of the Clark County Historical Society in 1998. In the 1920s, both steeples were removed, but they are scheduled to be replaced before the Historical Society's grand opening on July 4, 1999.

IMAGES
of America

SPRINGFIELD

Harry C. Laybourne

ARCADIA
PUBLISHING

ISBN 978-0-7385-4576-9

Published by Arcadia Publishing
Charleston, South Carolina

Printed in the United States of America

Library of Congress Catalog Card Number: 2006926055

For all general information contact Arcadia Publishing at:
Telephone 843-853-2070
Fax 843-853-0044
E-mail sales@arcadiapublishing.com
For customer service and orders:
Toll-Free 1-888-313-2665

Visit us on the Internet at www.arcadiapublishing.com

This book is dedicated to my family,
who has encouraged me in this project.

CONTENTS

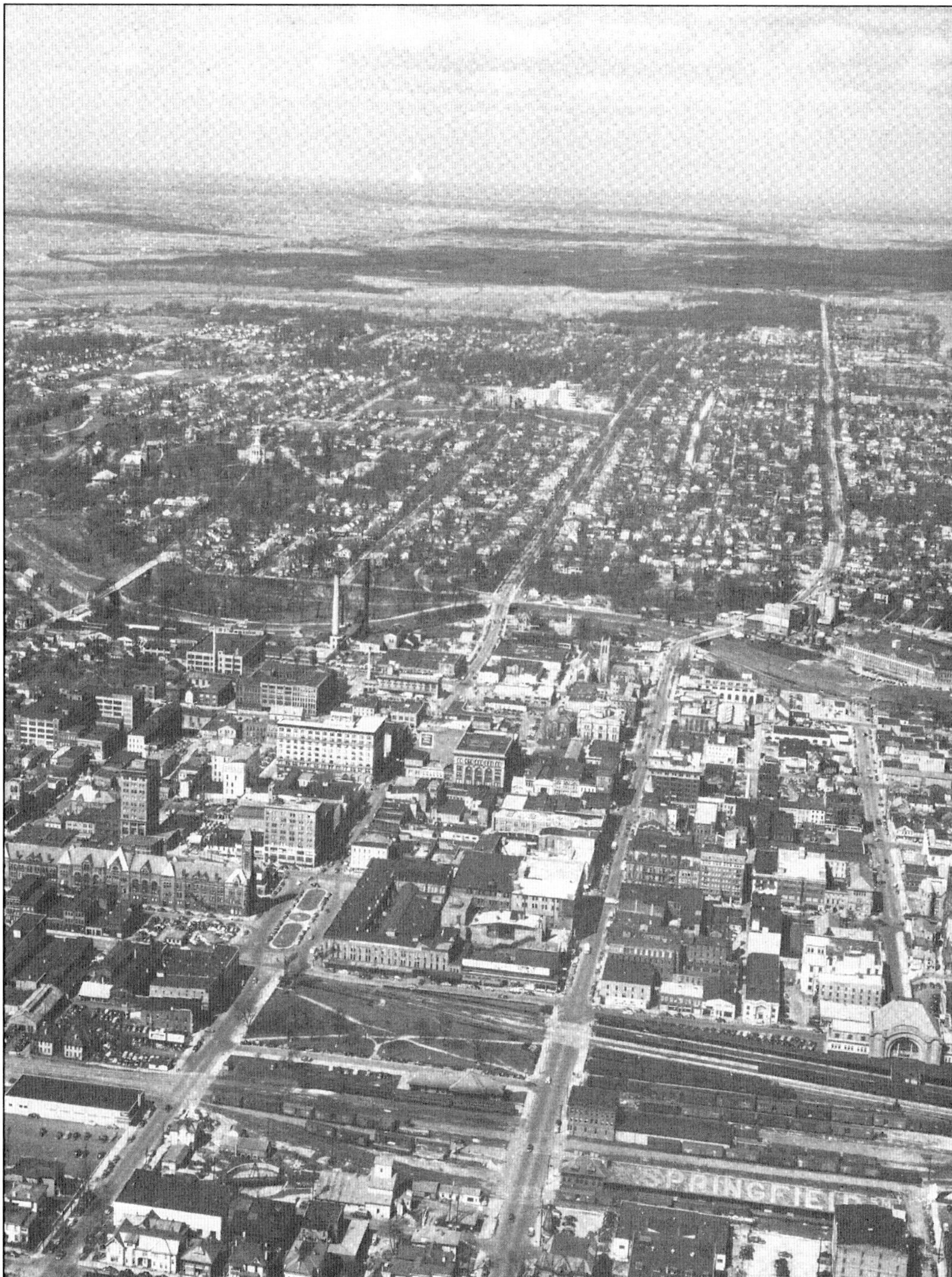

DOWNTOWN SPRINGFIELD IN THE 1930S. Note Pennsylvania Depot, Big Four Depot, Roundhouse, the Arcade, and the old City Hall.

INTRODUCTION

Springfield, Ohio, began its existence as a small, muddy, log cabin settlement. Strategically located on the path west and near ready sources of waterpower, Springfield grew quickly. Fertile land attracted farmers and waterways attracted industrialists. By 1803, the first mills, owned by James Demint and Simon Kenton, appeared on the banks of Buck Creek, and the village was linked to Dayton by wagon road.

By 1818, Clark County, named for General George Rogers Clark, was ready to assume its identity. Within nine years after becoming the county seat, Springfield had reached the population of a town and in another 23 years that of a full-fledged city.

In 1850, Springfield, with 5,108 inhabitants, became a city and was lit by gas lights. Industry continued to grow to international fame with the Champion Works and the James Leffel Company. Springfield's importance and popularity led to nationally familiar epithets, such as "the Reaper City," "the Rose City," and "the Home City."

Springfield also became famous for her personalities. Mother Stewart was an internationally recognized temperance crusader. P.P. Mast became well known for his *Farm and Fireside* magazine, which later became the basis for the Crowell-Collier Publishing Company. General Warren Keifer, veteran of the Civil War, became the first Speaker of the House from Ohio. And, Asa Bushnell, president of Warder, Bushnell and Glessner, served two terms as governor of Ohio from 1896 to 1900.

Springfield is now a city of 70,000 people. This book is by no means a comprehensive history, but rather represents a glimpse into the photographic past that made Springfield what it is today.

(Taken from the *Derr Road Inn Chronicle*)

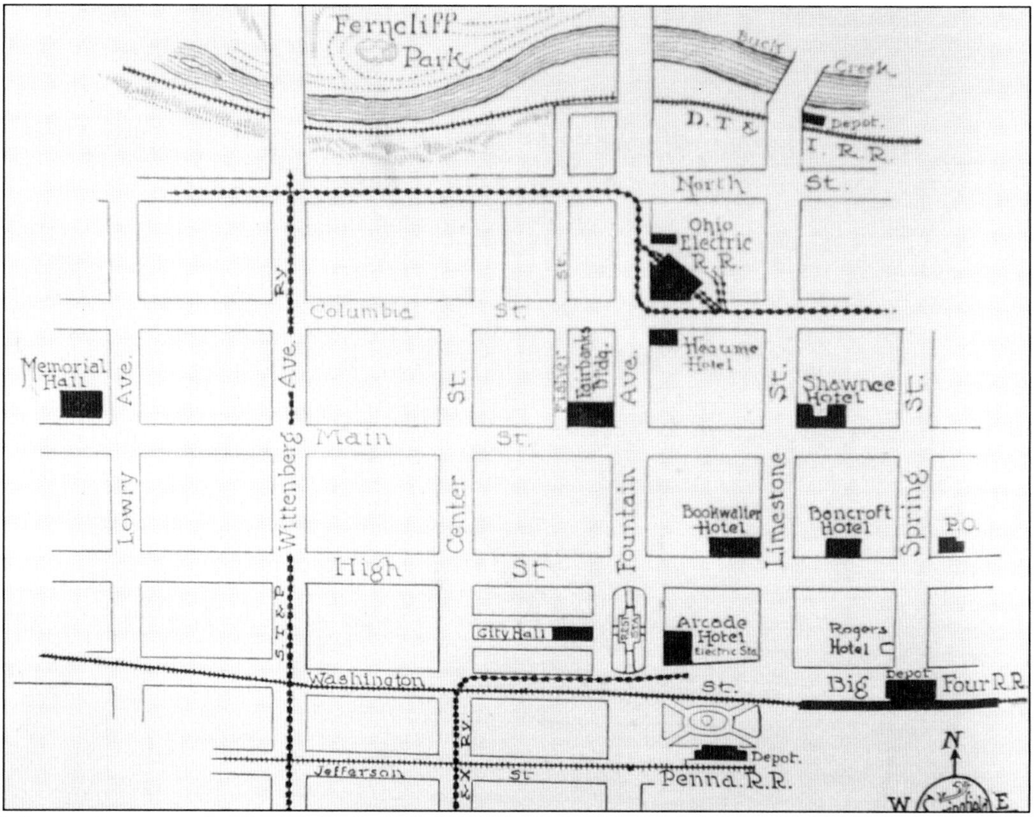

MAP OF DOWNTOWN SPRINGFIELD, C. 1905.

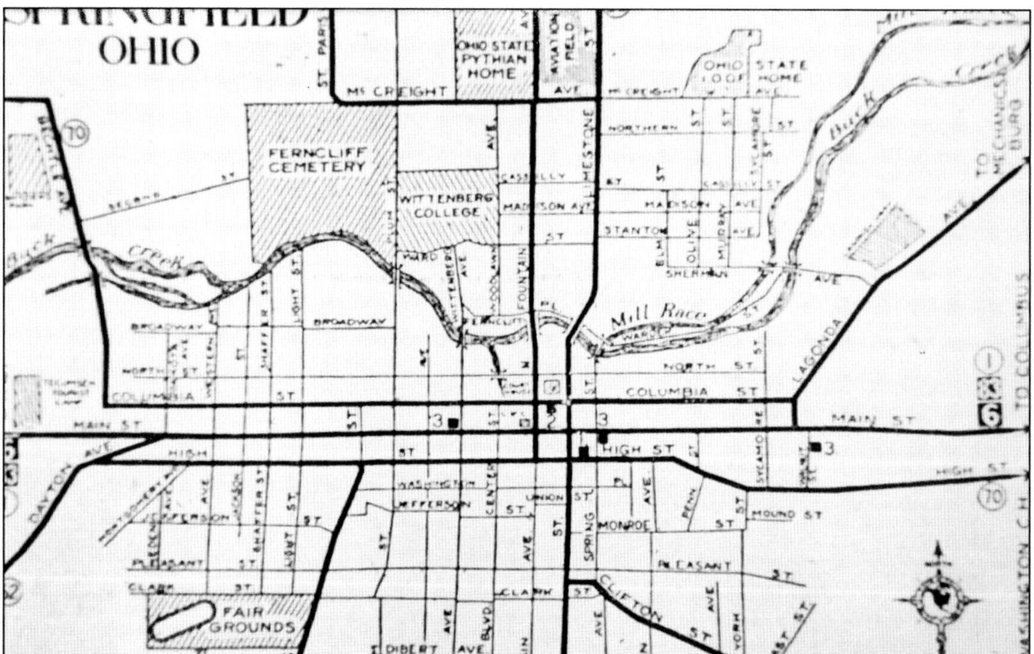

MAP OF DOWNTOWN SPRINGFIELD, C. 1910.

One

DOWNTOWN

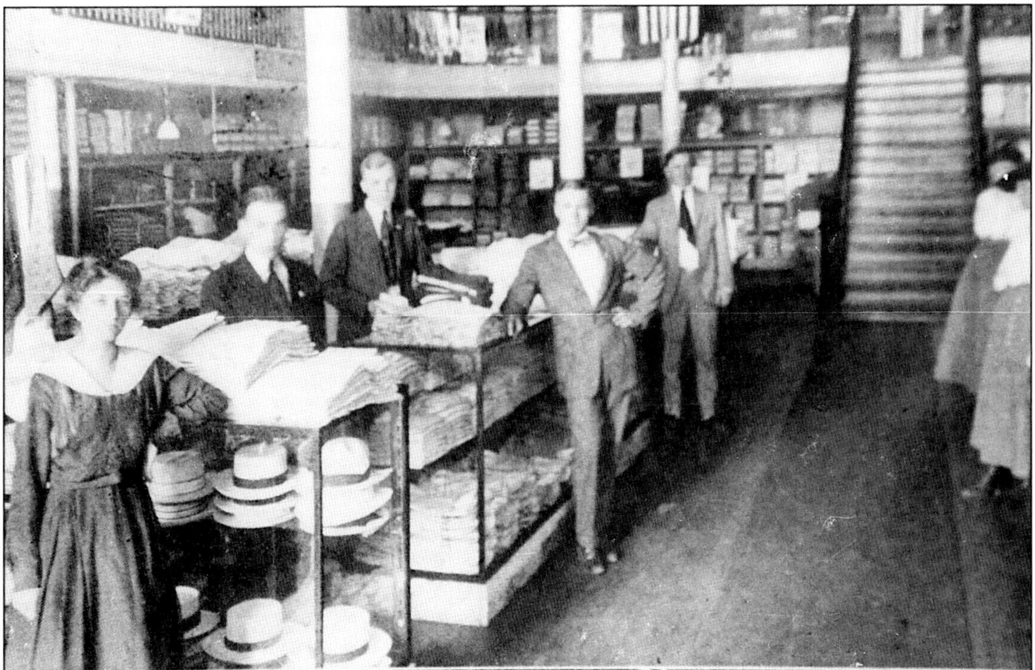

"THE HUB," 37-39 SOUTH FOUNTAIN AVENUE, SPRINGFIELD, OHIO

THE HUB, C. 1915. This was a popular men's clothing store downtown, located on the main floor of the Arcue Building on the northwest corner of High and Fountain Avenue.

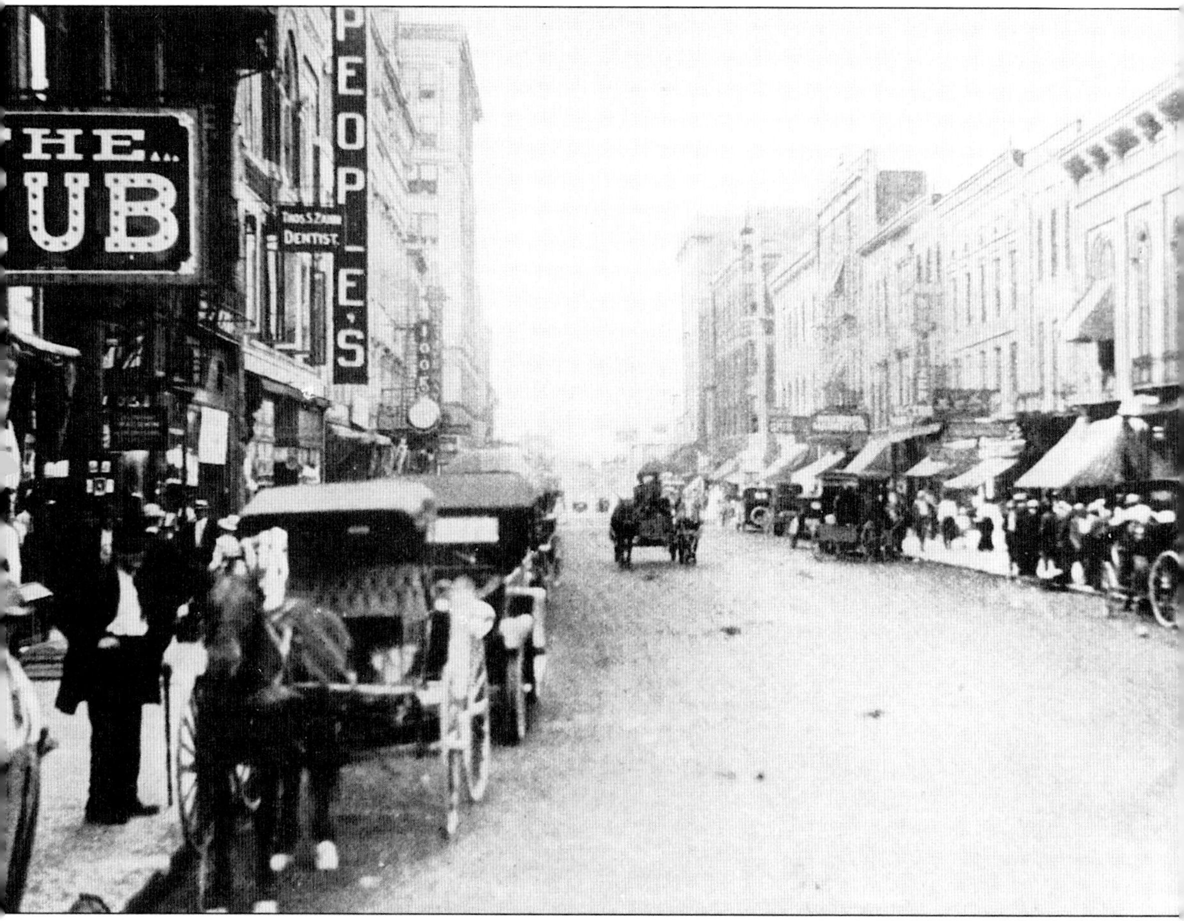

A Street View, Looking North from High Street on Fountain Avenue, c. 1910. Horse-drawn buggies were common in the early 1900s, lining the street as they carried passengers to the downtown stores and businesses. The Hub Clothing Store is pictured on the left.

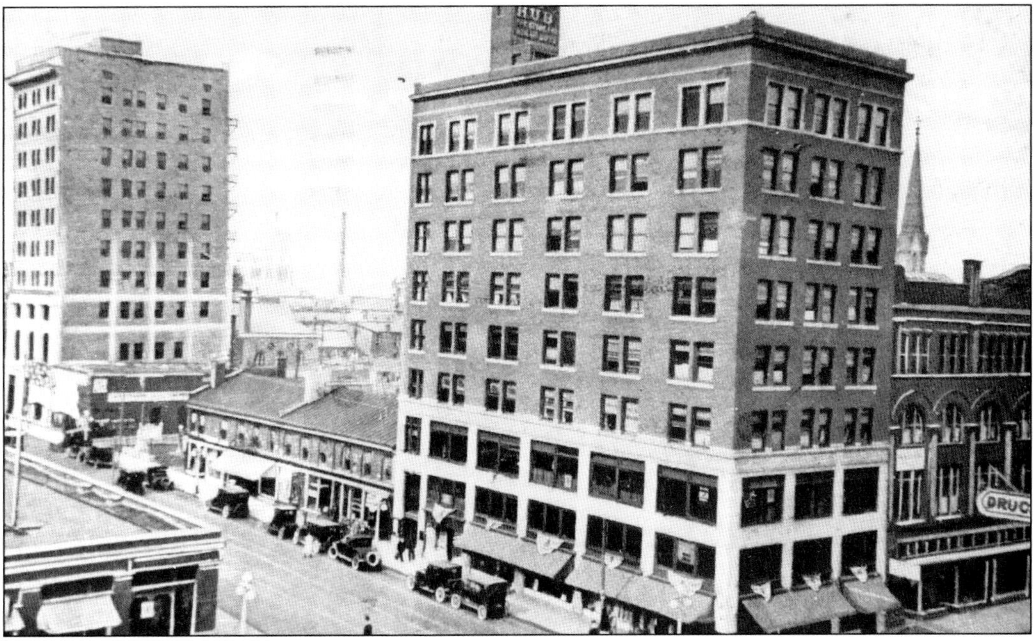

ARCUE BUILDING, LOCATED AT THE NORTHWEST CORNER OF FOUNTAIN AVENUE AND HIGH STREET, MID-1920S. The Tecumseh Building, which was formerly the Francis Drolla Building, is visible on the left.

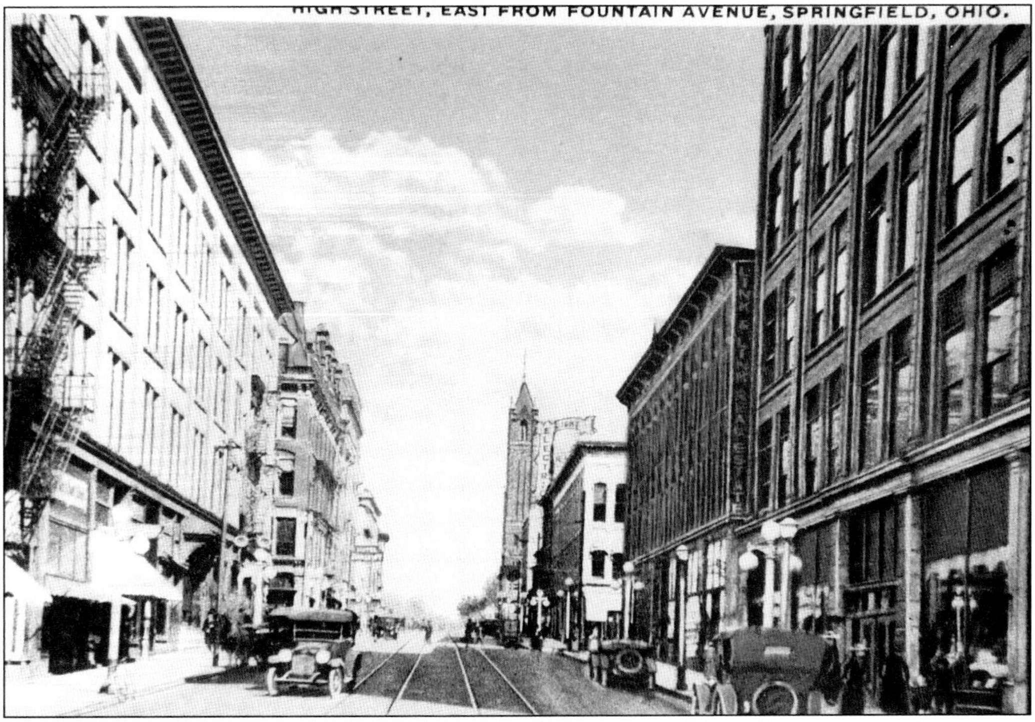

A STREET VIEW, LOOKING EAST FROM THE CORNER OF HIGH STREET AND FOUNTAIN AVENUE. St. Raphael's Church is visible in the background on the right. Notice the traction car tracks that once ran down High Street.

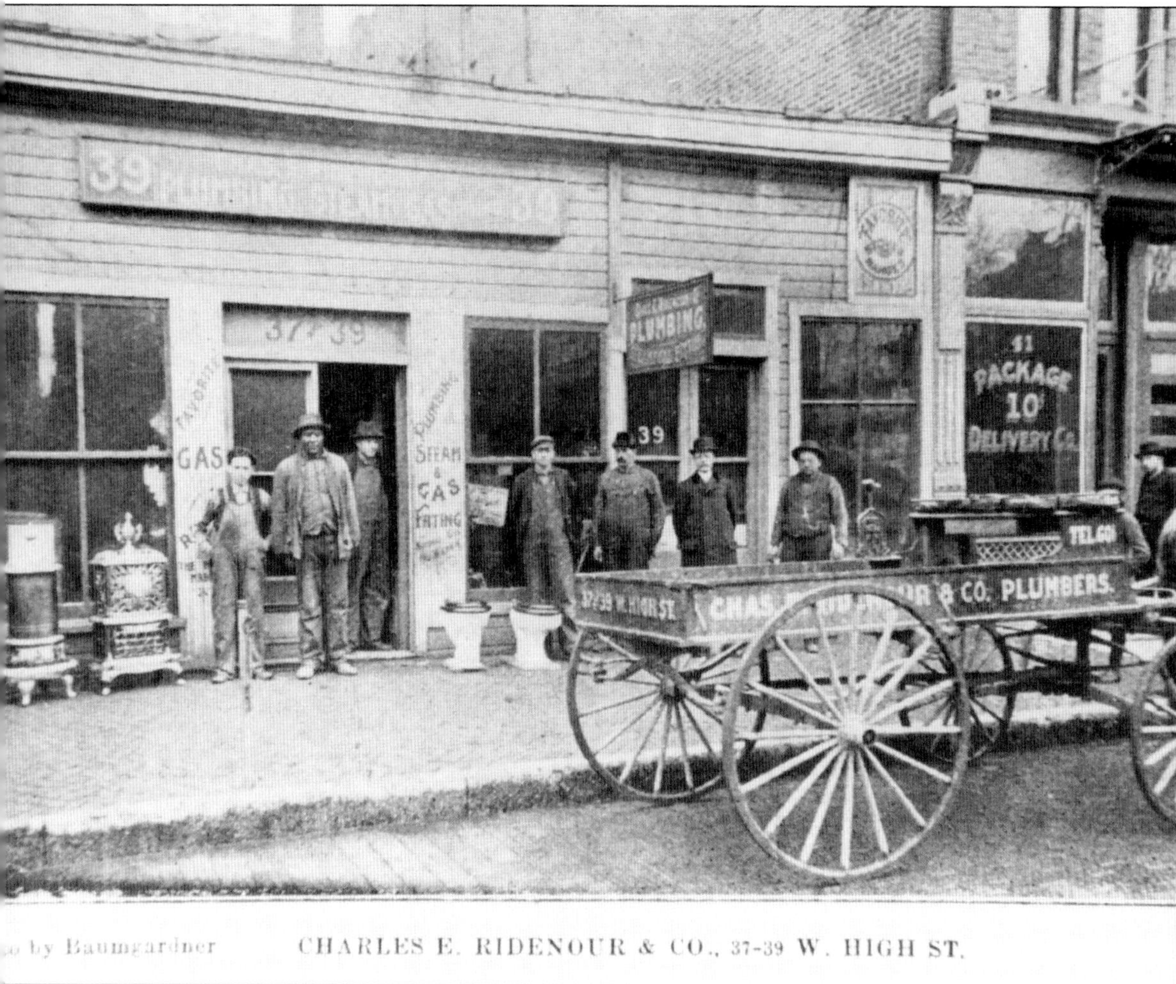

Charles E. Ridenour and Company, Located at 37–39 West High Street, Early 1900s. This plumbing, steam, and gas company employed many hard-working residents of Springfield.

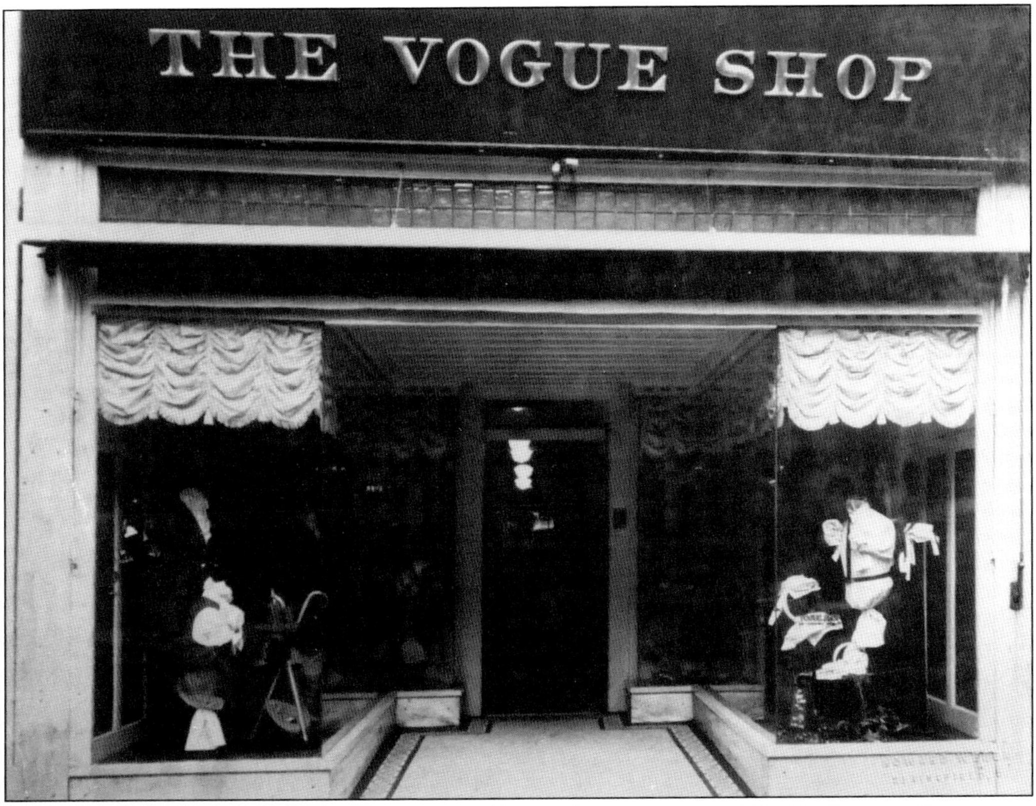

THE VOGUE SHOP, A MEN'S CLOTHING STORE LOCATED AT 20–22 SOUTH FOUNTAIN AVENUE, LATE 1930S.

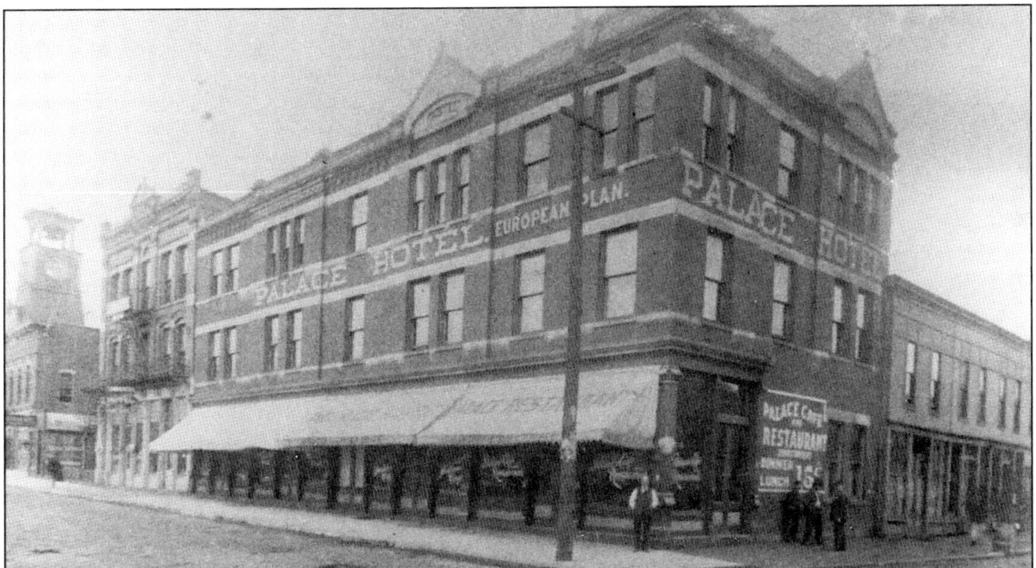

THE PALACE HOTEL, LOCATED ON THE SOUTHWEST CORNER OF SOUTH FOUNTAIN AVENUE AND WASHINGTON STREET, EARLY 1900S. Later, this became the Frances Hotel. According to the sign posted on the brick wall, lunch and dinner at the Palace Cafe cost only 15¢.

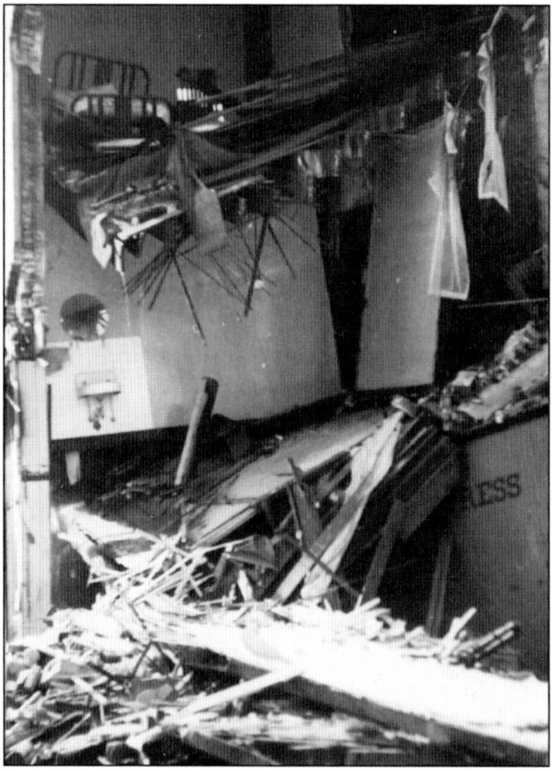

AFTERMATH OF A TRAIN ACCIDENT AT THE FRANCES HOTEL. In the late 1940s, the Frances Hotel, located on the southwest corner of Washington Street and Fountain Avenue, suffered great damage when a runaway train derailed into its walls. This photo shows part of the disaster left behind.

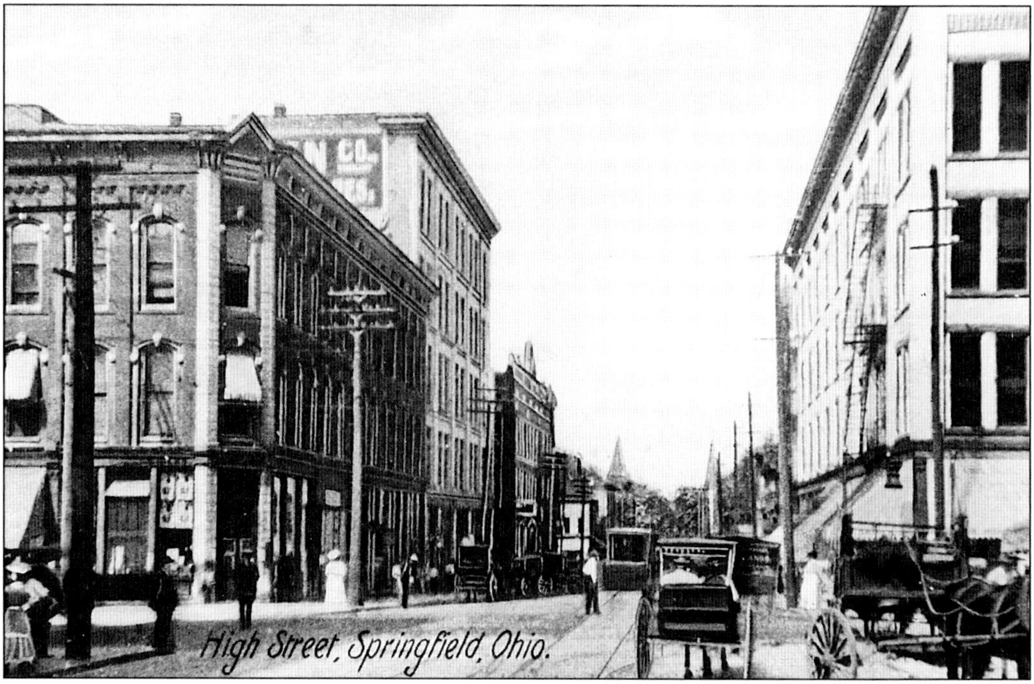

A STREET VIEW, LOOKING WEST ON EAST HIGH STREET FROM SOUTH LIMESTONE STREET, C. 1905. The building on the left is presently the site of the McAdams Building. The original Wren's Department Store Building appears on the left in the background.

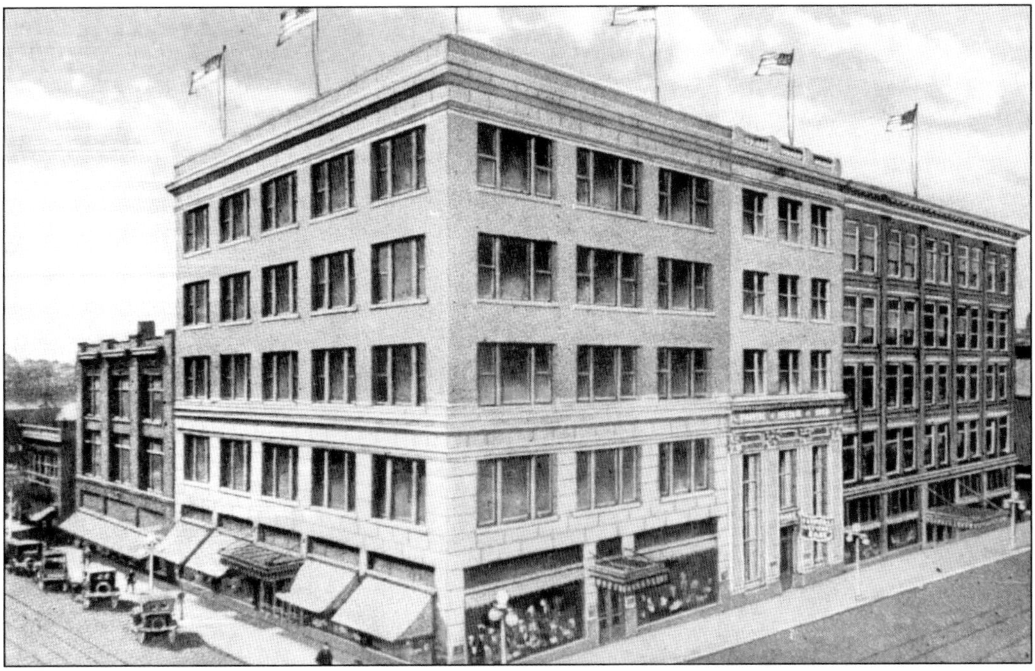

THE EDWARD WREN COMPANY DEPARTMENT STORE, 1915. At this time, Wren's occupied both buildings, with the Farmer's National Bank located in the center.

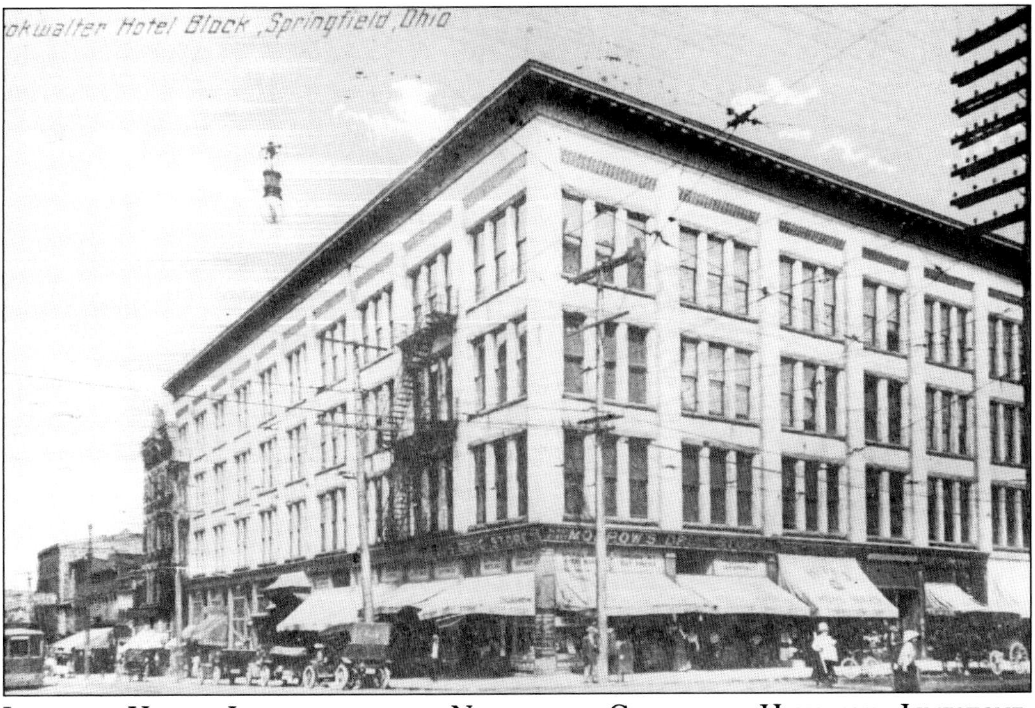

LAGONDA HOUSE, LOCATED AT THE NORTHWEST CORNER OF HIGH AND LIMESTONE, C. 1900. This hotel, which opened in 1869 and was destroyed by fire in 1895, had 140 rooms and cost $130,000 to build. After the fire, it was rebuilt as the Bookwalter Hotel with 120 rooms and thrived until 1940, when it was torn down to make way for the new Woolworth's Store.

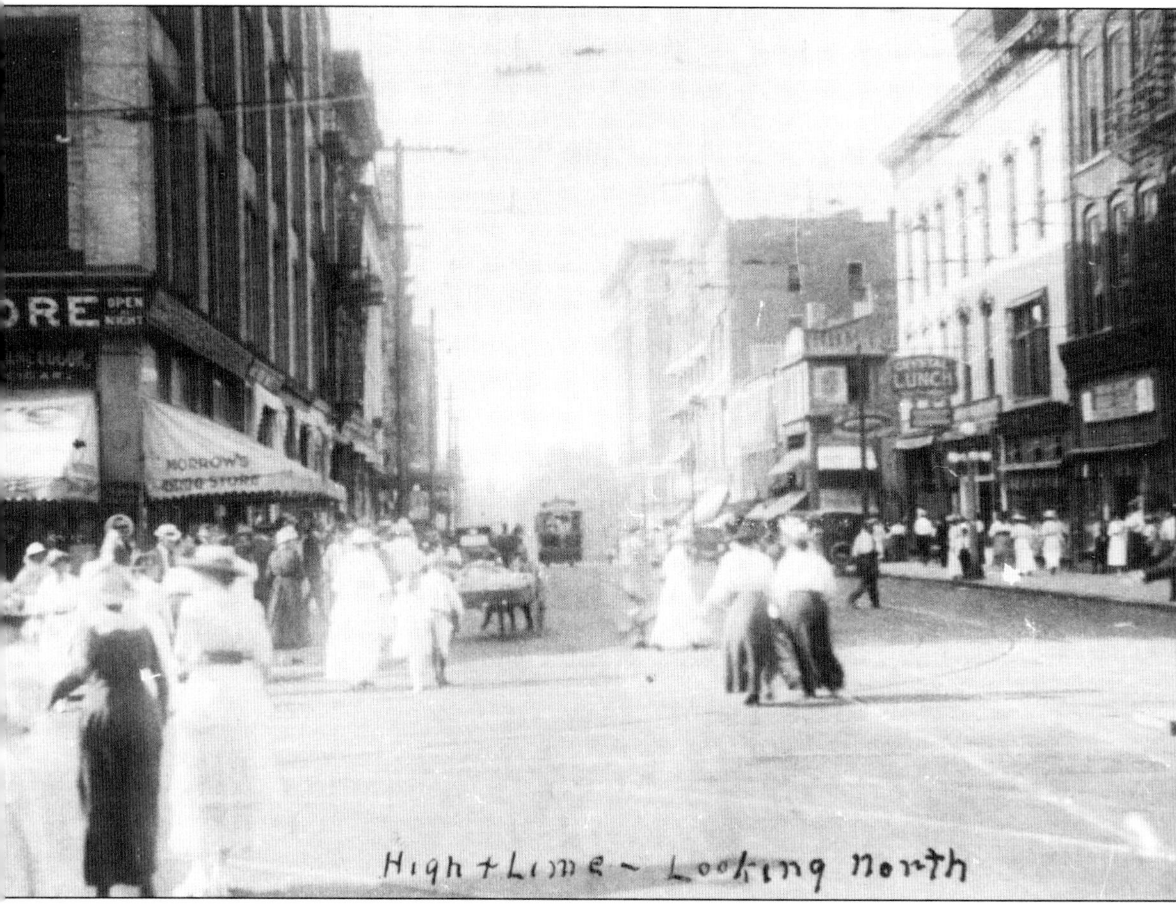

A STREET VIEW, LOOKING NORTH ON SOUTH LIMESTONE STREET FROM EAST HIGH STREET, C. 1910. The Crystal Restaurant is visible on the right side of the street. Note the policeman standing on the far right directing traffic and the oncoming trolley car.

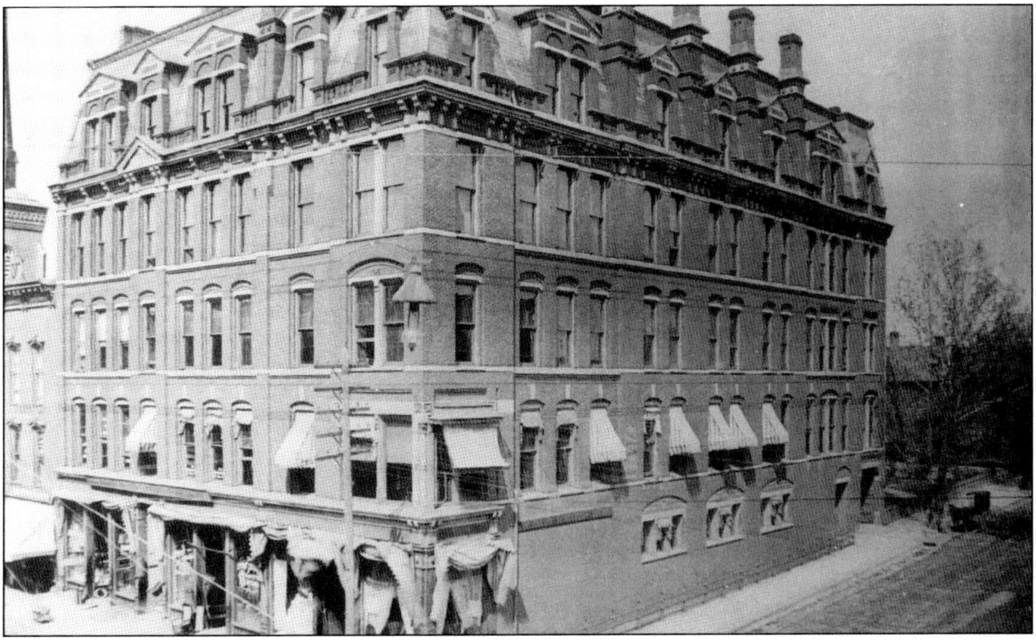

THE MITCHELL BUILDING, LOCATED ON THE NORTHEAST CORNER OF SOUTH LIMESTONE AND EAST HIGH STREET. Previously, the First Baptist Church occupied this site until they sold it to Mr. Mitchell for $25,000 in gold. The new Baptist church was built on Miller Street and South Fountain Avenue. The steeple in the rear of this photo is the Second Presbyterian Church, which later became the Boston Store.

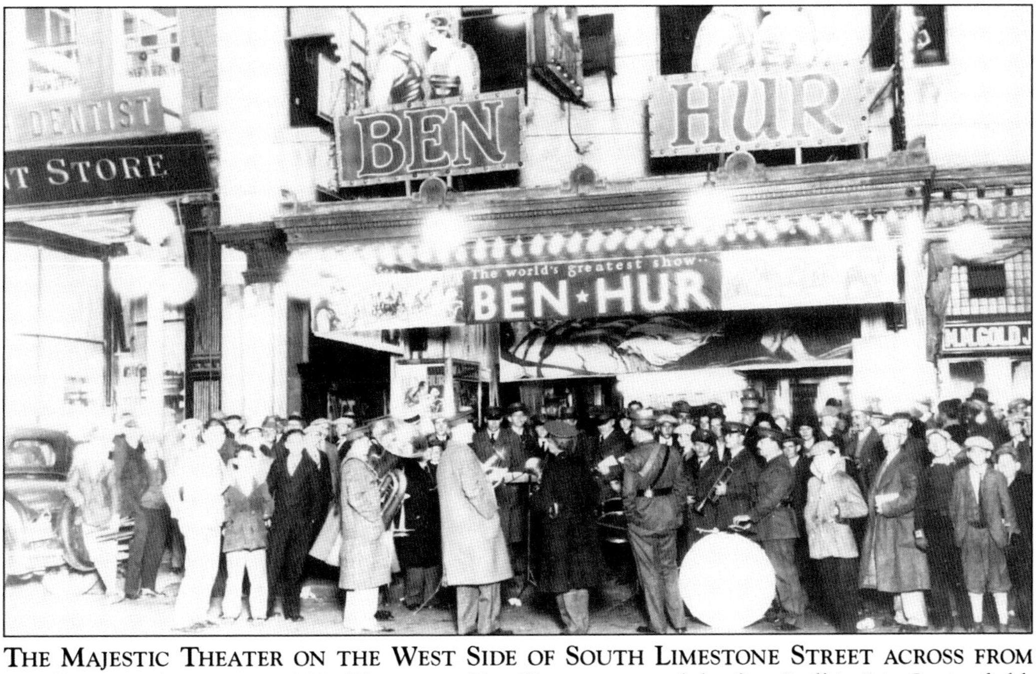

THE MAJESTIC THEATER ON THE WEST SIDE OF SOUTH LIMESTONE STREET ACROSS FROM THE BOSTON STORE, C. 1928. The movie *Ben Hur* was one of the first "talkies" in Springfield; therefore, its arrival received great fanfare, including a live band outside the theater to entertain the crowds. The building pictured to the left was Woolworth's Five and Dime Store.

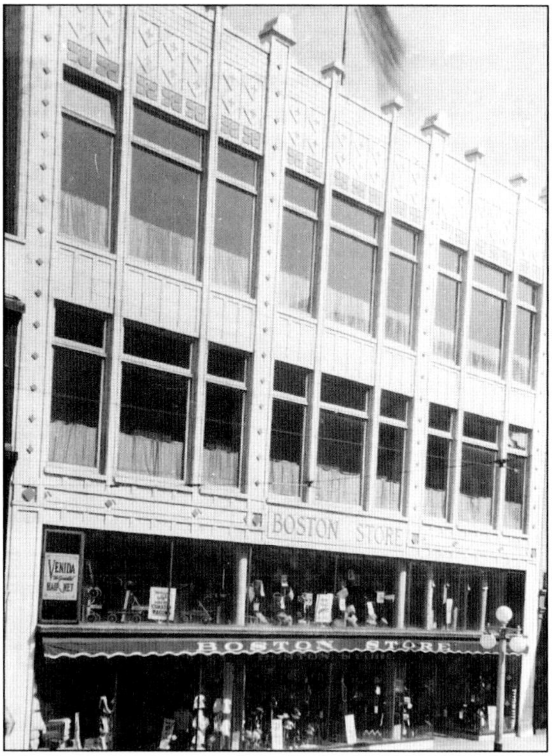

The Boston Store on South Limestone Street in the 1920s. The Boston Store sold various household items to residents of Springfield.

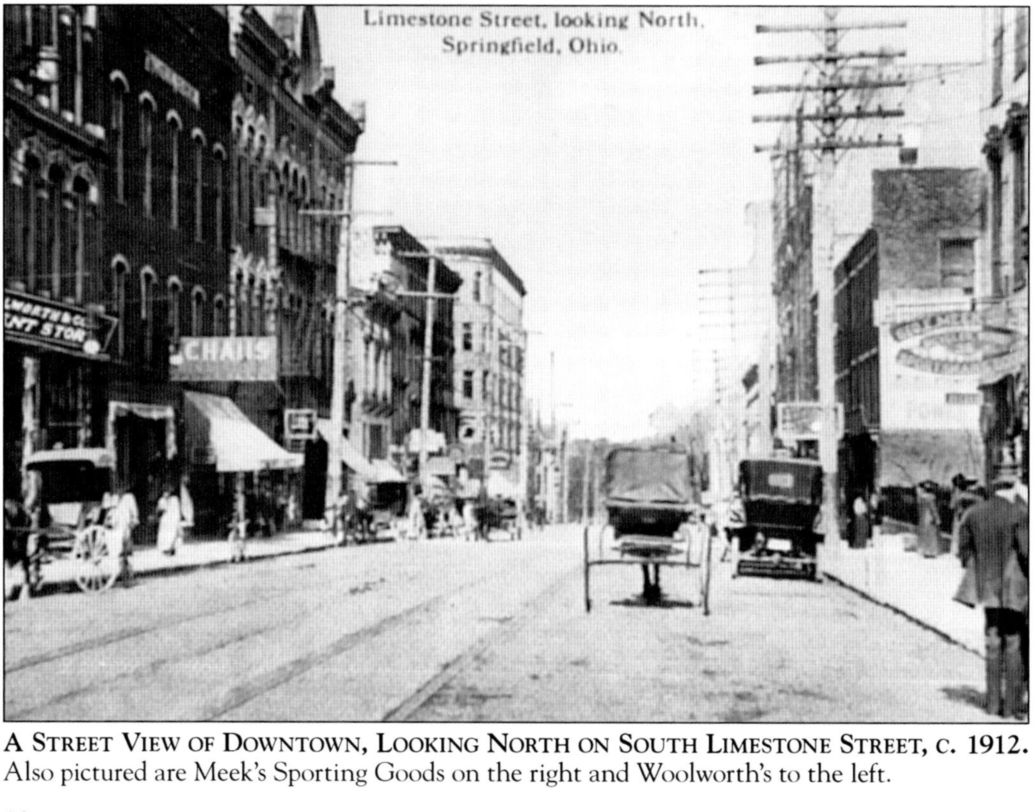

A Street View of Downtown, Looking North on South Limestone Street, c. 1912. Also pictured are Meek's Sporting Goods on the right and Woolworth's to the left.

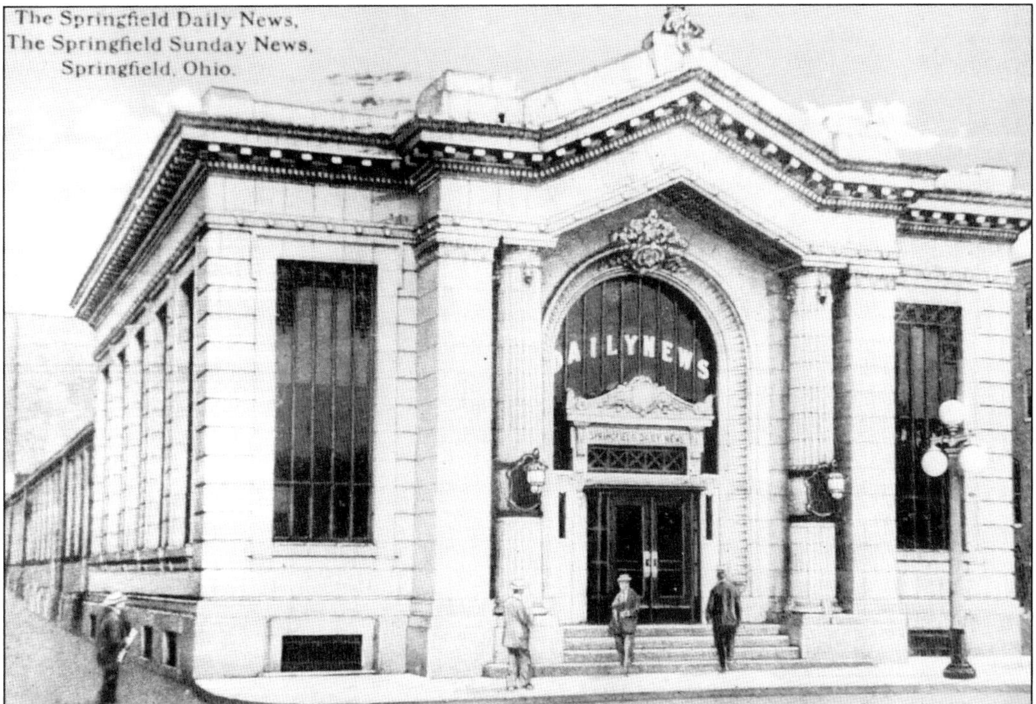

THE SPRINGFIELD DAILY NEWS BUILDING, LOCATED ON THE NORTH SIDE OF EAST WASHINGTON STREET, EAST OF SOUTH LIMESTONE STREET, C. 1917. Many people remember how the ball scores were posted on the top of this building after each game.

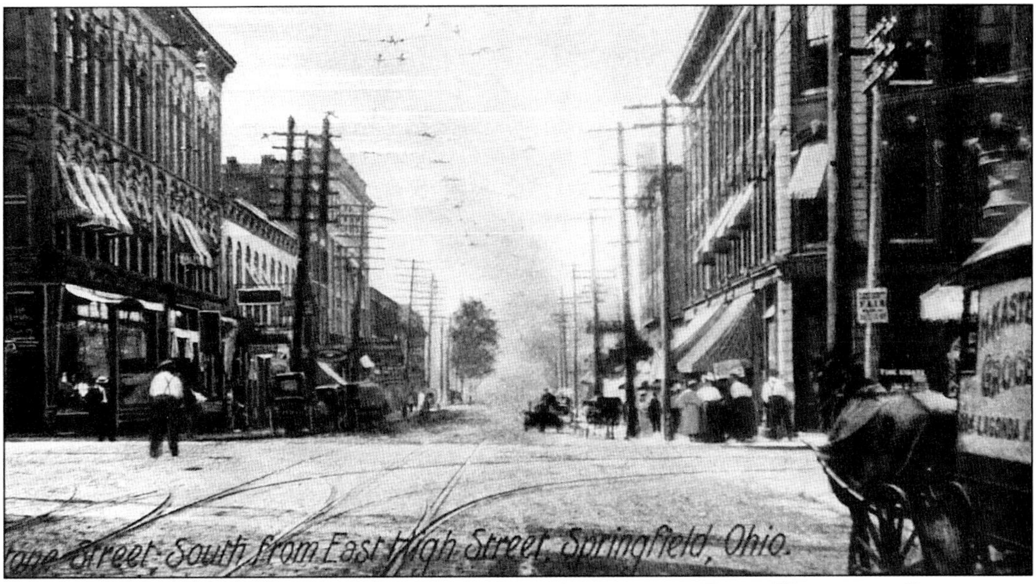

A STREET VIEW, LOOKING SOUTH FROM THE CORNER OF EAST HIGH AND LIMESTONE STREET. The building on the right is now the McAdams Building. The marquee in the right background belonged to the Grand Opera House. Later, this was the site of the Columbia Theater, which eventually collapsed into Mill Run and was rebuilt by Gus Sun as the Regent Theater.

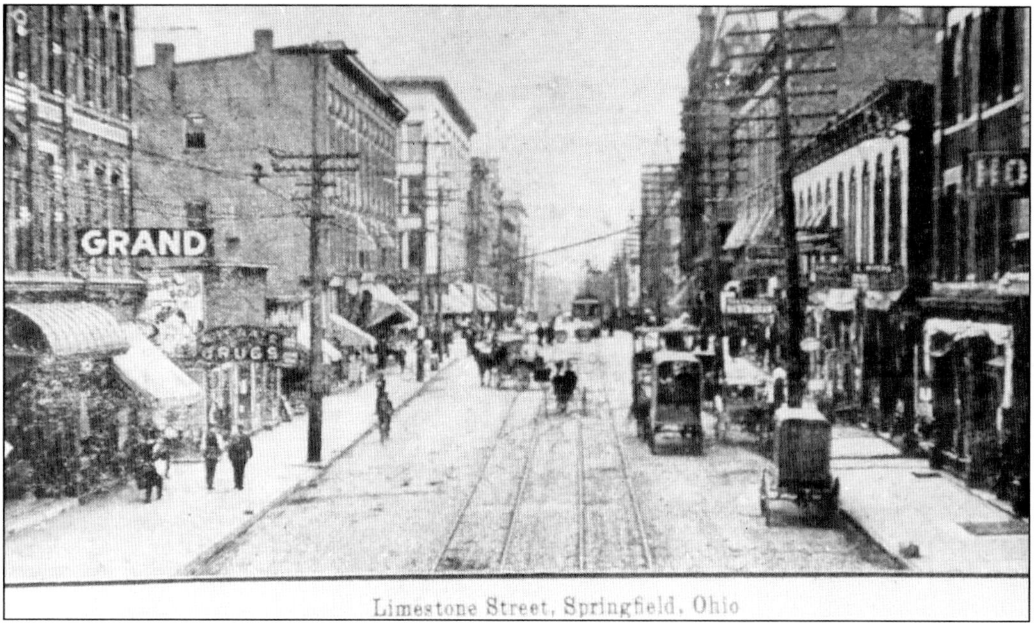

A Street View, Looking North on South Limestone Street from East Washington Street, c. 1905. The Grand Opera House, which seated 1,200 people, is on the left. Today this building is the Regent Theater.

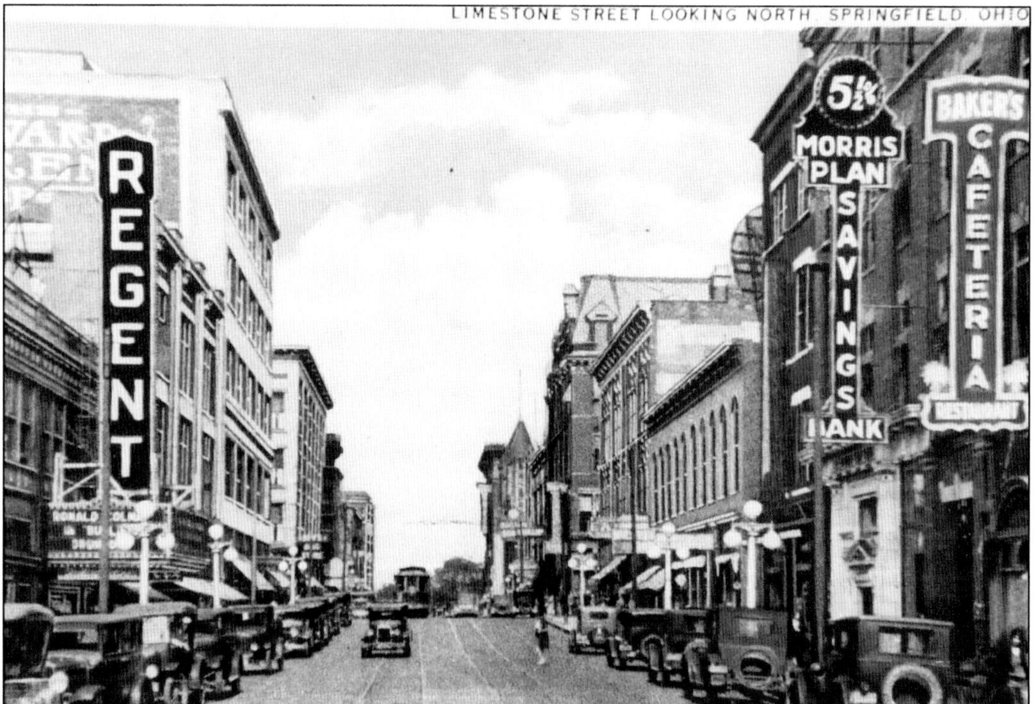

A Street View, Looking North on South Limestone from East Washington Street, c. 1925. At the time, the newly built Regent Theatre was playing *Bulldog Drummond*, starring Ronald Colman. Baker's Cafeteria is visible on the right.

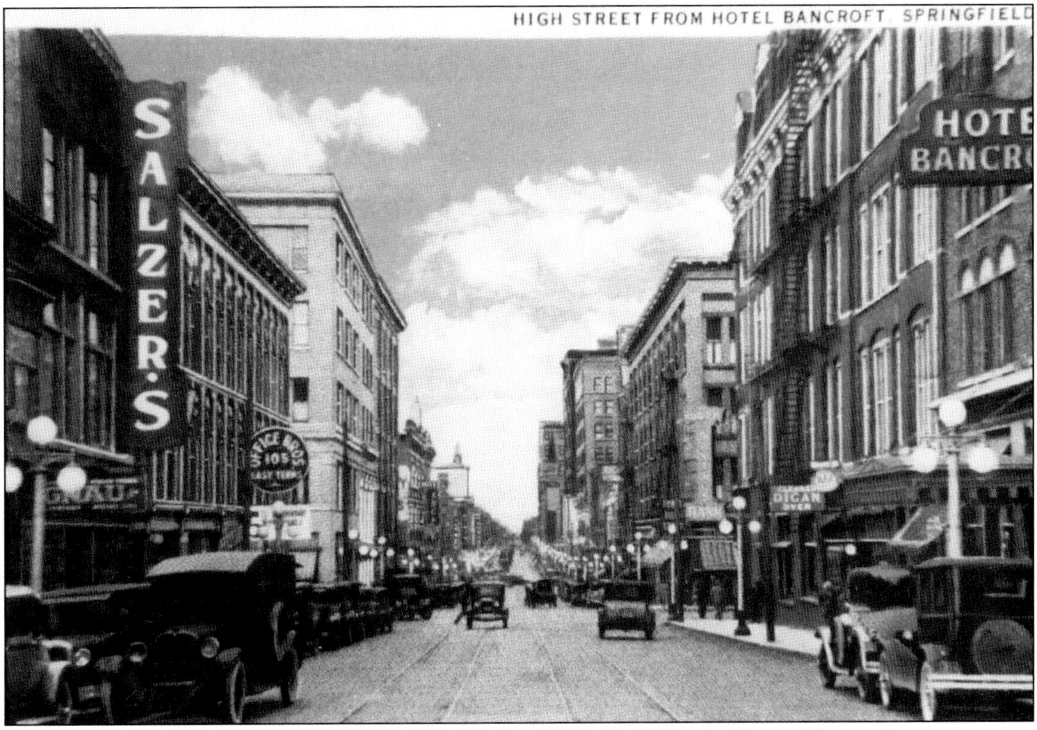

HOTEL BANCROFT AND SALZER'S FURNITURE, LOCATED ON EAST HIGH STREET NEAR LIMESTONE STREET, EARLY 1940S. Later, this building housed Reco Sporting Goods. This postcard was purchased in Florida by Roger Devers.

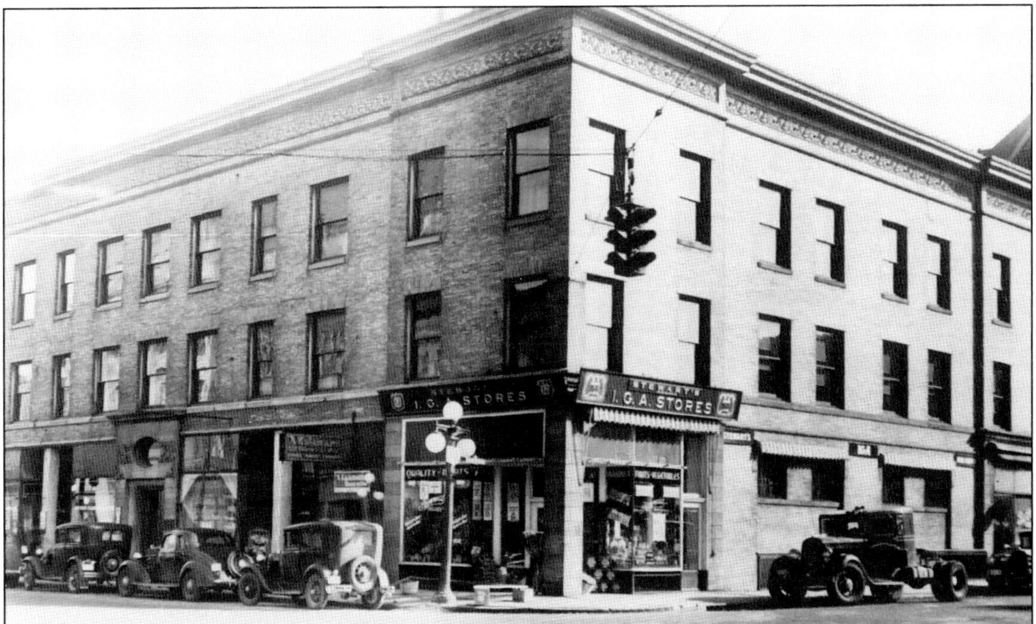

THE WINWOOD BUILDING ON THE SOUTHEAST CORNER OF WEST HIGH AND SOUTH CENTER STREET, C. 1930S. An IGA Grocery Store is visible on the right street corner. Later, this building was occupied by Barnitz Studio.

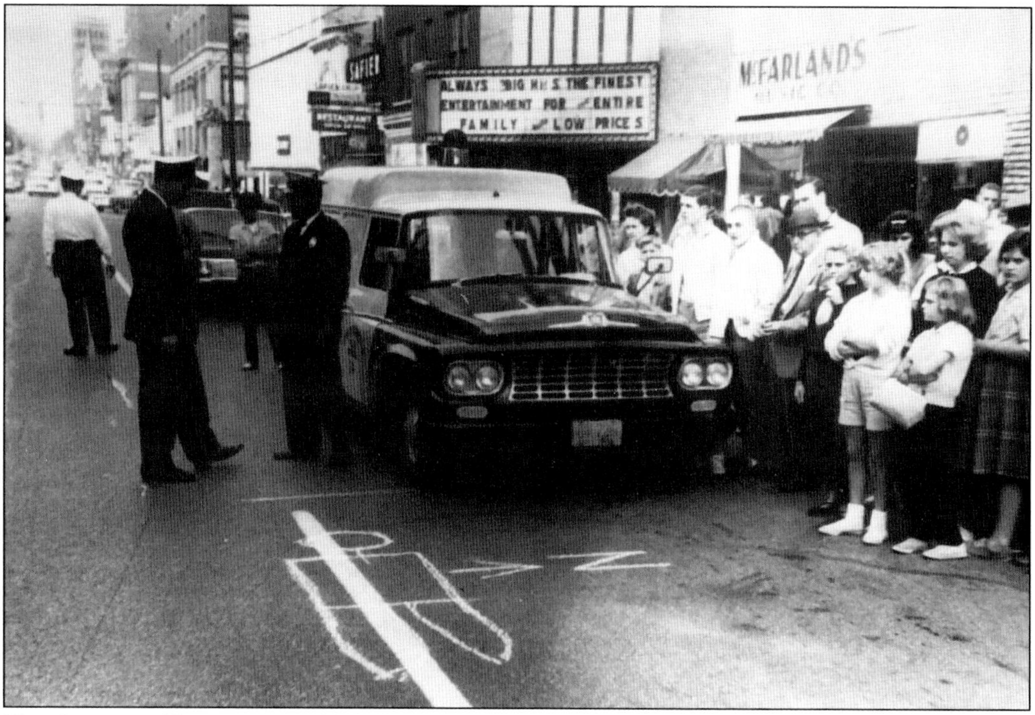

THE LIBERTY THEATER ON EAST HIGH STREET ACROSS FROM THE ARCADE, 1960. Their marquee advertised, "the finest entertainment for the entire family at low prices."

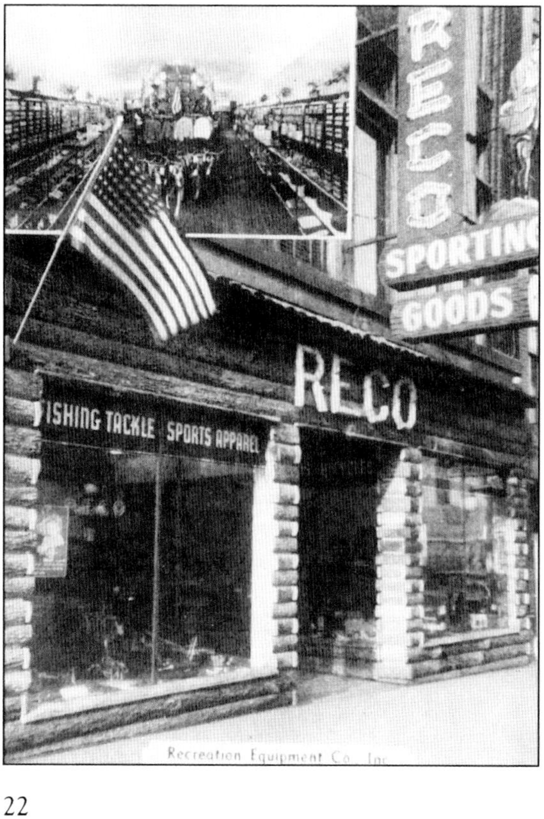

RECO SPORTING GOODS, LOCATED AT 16–18 EAST HIGH STREET, C. 1940S. This rustic store was well known for selling sporting equipment and recreational clothes.

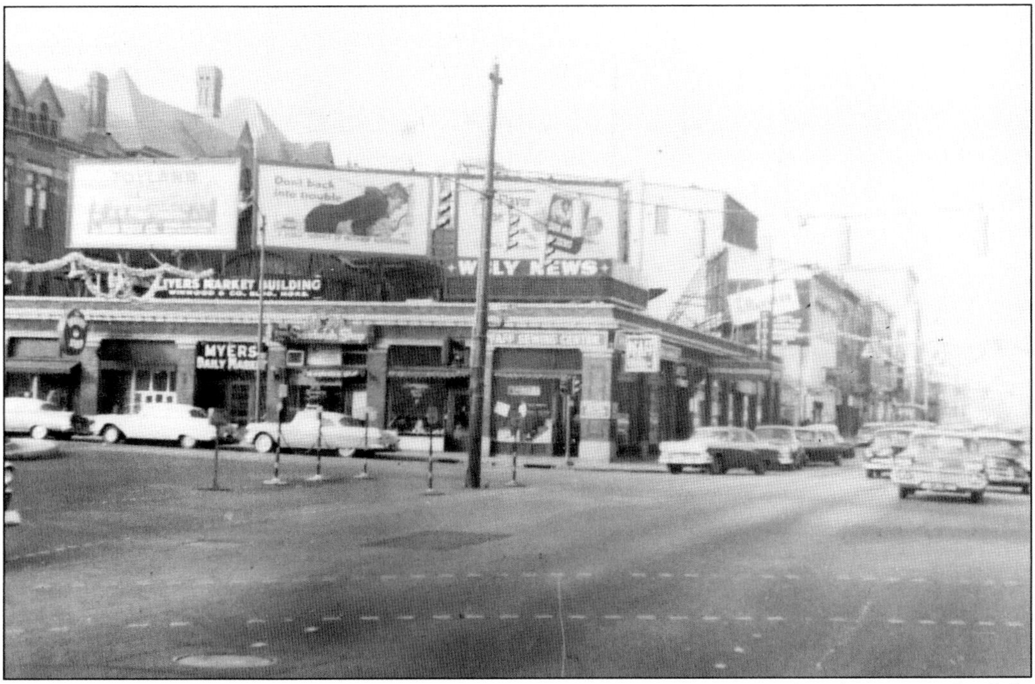

CORNER OF HIGH STREET AND SOUTH FOUNTAIN AVENUE, 1974. Marketplace is on the left and Myer's Daily Market is pictured to the right.

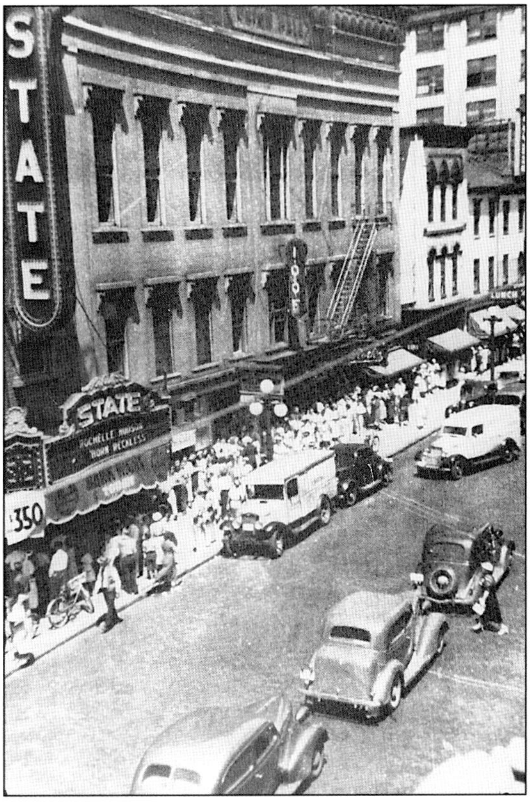

CROWDS ON SOUTH FOUNTAIN AVENUE FOR THE STATE THEATER, 1940S. On this day, people were lined up along South Fountain Avenue to see Rochelle Hudson starring in *Born Reckless.*

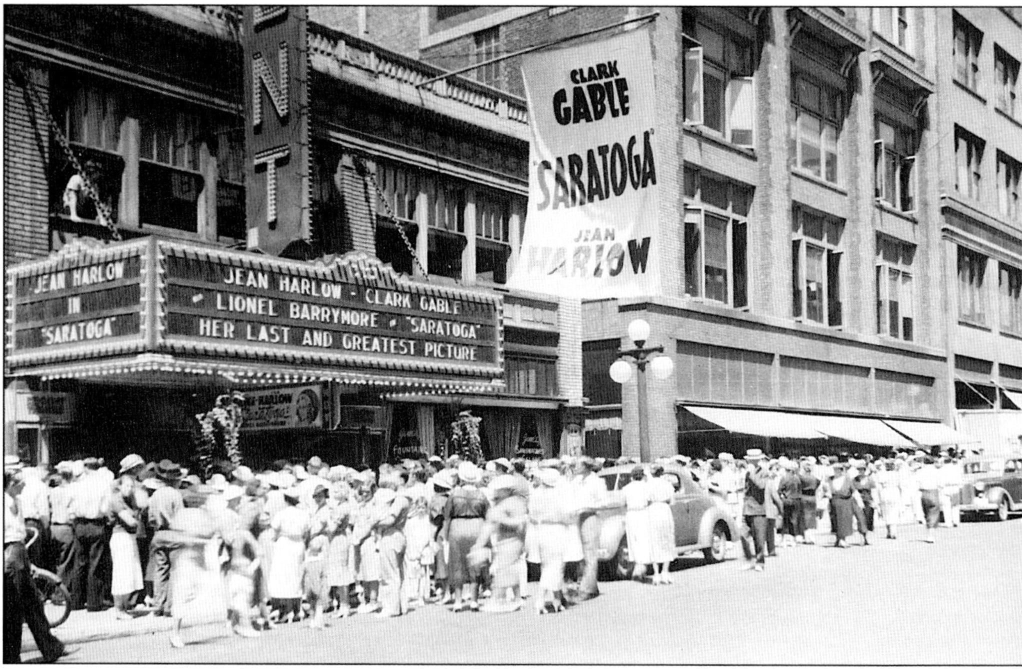

REGENT THEATER ON SOUTH LIMESTONE STREET, 1940S. A popular movie *Saratoga*, starring Clark Gable and Jean Harlow, was the cause for a large attendance on this particular day.

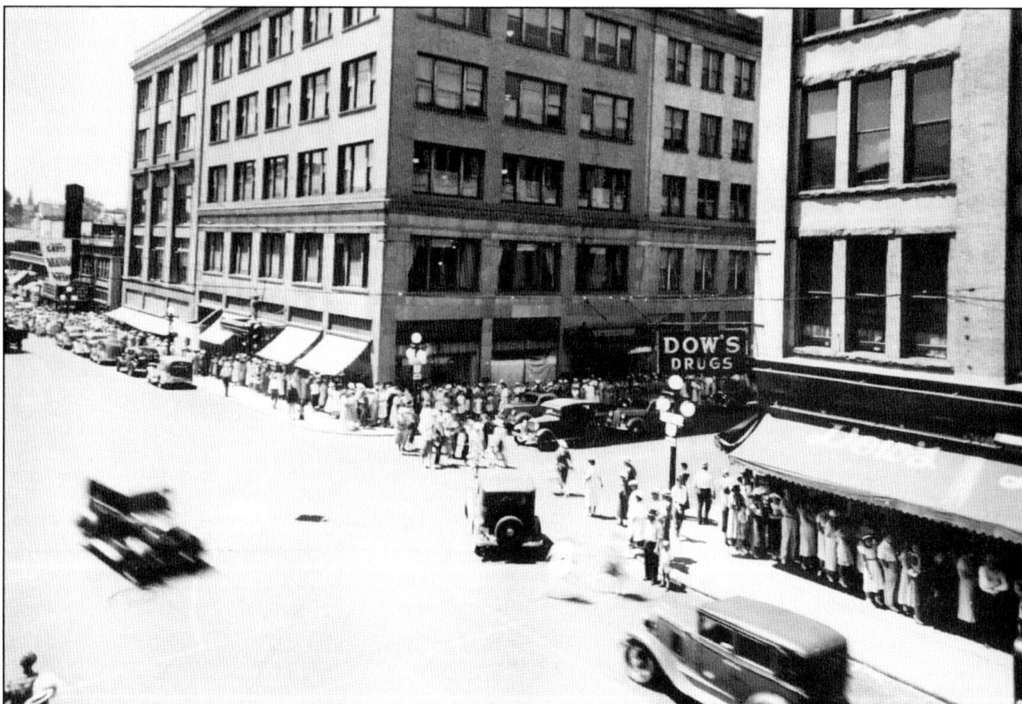

CROWDS LINED UP AT THE CORNER OF WREN'S DEPARTMENT STORE FOR THE REGENT THEATER, C. 1940S. Lines also formed regularly in front of Dow's Drug Store to go to the Majestic Theater.

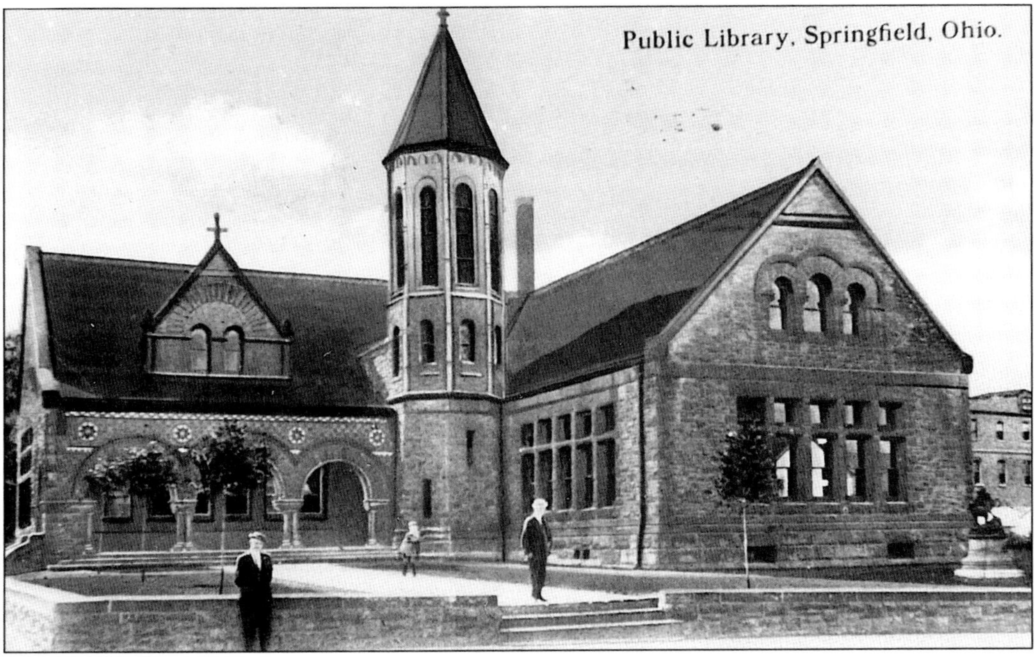

WARDER PUBLIC LIBRARY, LOCATED ON THE SOUTHWEST CORNER OF SPRING AND HIGH STREET. The library was built in 1890 at a cost of $125,000 and donated to the city by industrialist Benjamin Warder. In 1989, it became the Literacy Center because a new library was built at a different location.

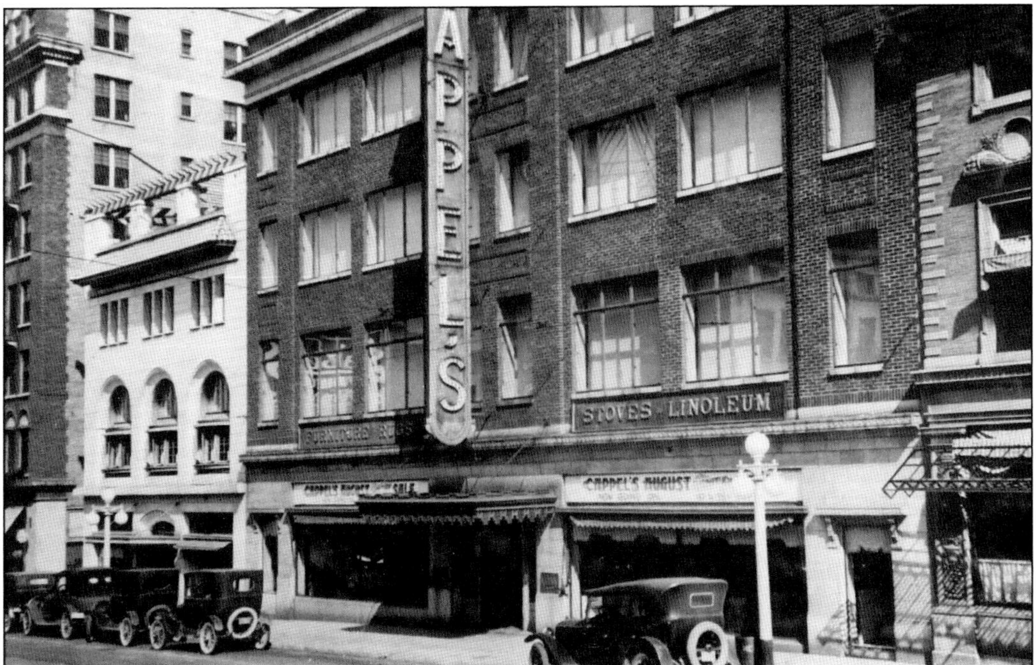

CAPPEL'S, A POPULAR FURNITURE STORE LOCATED AT 124–130 EAST HIGH STREET, MID 1920S.

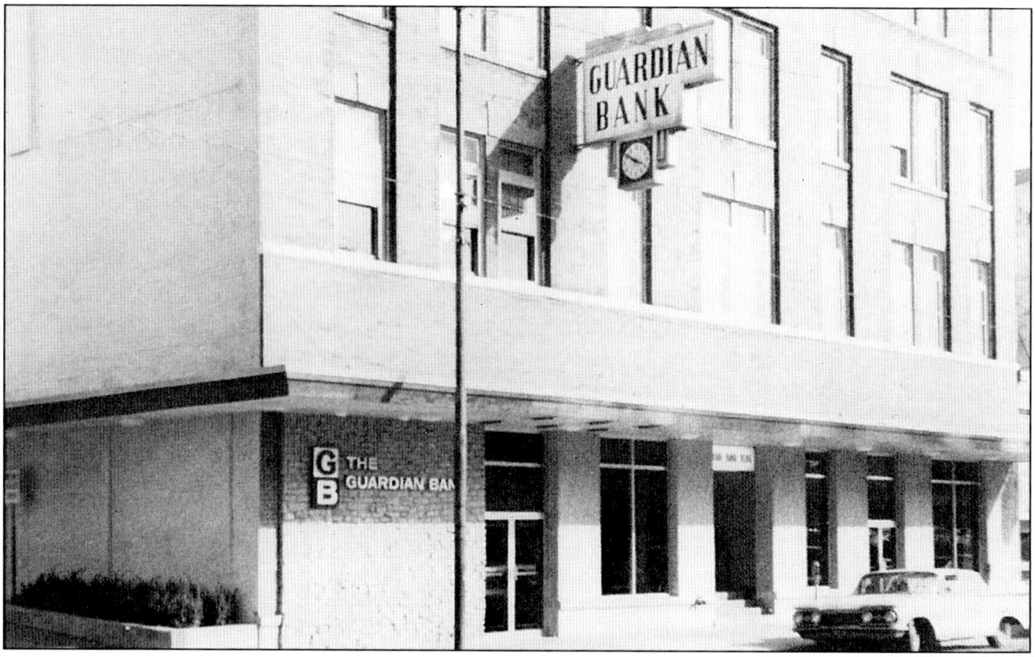

GUARDIAN BANK (FORMERLY MORRIS PLAN), LOCATED AT 120 SOUTH LIMESTONE STREET, C. 1960S. Today, it is Security Bank and located on the northeast corner of South Limestone and East High Street.

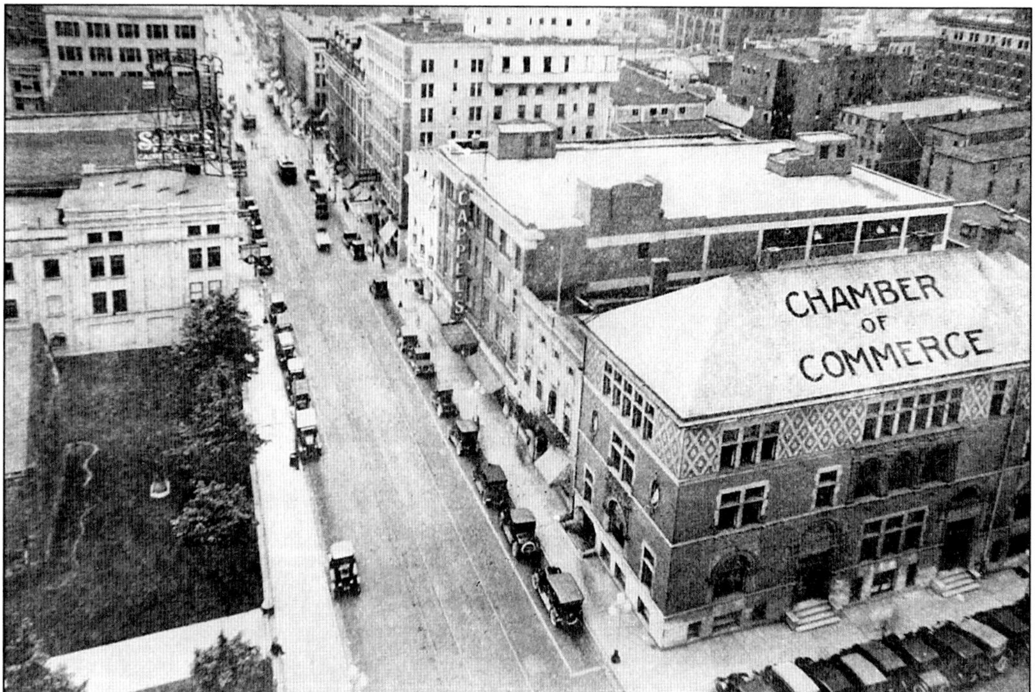

A STREET VIEW OF DOWNTOWN FROM ST. RAPHAEL'S CHURCH, C. 1920S. On the right is the Chamber of Commerce Building, next to Cappel's Furniture. Pictured to the left is the Ohio Edison Company, previously Springfield Light, Heat, and Power Company.

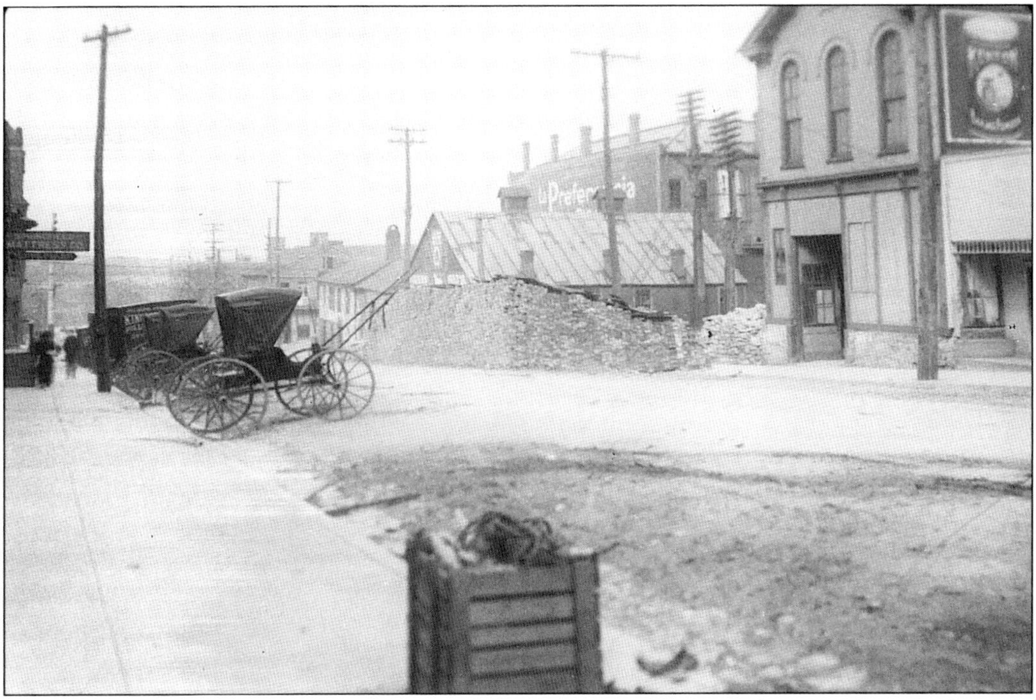

The Springfield Mattress Company, Located on the Left Side of Spring Street, c. 1890. This view was taken looking north between Main and High Street. The Mattress Company's sign is visible on the far left near the carriages.

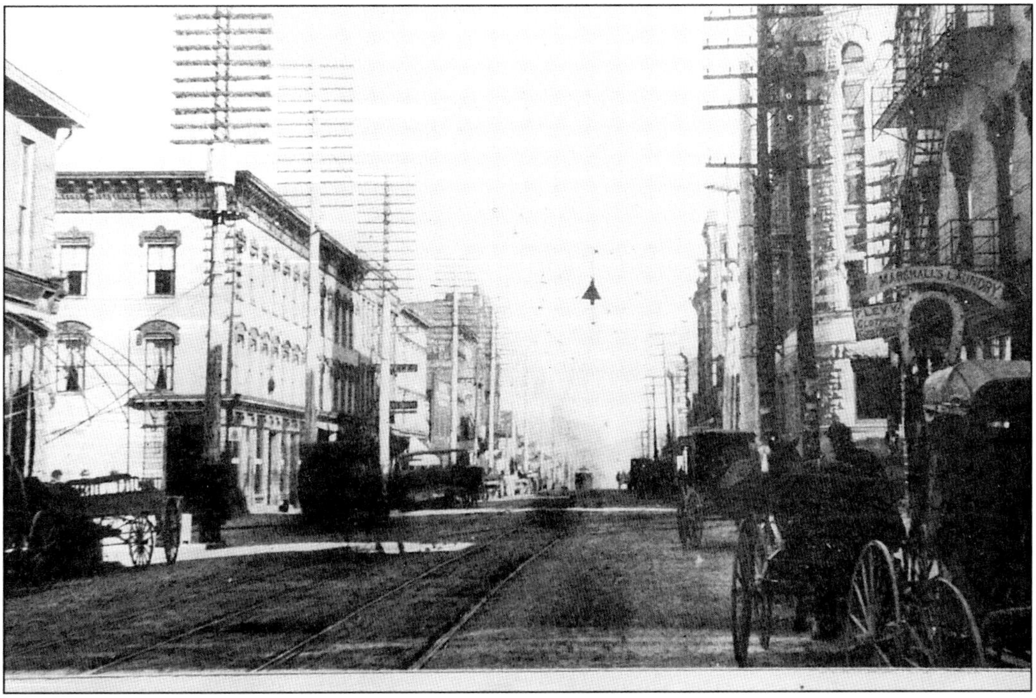

Main Street Looking East at the Corner of Limestone Street, 1915. The old M & M Savings and Loan is on the right. The Cherry Hotel is on the left.

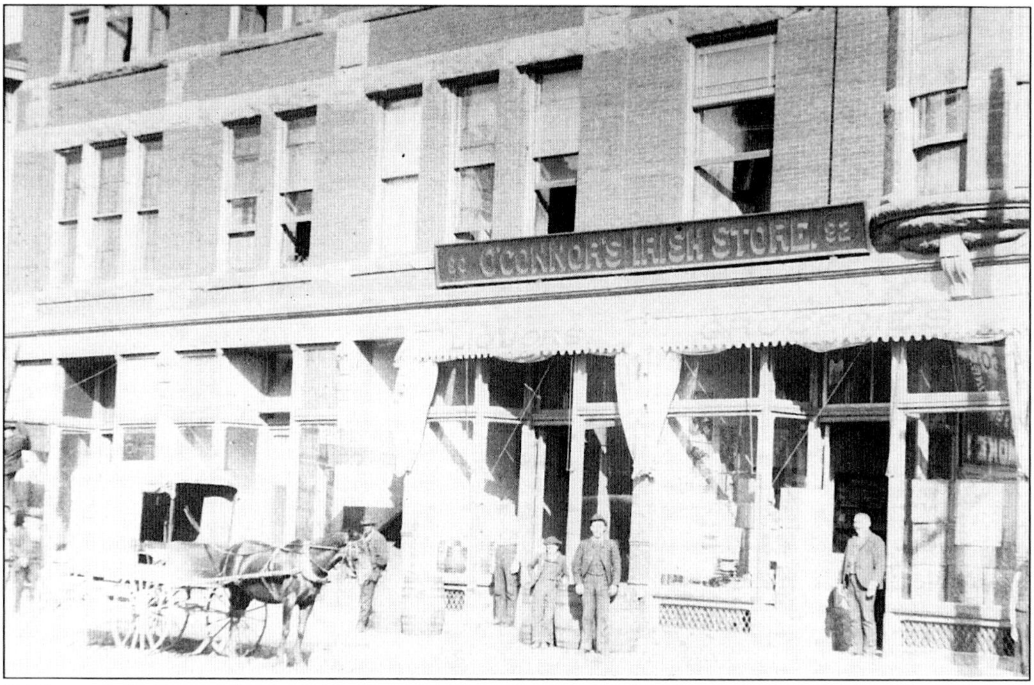

O'CONNOR'S IRISH STORE, LOCATED ON THE NORTHWEST CORNER OF EAST MAIN AND SPRING STREET, C. 1920S. Among other household items, this store sold liquor and groceries. Later, Springfield Rug and Furniture occupied this location.

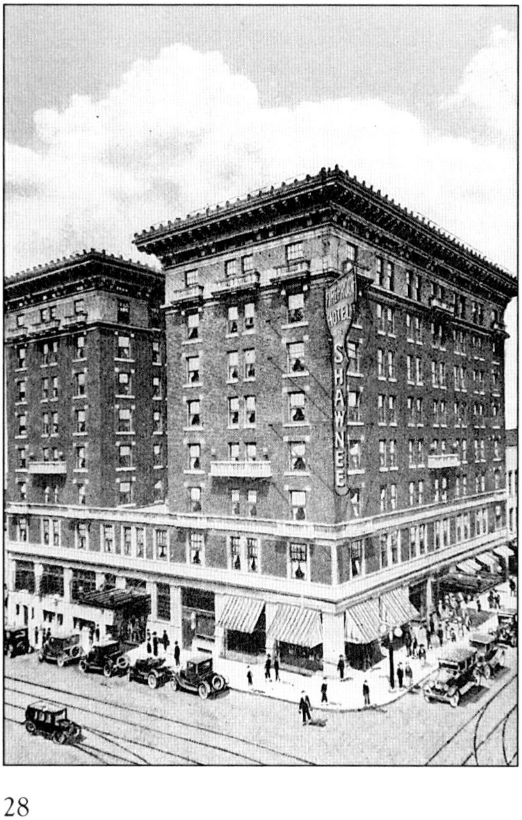

SHAWNEE HOTEL, BUILT IN 1916 AND LOCATED ON THE NORTHEAST CORNER OF MAIN AND LIMESTONE. Today, this is the City Place Apartments. Previous names included St. James, Murray Cherry, and Willis House.

Springfield National Bank, Located at the Southeast Corner of Main and Limestone, Early 1900s. The building was known as the Gotwald Building, and later as the M & M Federal Savings and Loan Association.

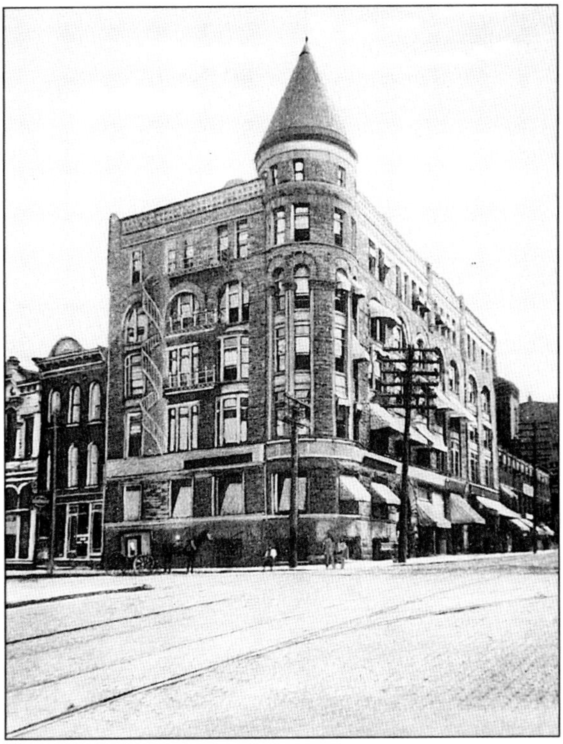

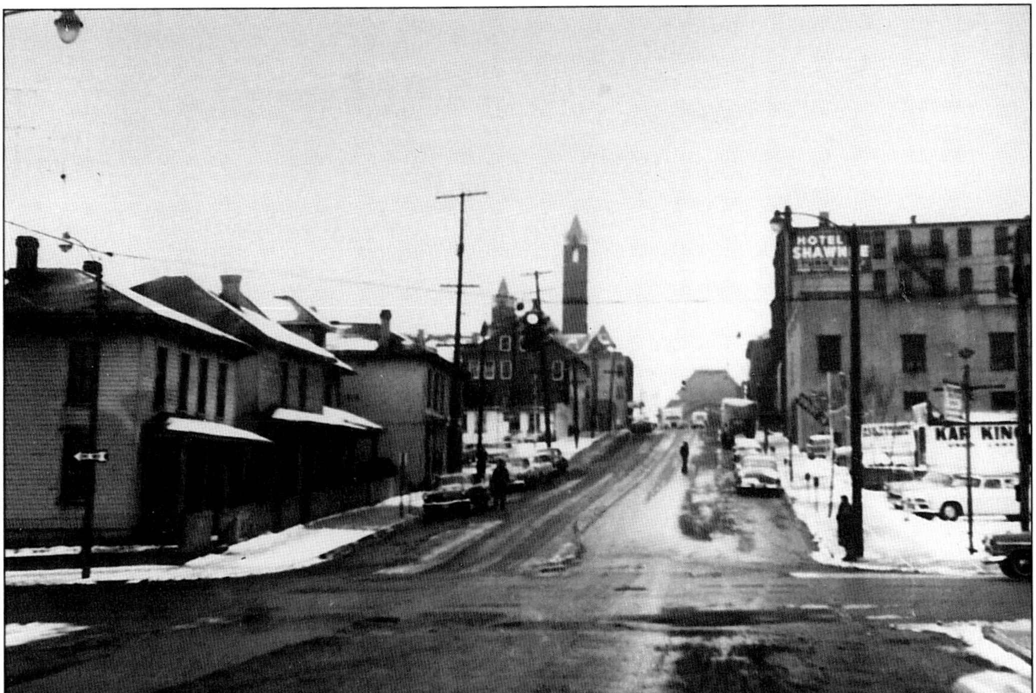

View of the Corner of North Spring Street and East Columbia Street, 1960. This photo, taken ten years before the Spring Street Overpass was built, shows St. Raphael's Church and the Big Four Depot in the background. The Hotel Shawnee is on the right.

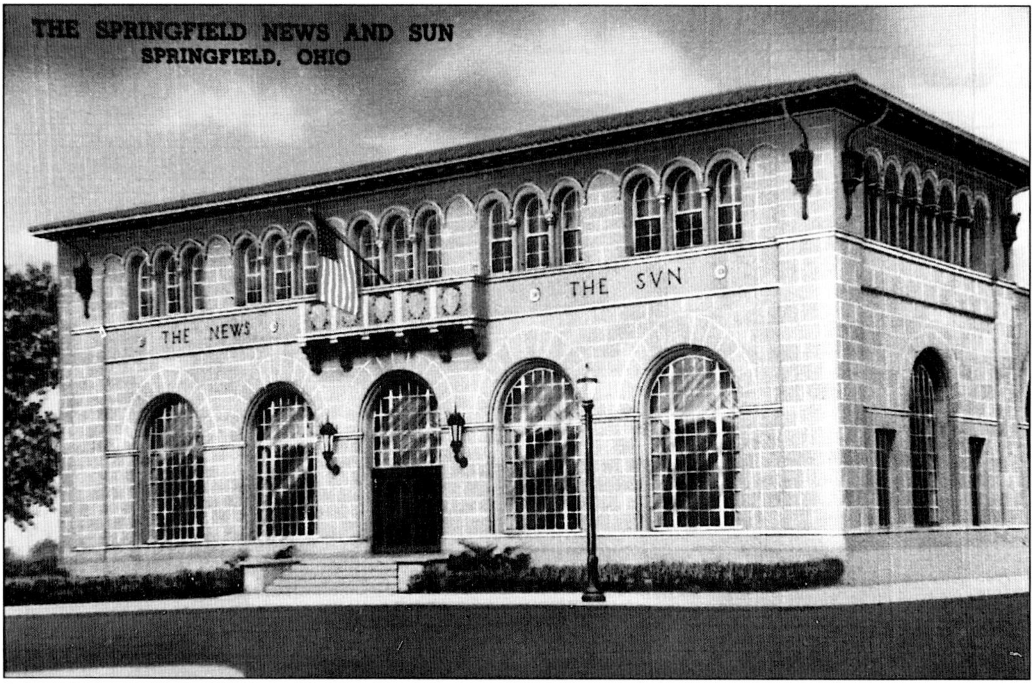

SPRINGFIELD NEWS AND SUN BUILDING, BUILT IN 1929 AND LOCATED ON THE NORTHEAST CORNER OF NORTH LIMESTONE AND EAST NORTH STREET.

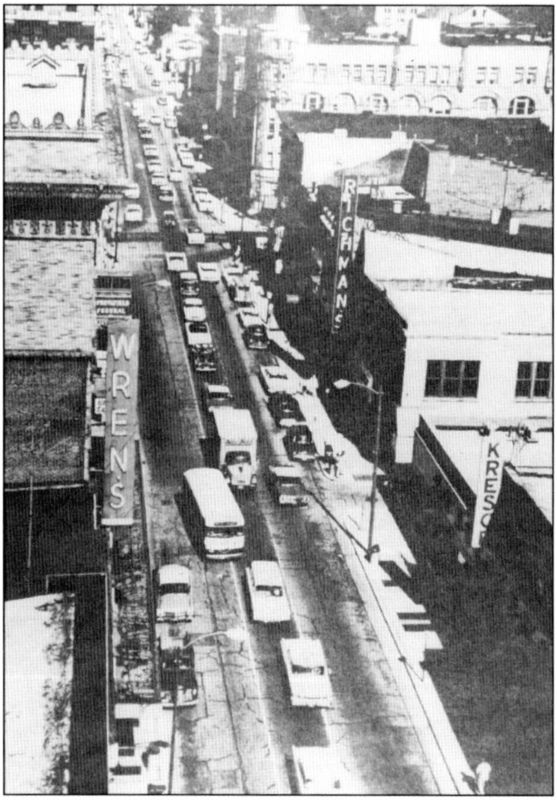

A VIEW FROM THE FIRST NATIONAL BANK BUILDING LOOKING EAST ON EAST MAIN STREET, C. 1950S. This scene also shows Wren's Department Store and Richmans Men's Store.

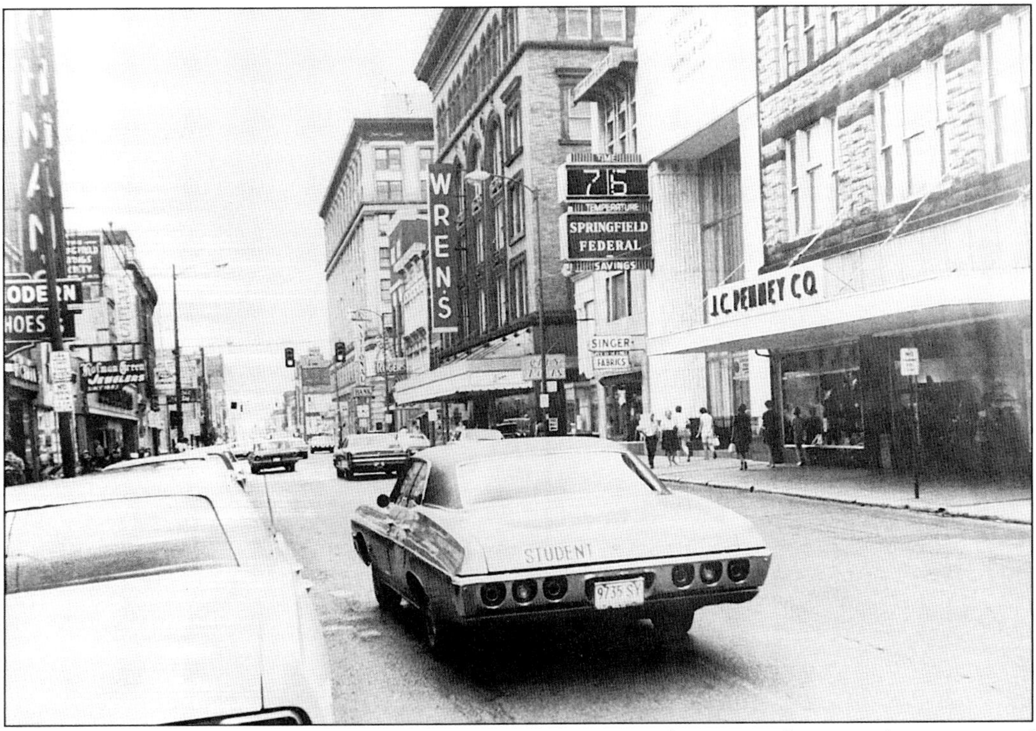

VIEW OF EAST MAIN STREET, LOOKING WEST, C. 1960S. This particular view shows many of the downtown businesses, including J.C. Penney's, Springfield Federal Savings and Loan, and Wren's Department Store.

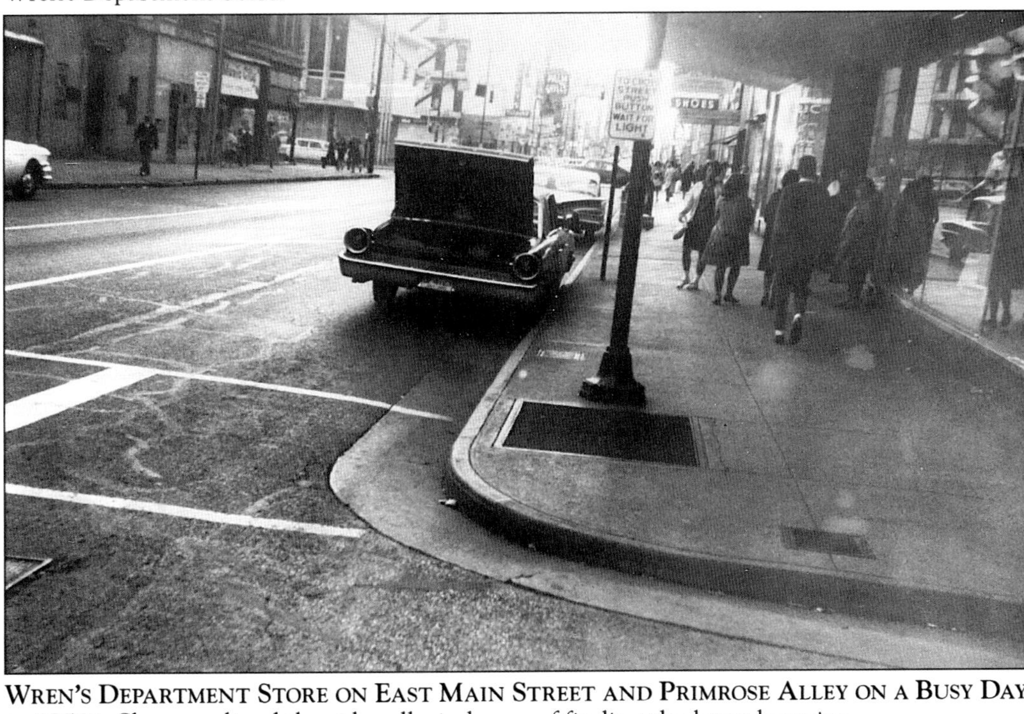

WREN'S DEPARTMENT STORE ON EAST MAIN STREET AND PRIMROSE ALLEY ON A BUSY DAY, C. 1950S. Shoppers lined the sidewalks in hopes of finding the latest bargains.

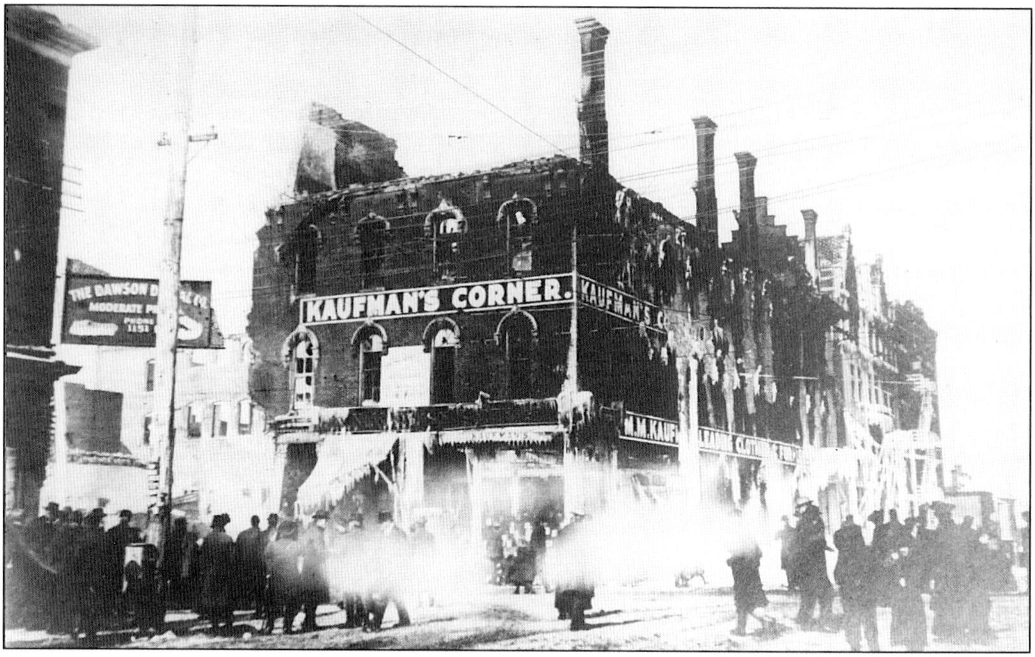

A VIEW AFTER THE FIRE OF BLACK'S OPERA HOUSE, LOCATED ON THE NORTHWEST CORNER OF MAIN STREET AND FOUNTAIN AVENUE. Built in 1869, the structure cost $100,000 and was destroyed by a fire in February 1903. It seated 1,000 people on the second floor, with business offices occupying the first floor.

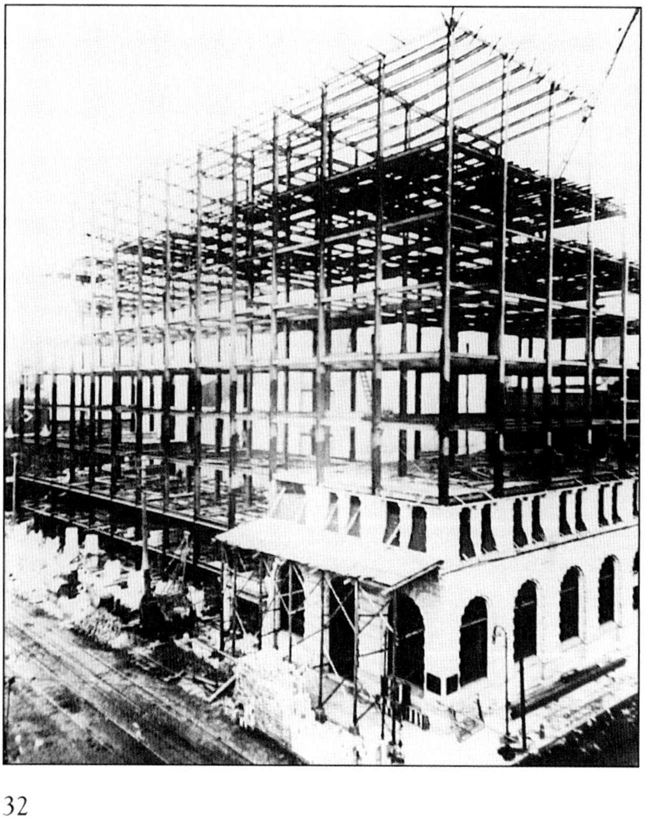

FAIRBANKS BUILDING, LOCATED ON THE NORTHWEST CORNER OF MAIN AND FOUNTAIN AVENUE. This building, also known as the First National Bank Building, was built around 1906 to replace Black's Opera House after it burned down in the fire. This is now the site of BancOhio.

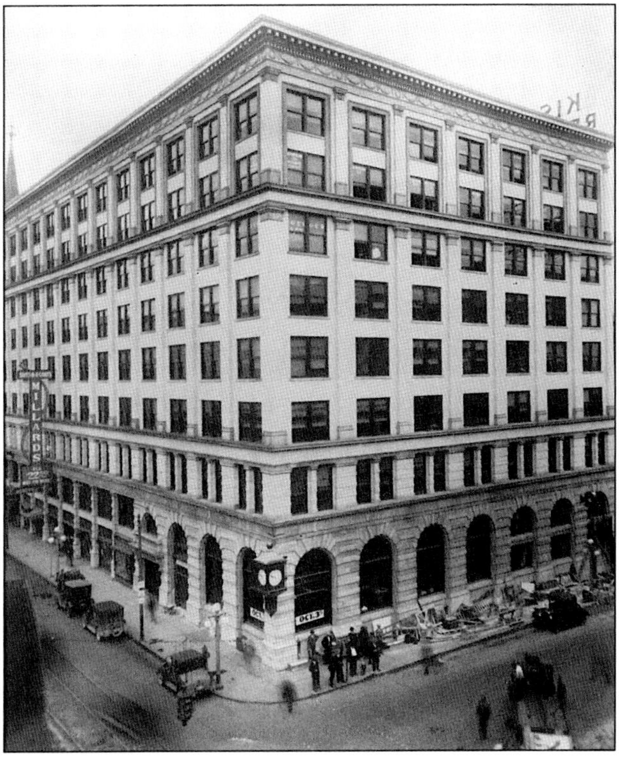

THE FIRST NATIONAL BANK (NOW BANCOHIO), LOCATED IN THE FAIRBANKS BUILDING, 1927. Prior to their move on October 3, 1927, to the Fairbanks Building, the bank spent many years at 22 East Main Street in the Bushnell Building.

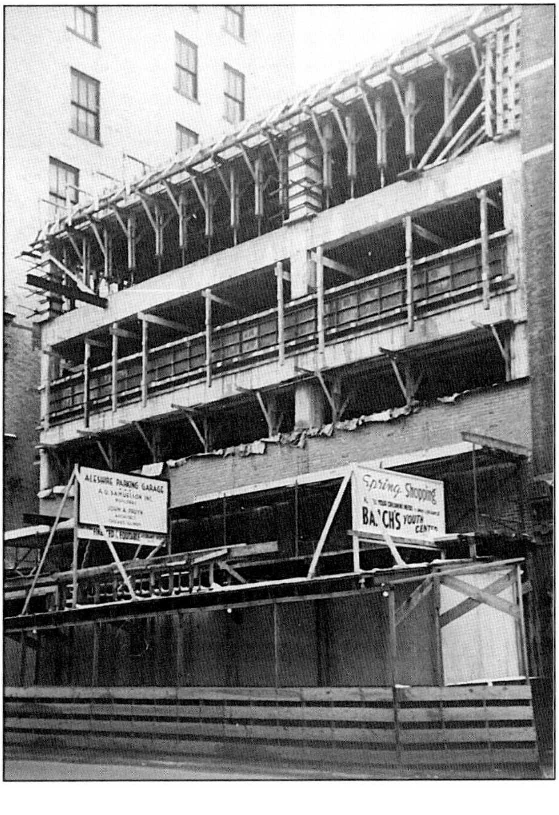

ALESHIRE PARKING GARAGE ON NORTH FOUNTAIN AVENUE. After World War II, Mr. Aleshire built this garage behind the First National Bank Building where the old YMCA was previously located. It was demolished in the 1960s and is now a drive-through for BancOhio.

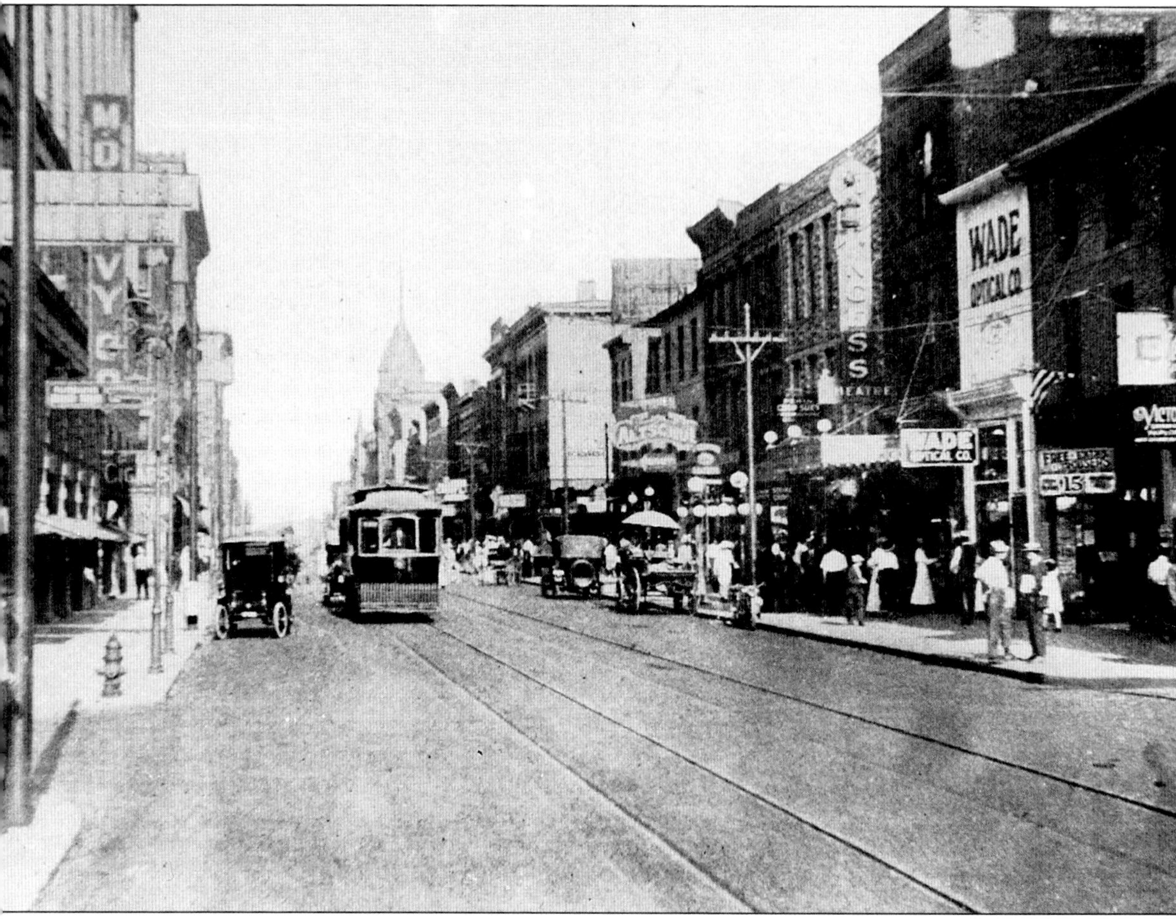

A STREET VIEW OF WEST MAIN STREET LOOKING EAST FROM FISHER STREET, C. 1917. The Fairbanks Theater is on the left across from the Princess Theater on the right.

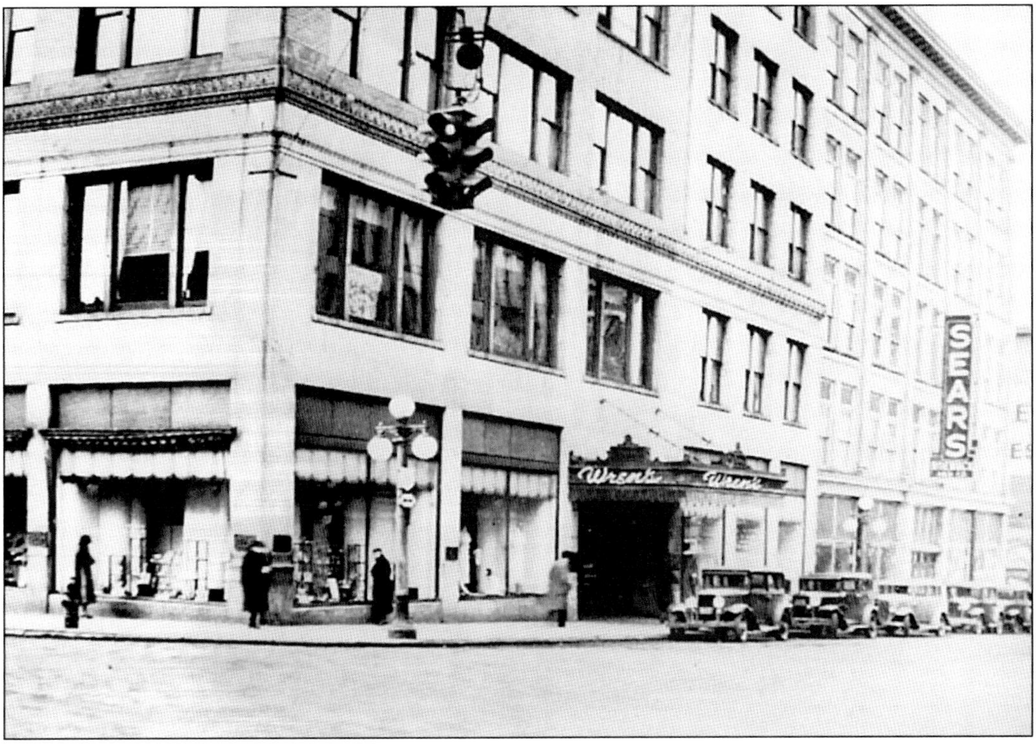

TODAY'S MCADAMS BUILDING, LATE 1930S. From 1903 through the 1930s, Wren's Department Store occupied the entire building. By the time this photo was made, however, Wren's had begun leasing part of the building to Sears. Note the window shoppers that are absent today.

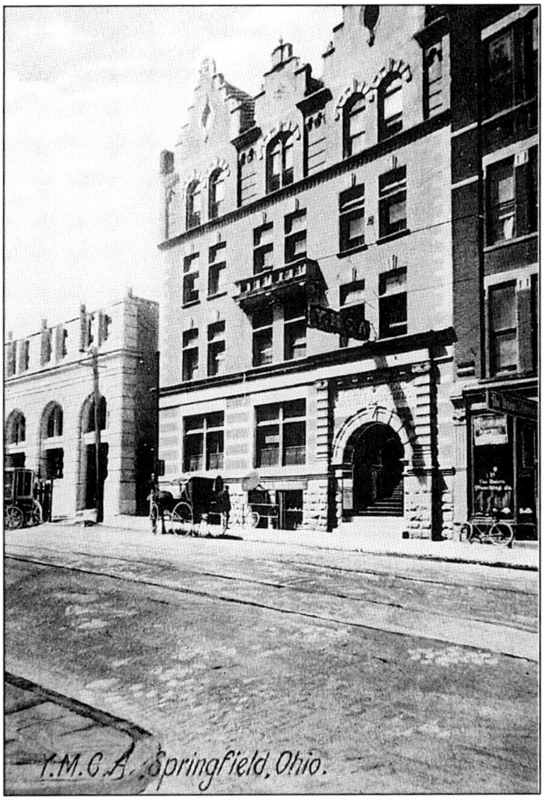

SPRINGFIELD'S FIRST YMCA, BUILT AND DEDICATED ON SEPTEMBER 17, 1901. It closed in 1939 when the Central YMCA was built on the southwest corner of North and Limestone. In 1991, this site became a bank drive-through.

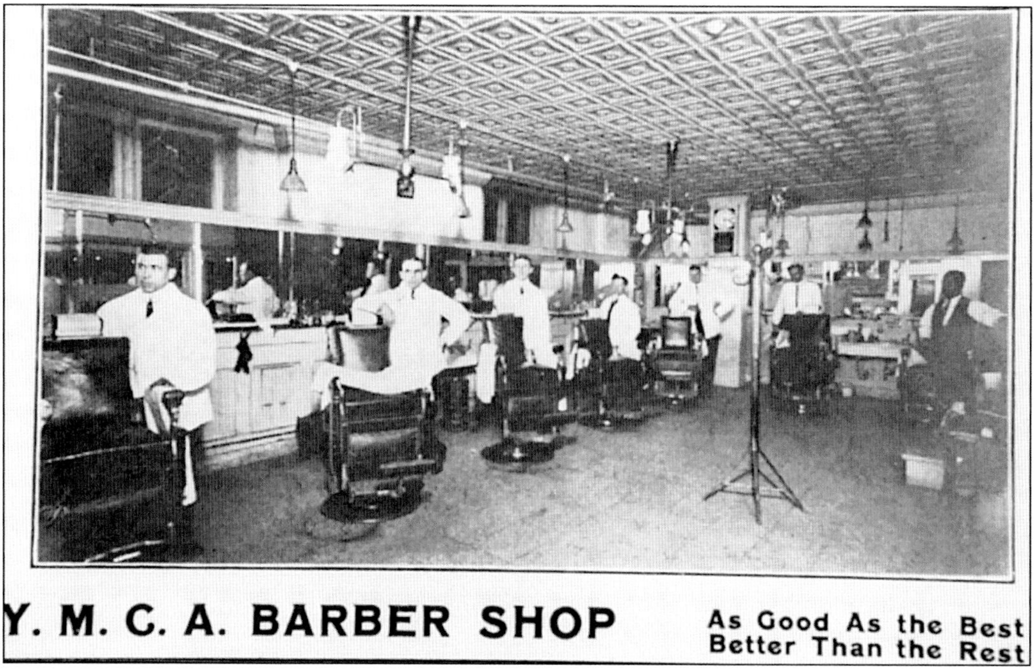

INTERIOR OF THE YMCA BARBER SHOP, LOCATED AT 15 NORTH FOUNTAIN AVENUE, 1915. In this scene, several barbers stood ready by their chairs, boasting that they were "as good as the best, better than the rest."

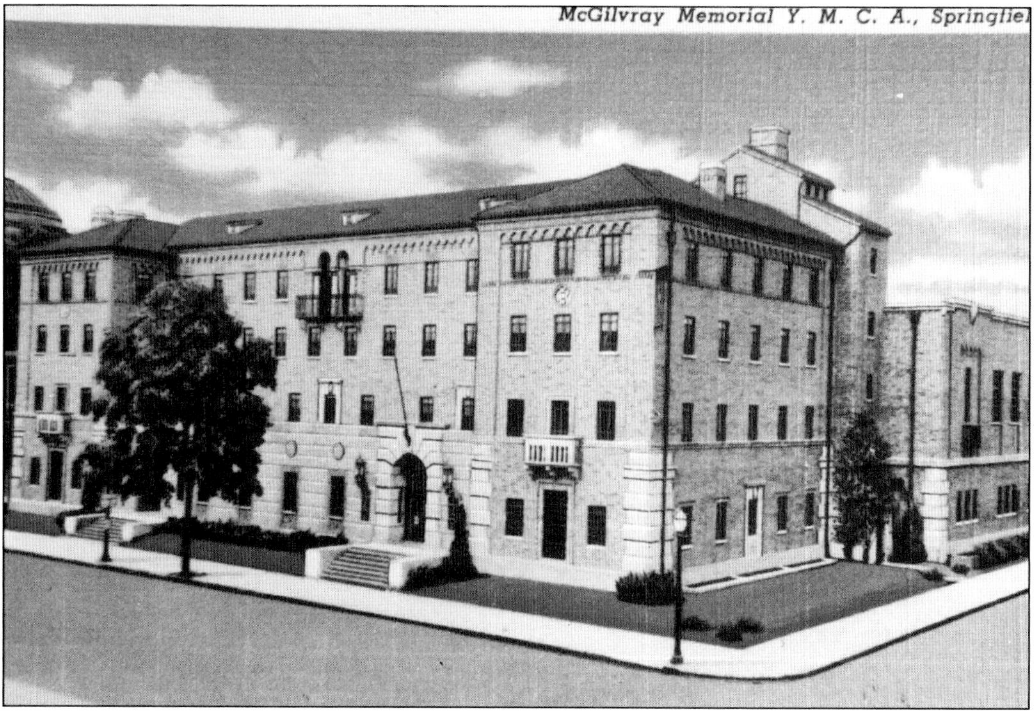

MCGILVRAY YMCA, BUILT OCTOBER 8, 1939. It was demolished in January 1990, and today it serves as a parking lot.

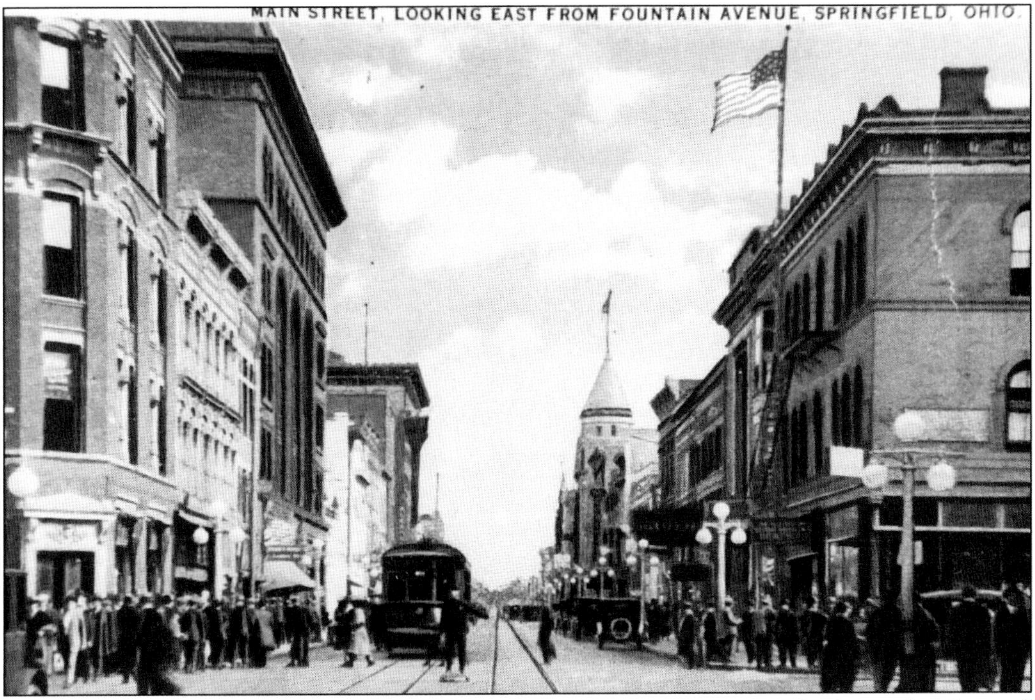

MAIN STREET LOOKING EAST FROM FOUNTAIN AVENUE, C. 1920. The Lagonda National Bank is on the left with the Bushnell Building visible in the background.

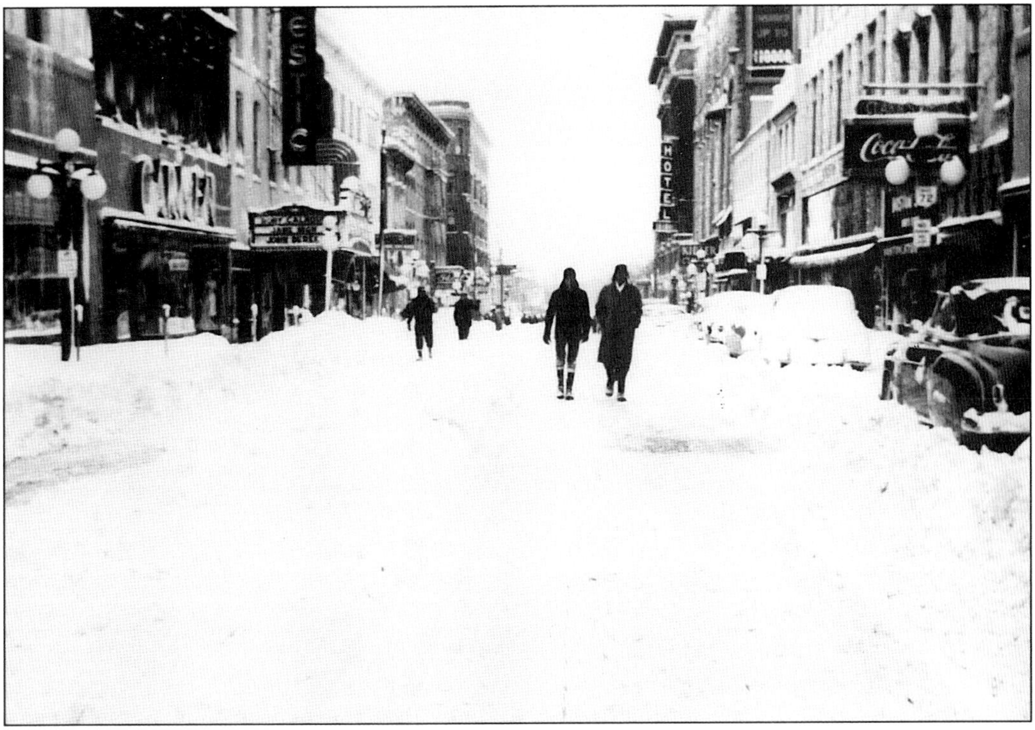

THE BIG SNOW OF NOVEMBER 1950 LOOKING NORTH ON SOUTH LIMESTONE STREET. The Majestic Theater's entrance is buried under the snowbanks on the left.

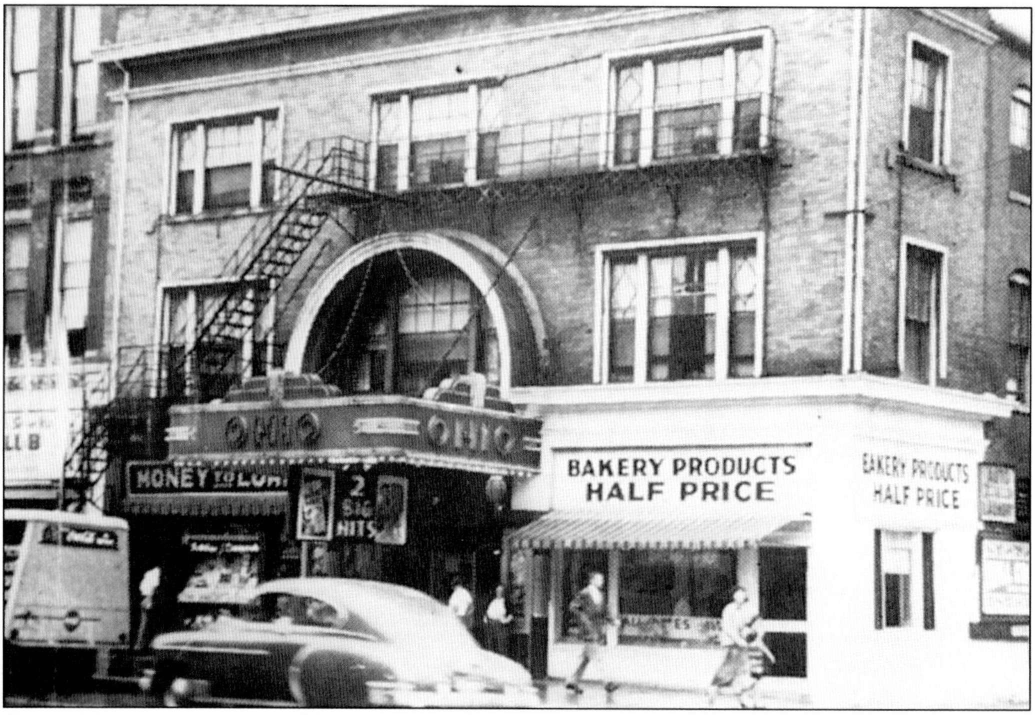

OHIO THEATER ON THE NORTHWEST CORNER OF WEST MAIN AND CENTER STREET, c. 1955. This was first the Wigwam, and then it became the Band Box Theater.

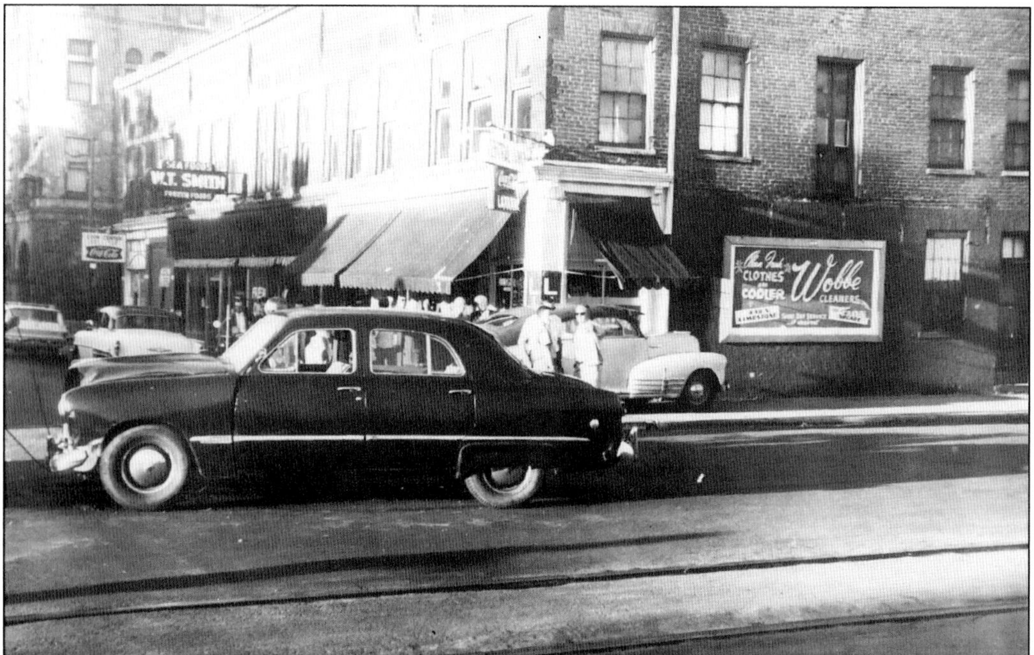

NORTHEAST CORNER OF WEST WASHINGTON STREET AND SOUTH CENTER STREET, LATE 1950s. This view shows Central Lunch on the corner and W.T. Smith's Fish Market in the background.

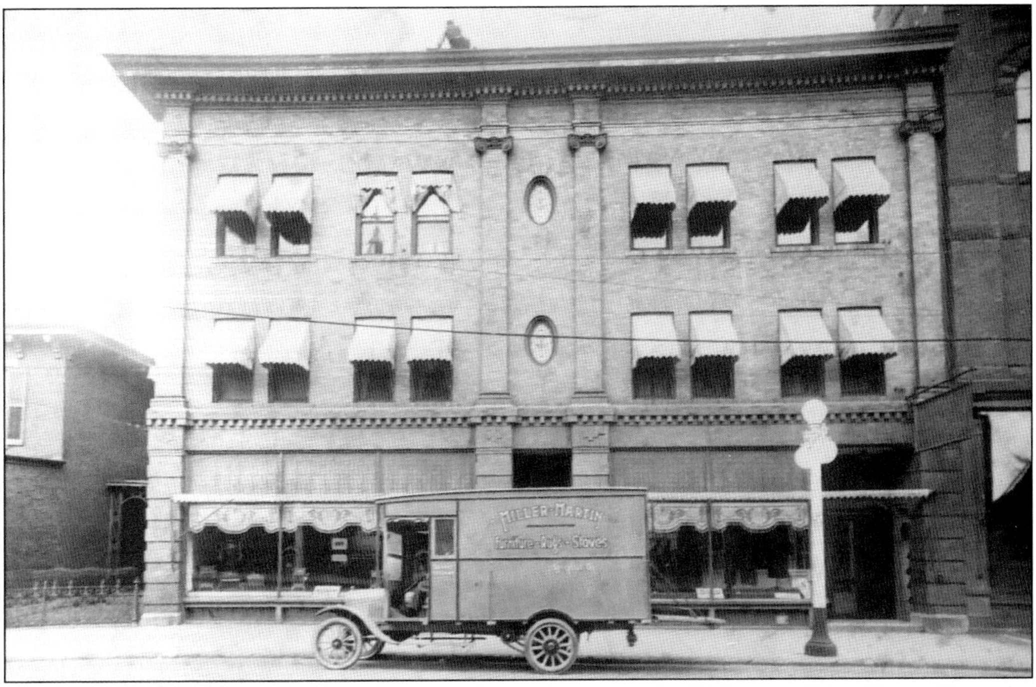

CENTRAL RUG, C. 1917. This business was located next to the Delscamp Paint Store. Note the man on the roof posing for the photo!

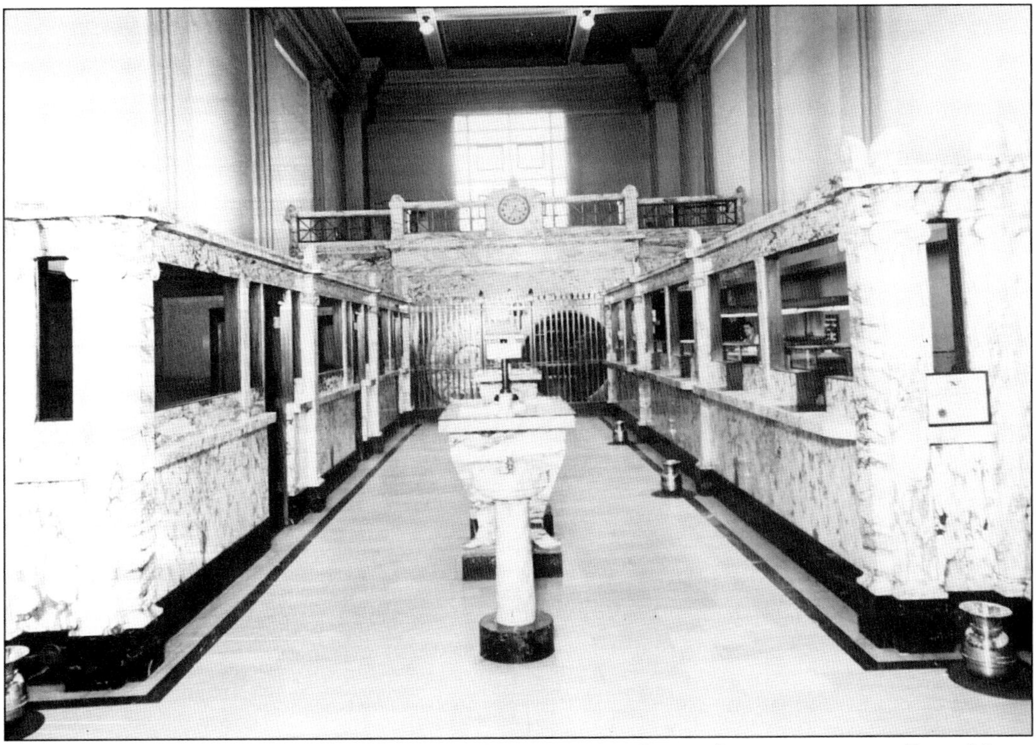

THE OLD LOBBY OF SPRINGFIELD FEDERAL SAVINGS AND LOAN ASSOCIATION ON EAST MAIN STREET, C. 1940S.

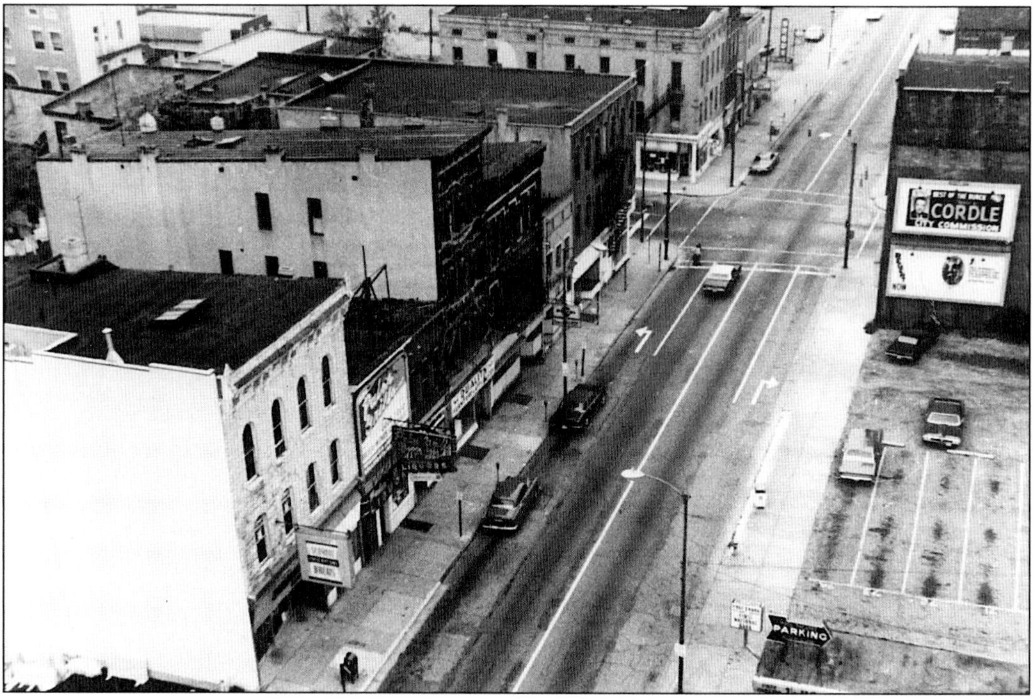

VIEW FROM THE FIRST NATIONAL BANK BUILDING ON WEST MAIN STREET, C. 1960S. This photo also shows Schmidt's Drug Store, Palm Grill's Restaurant, and the Subway.

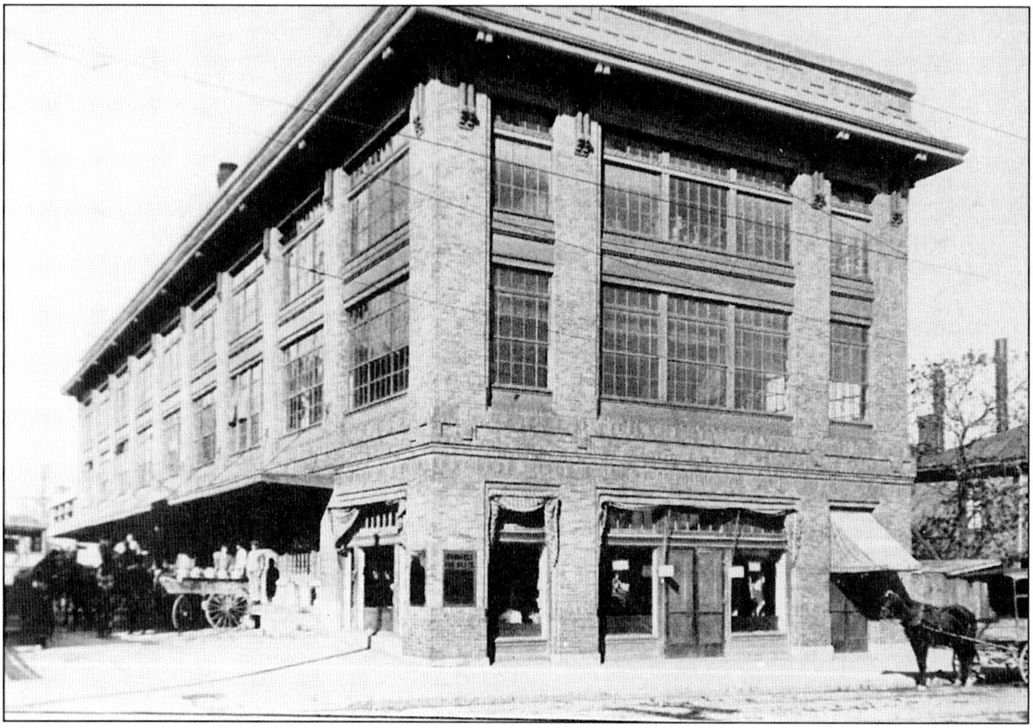

SPRINGFIELD PURE MILK COMPANY, LOCATED AT 125–129 NORTH FOUNTAIN AVENUE, 1915. Later, it became Borden's Dairy, and today it is the site of Huntington National Bank.

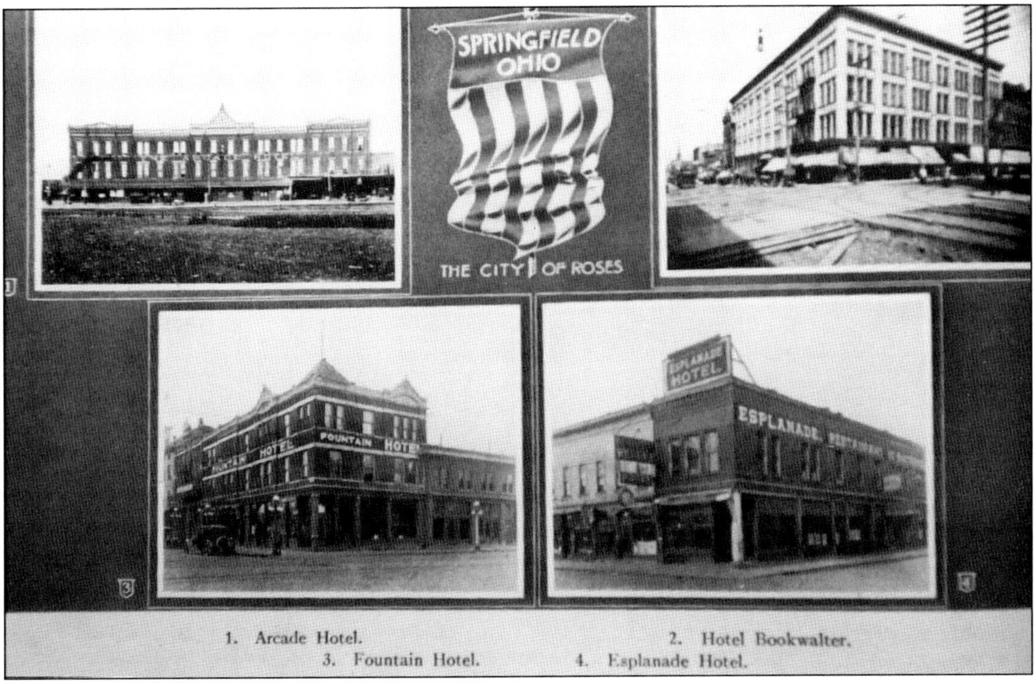

SPRINGFIELD, CITY OF ROSES POSTCARD, 1915. The building are as follows, clockwise from top left: Arcade Hotel (located on the northeast corner of Fountain and Washington), Bookwalter Hotel (on the northwest corner of High and Limestone Street), Esplanade Hotel (located on the southwest corner of Fountain and South Market), and Fountain Hotel (located on the southwest corner of Fountain and Washington).

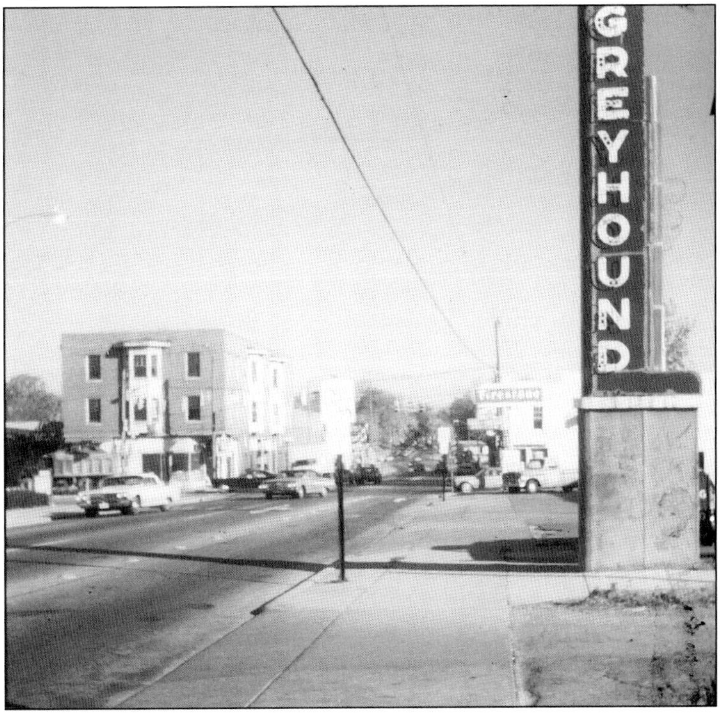

VIEW LOOKING NORTH ON NORTH FOUNTAIN AVENUE, 1970. On the right is the Firestone Store and the Greyhound Bus Terminal.

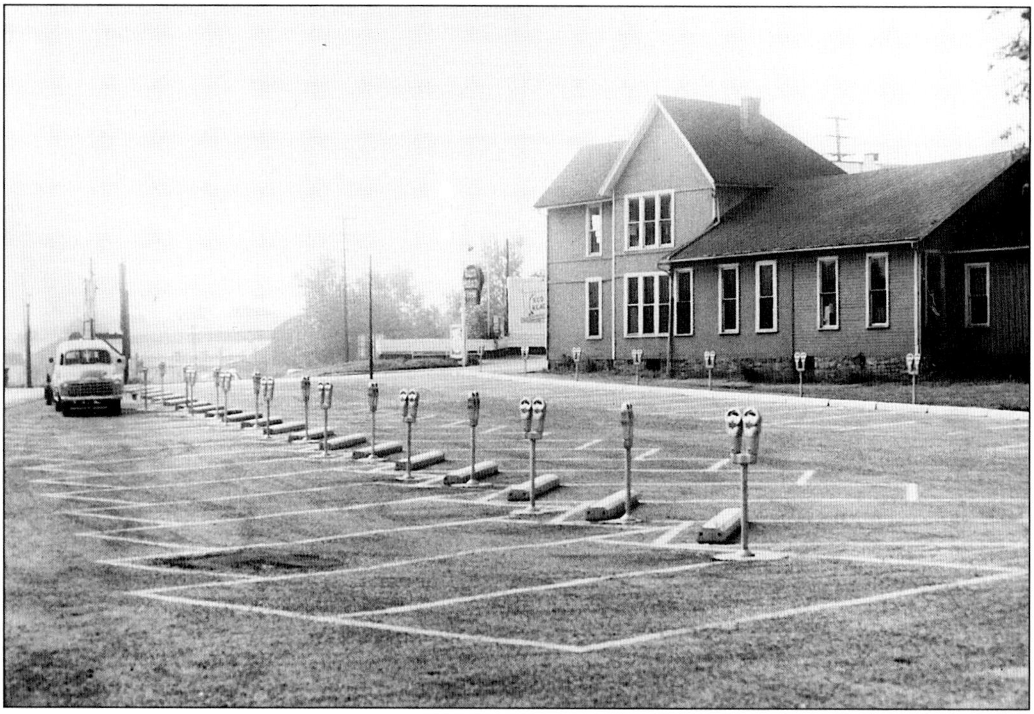

SITE OF TODAY'S RIVERBEND BUILDING. Do you remember this city parking lot on the west side of North Limestone Street? This photograph was taken in the 1960s.

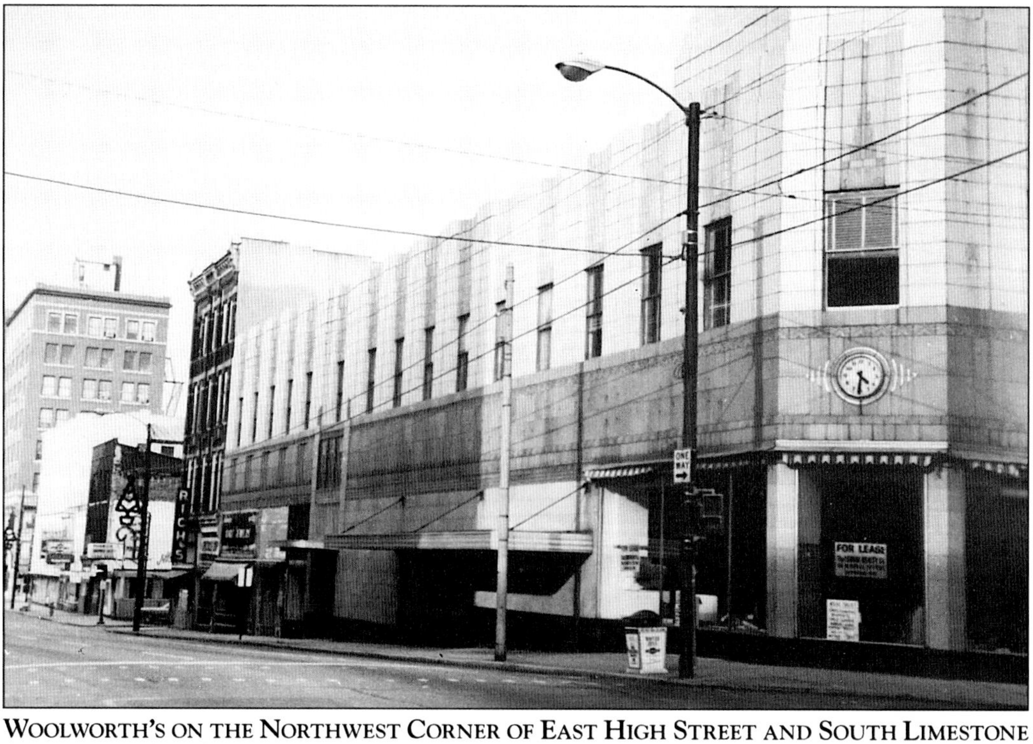

WOOLWORTH'S ON THE NORTHWEST CORNER OF EAST HIGH STREET AND SOUTH LIMESTONE STREET. Woolworth's moved to the Mall in 1971.

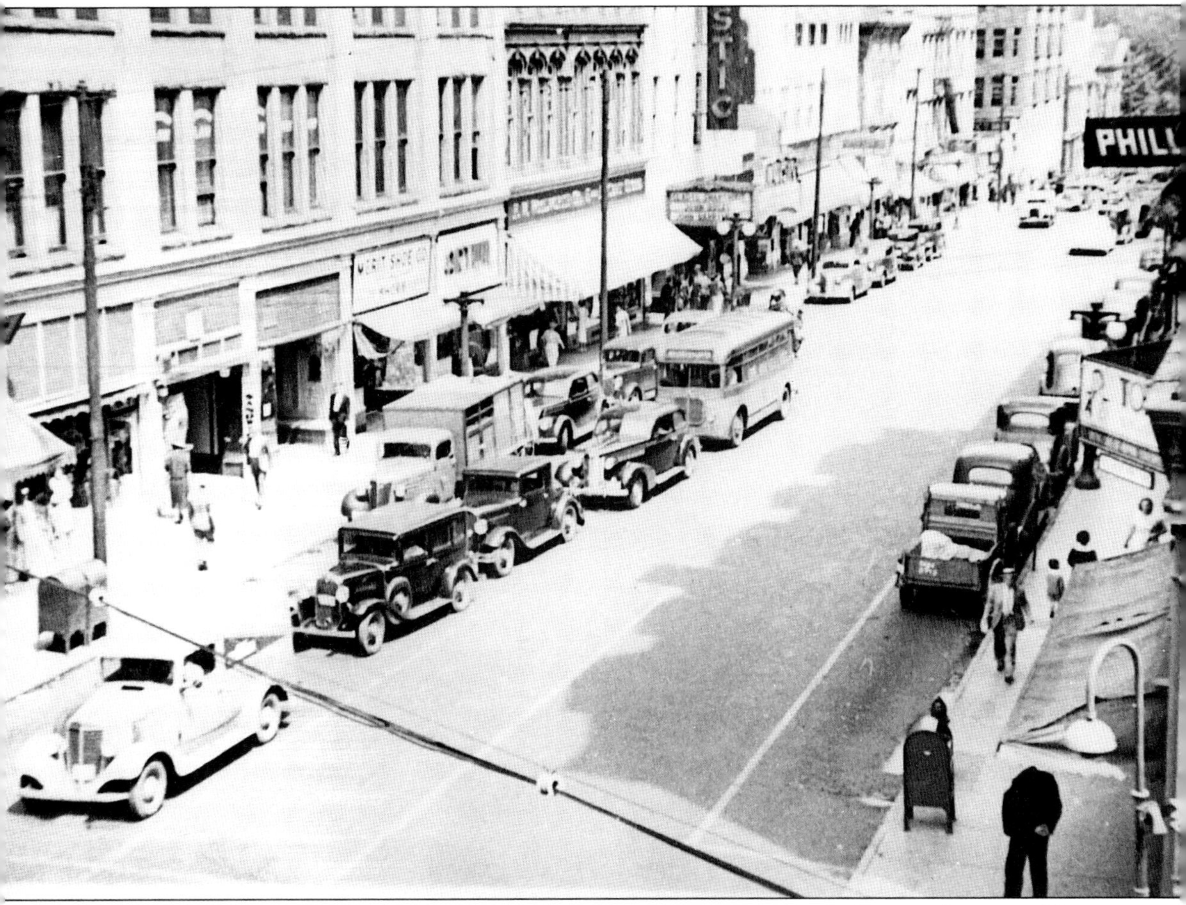

LOOKING NORTH ON SOUTH LIMESTONE STREET FROM EAST HIGH STREET, EARLY 1930S. The Majestic Theater and Phillip's Dress Shop are also pictured.

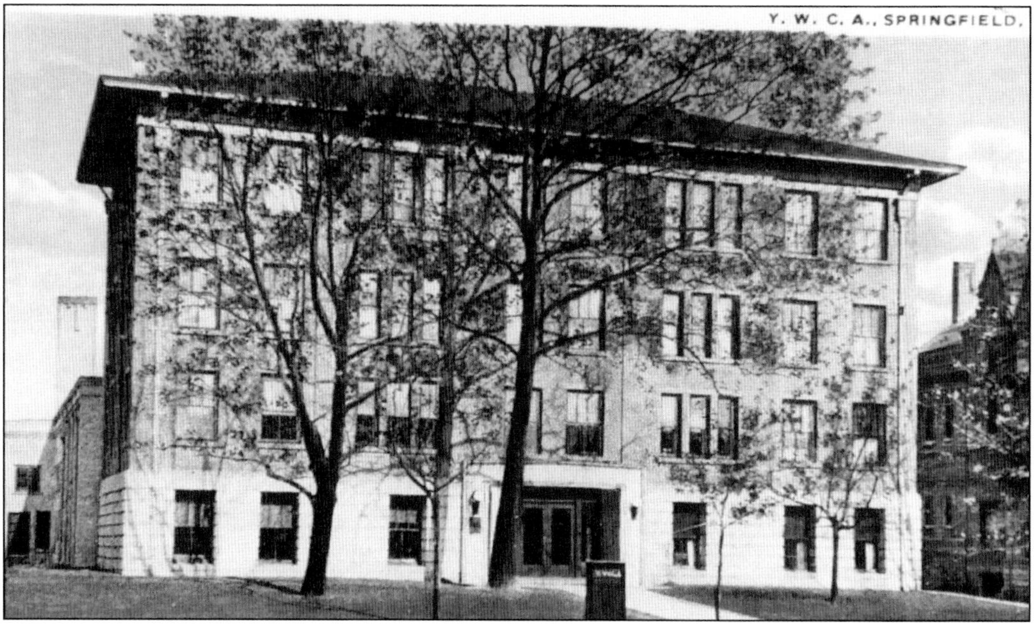

The YWCA at 250 East High Street. Their long history included being a school, a female seminary, and finally a women's "Y." Eventually they merged with the YMCA to become a Family "Y." This building was torn down in May 1992 to pave a new parking lot for the High Street Methodist Church.

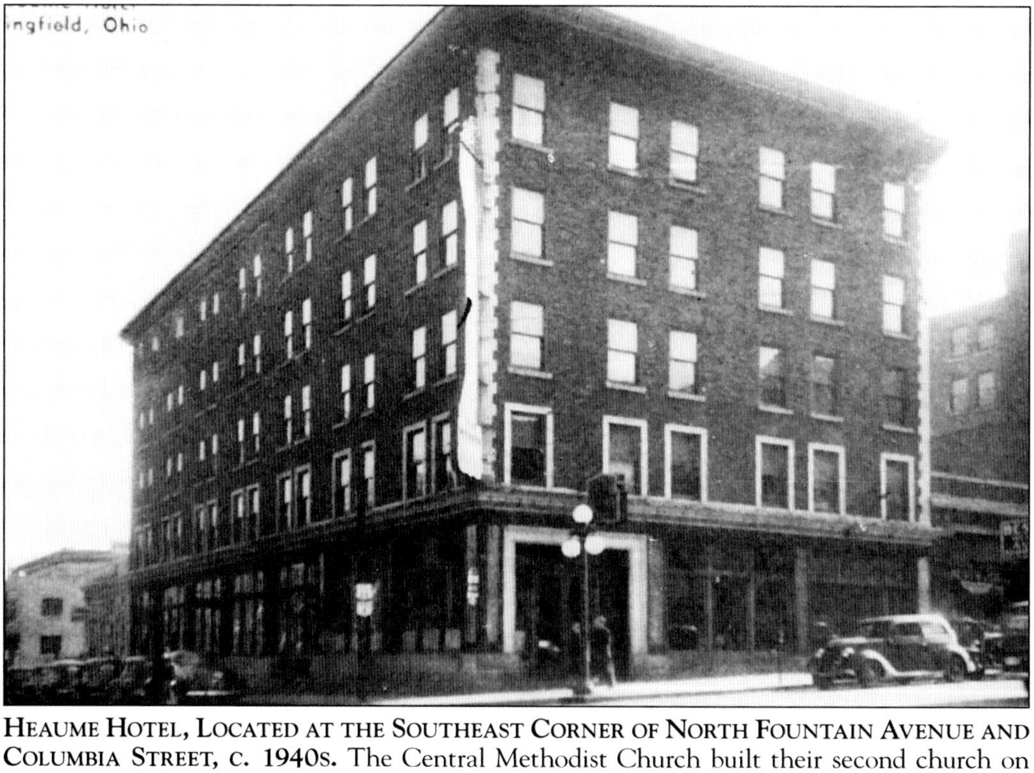

Heaume Hotel, Located at the Southeast Corner of North Fountain Avenue and Columbia Street, c. 1940s. The Central Methodist Church built their second church on this site in 1833.

THE OHIO EDISON COMPANY, LOCATED AT 125 EAST HIGH STREET, C. 1930S. The company headquarters was located here a long time before they moved in with Clark State Community College at the southeast corner of East High and South Limestone. This particular building was torn down in June 1992.

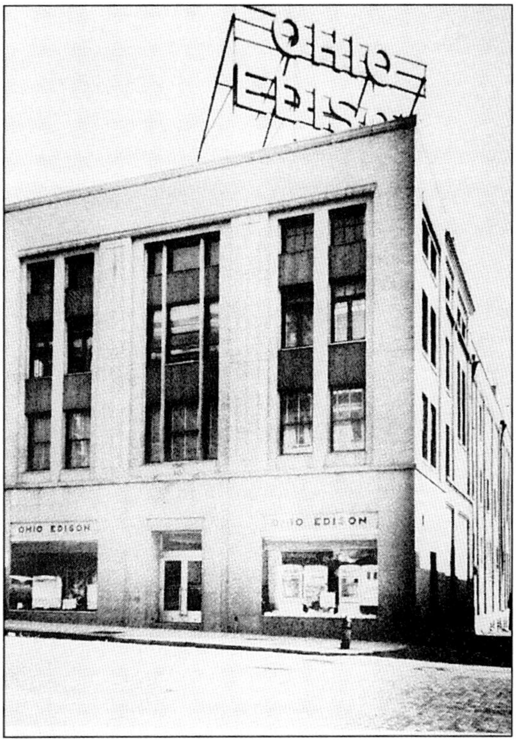

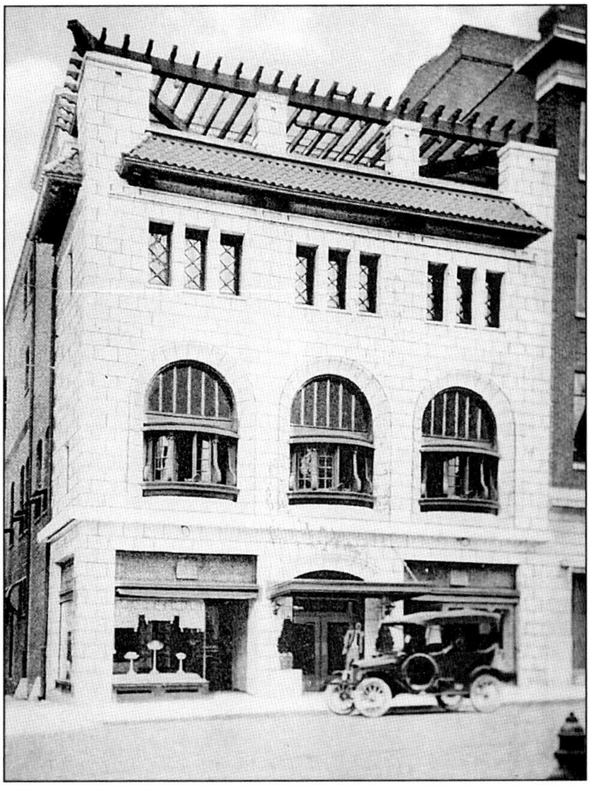

THE KNIGHTS OF COLUMBUS BUILDING, LOCATED AT 122 EAST HIGH STREET, C. 1920S. This building is now a parking lot for Security National Bank.

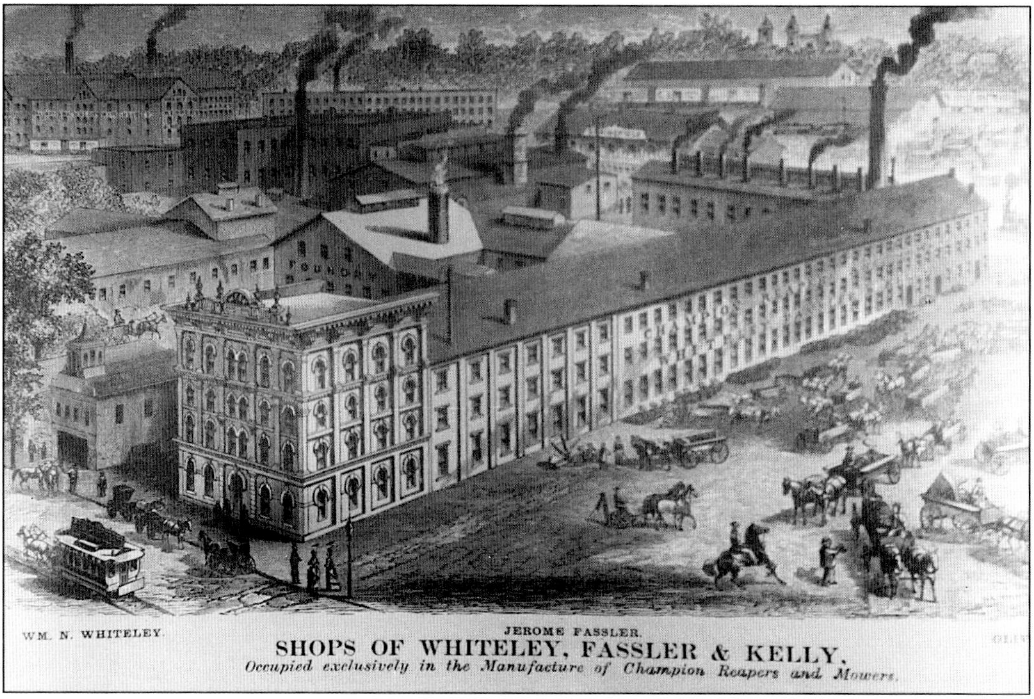

WHITELEY, FASSLER AND KELLY COMPANY SHOPS, LOCATED ON THE SOUTHEAST CORNER OF FOUNTAIN AND HIGH STREET. From 1856 to 1882, this company employed 700 men to build farm equipment. In 1883, Mr. Kelly remodeled the building and made additions which eventually became the Arcade.

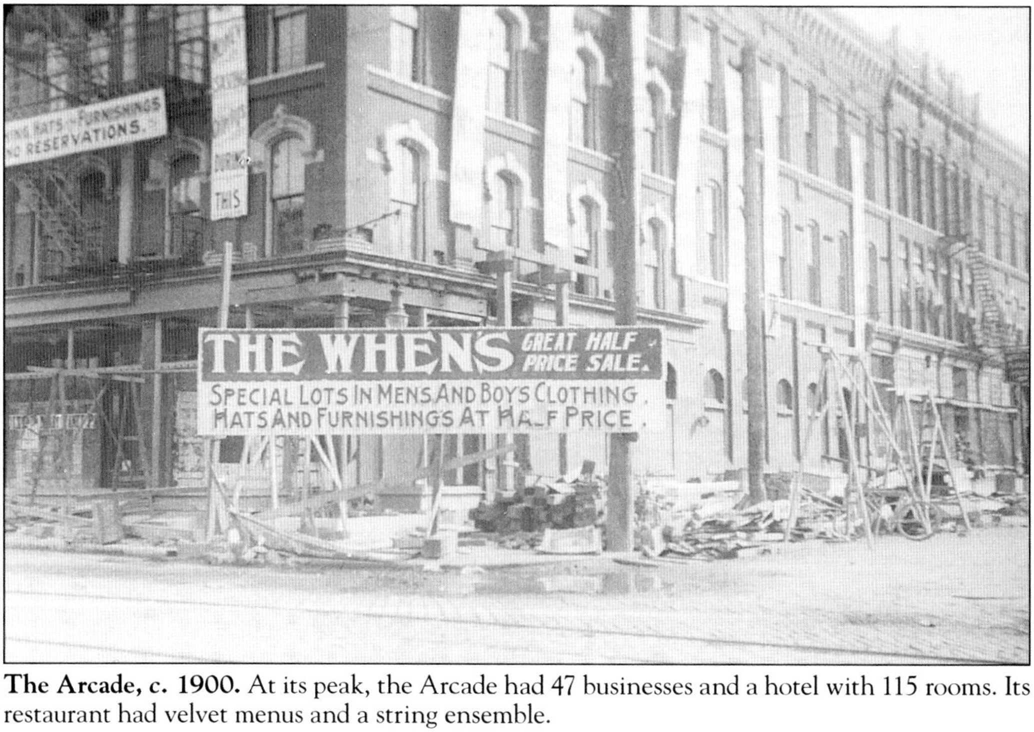

The Arcade, c. 1900. At its peak, the Arcade had 47 businesses and a hotel with 115 rooms. Its restaurant had velvet menus and a string ensemble.

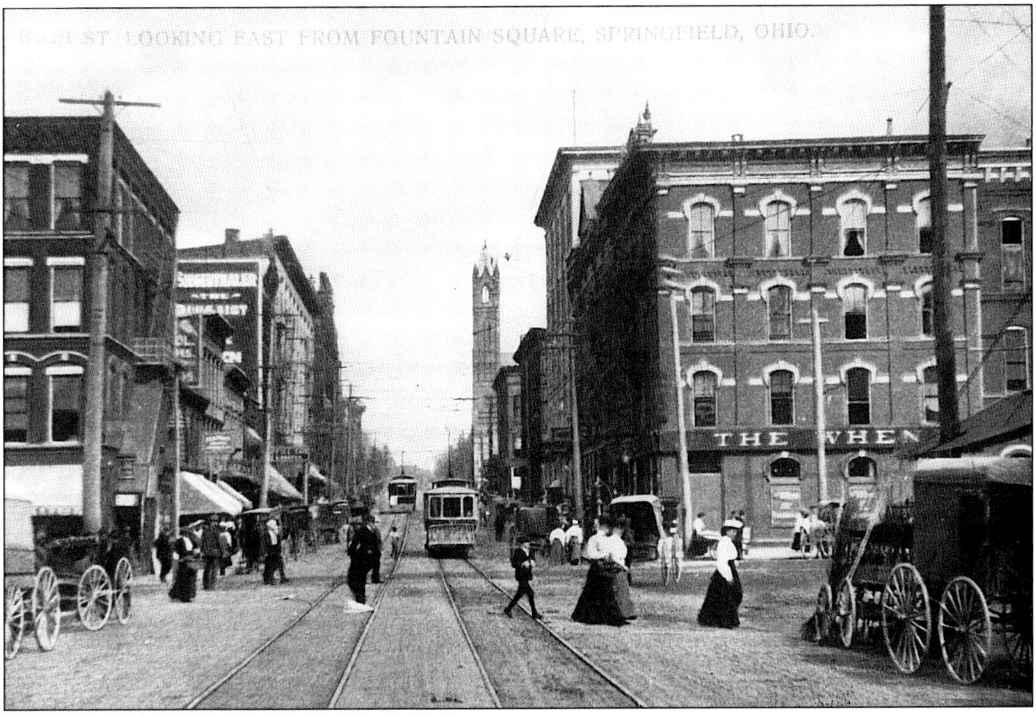

A STREET VIEW, LOOKING EAST ON HIGH STREET, c. 1908. This view from Fountain Square shows the Arcade on the right and St. Raphael's Catholic Church in the background.

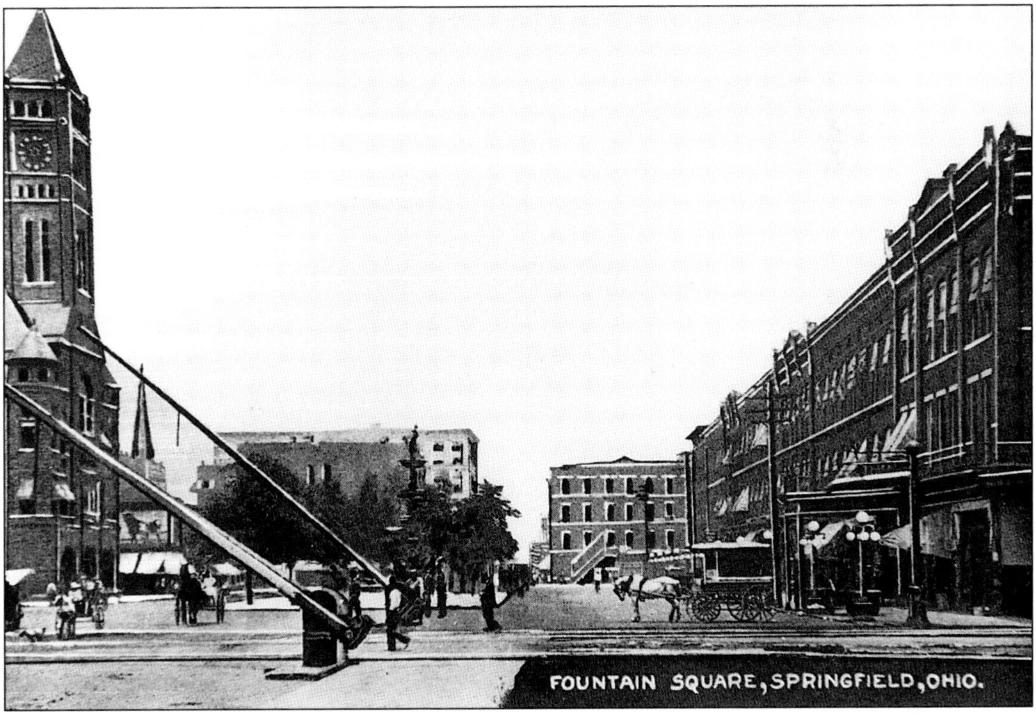

FOUNTAIN SQUARE, EARLY 1900. The structures on the left side of the photo are the crossing gates at the railroad and interurban tracks on Washington Street and Fountain Avenue.

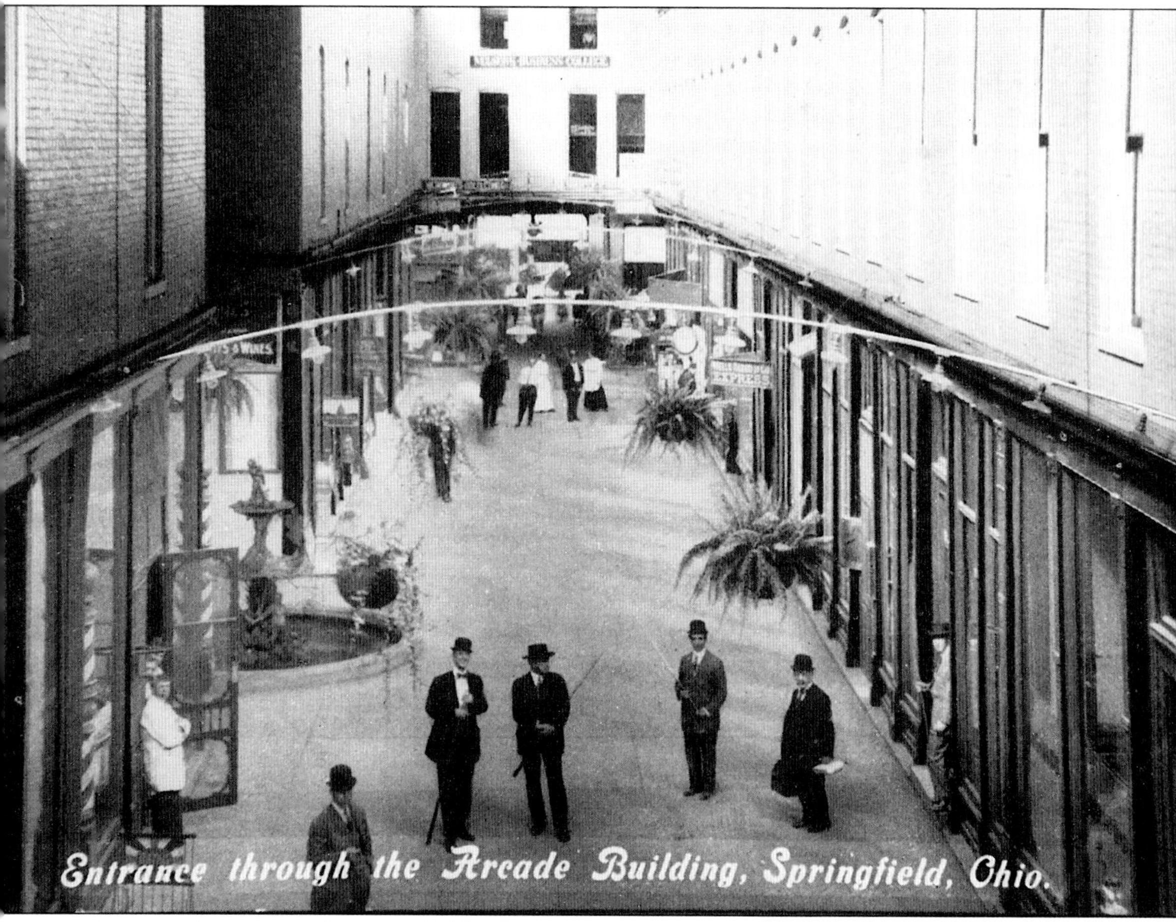

ARCADE CONCOURSE AREA, C. 1910. This concourse area included a fountain with large goldfish.

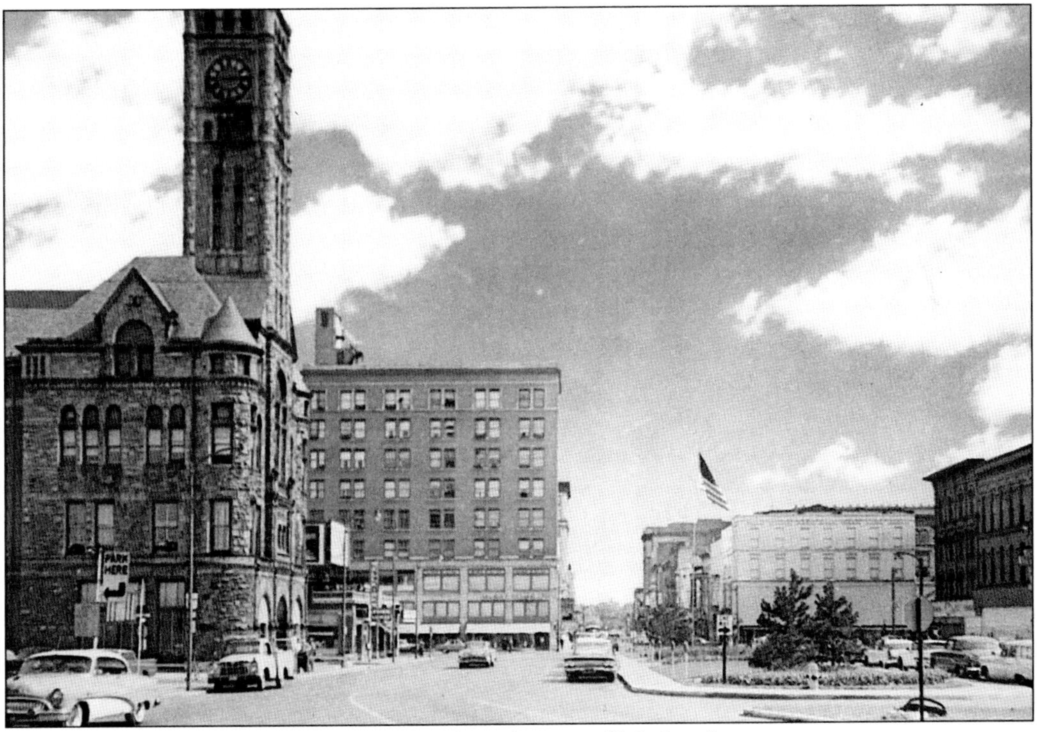

OLD CITY HALL, 1960S. This is the modern-day site of Marketplace.

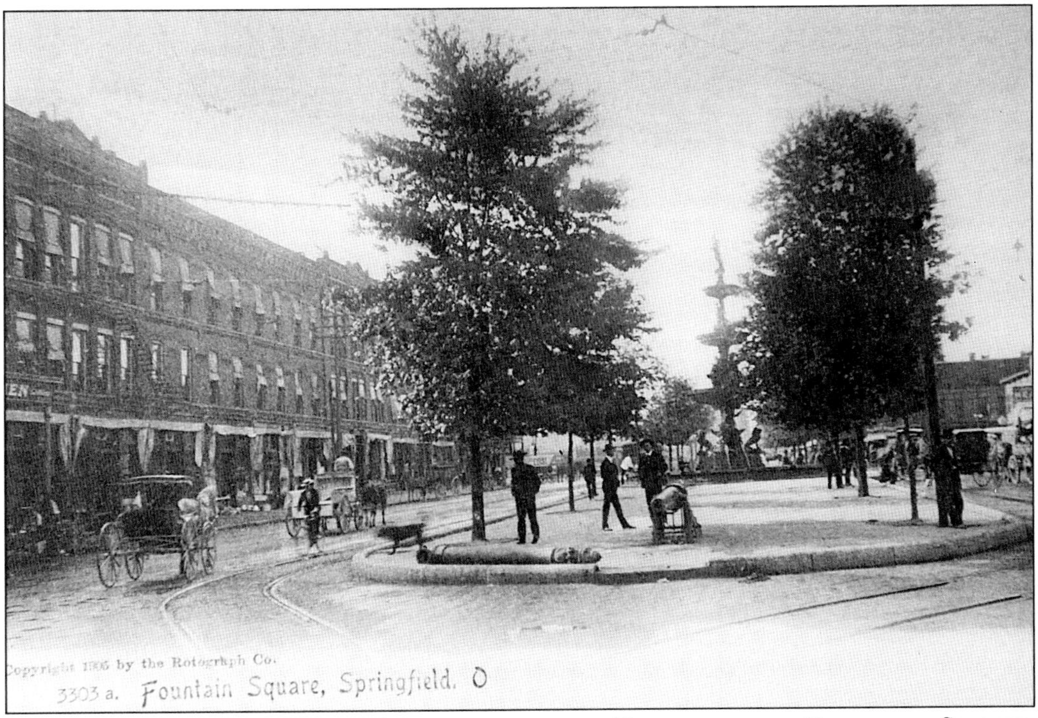

TROLLEY CARS AND BUGGIES SURROUNDING THE ESPLANADE AT FOUNTAIN SQUARE, EARLY 1900S.

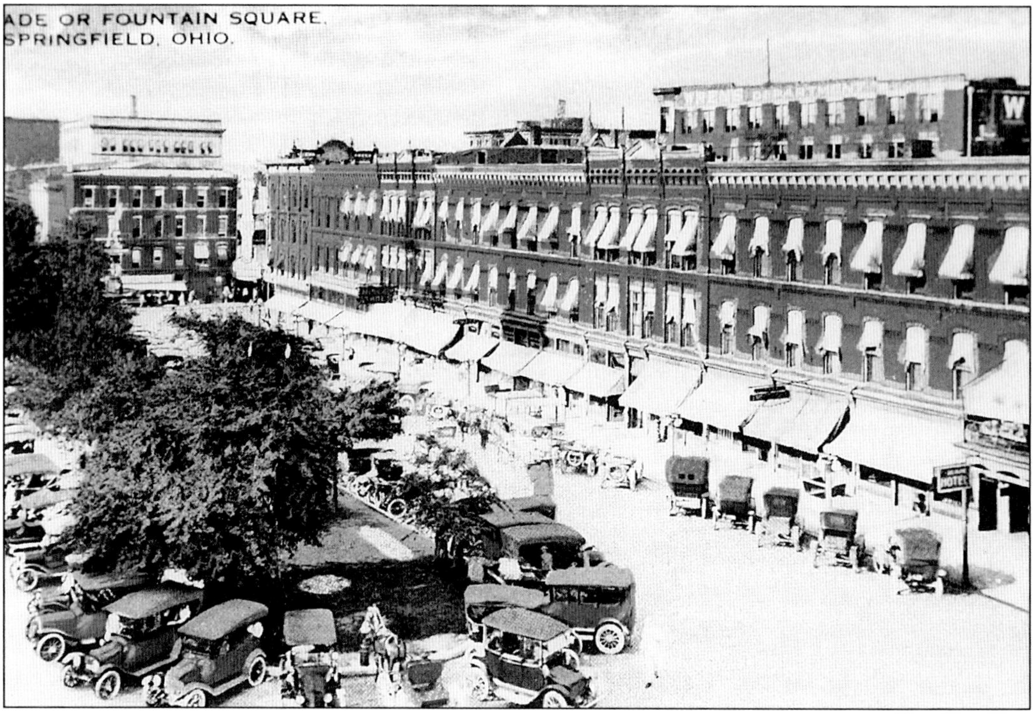

ARCADE, EARLY 1920S. This view shows the Esplanade crowded with early autos and a few buggies and horses.

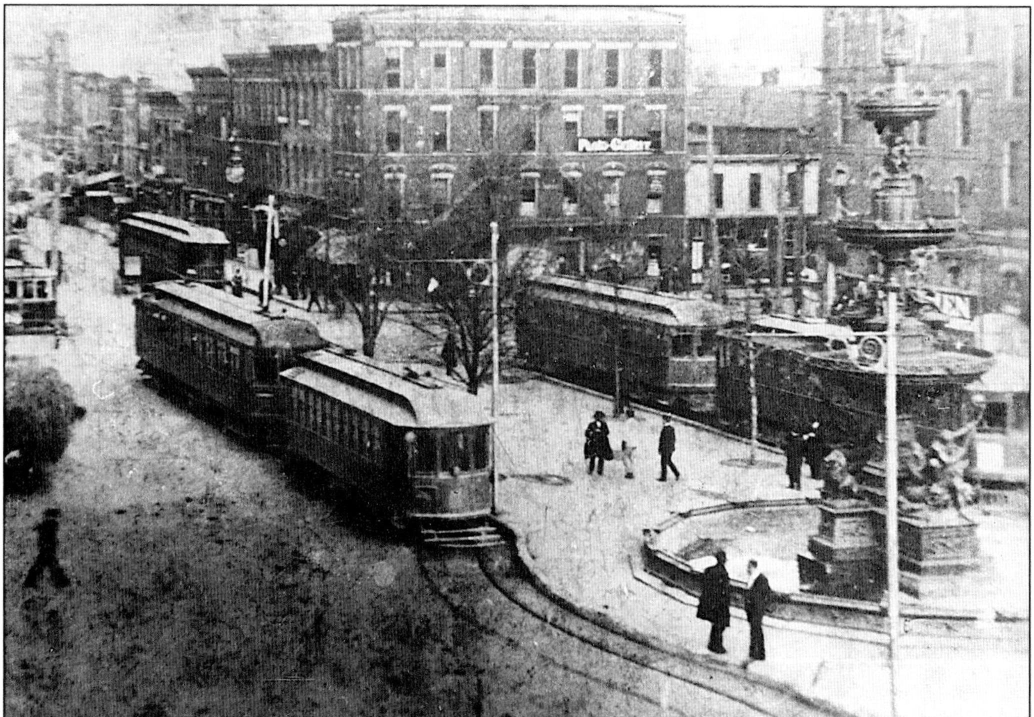

THE ESPLANADE WITH TRACTION CARS ON BOTH SIDES, C. 1910.

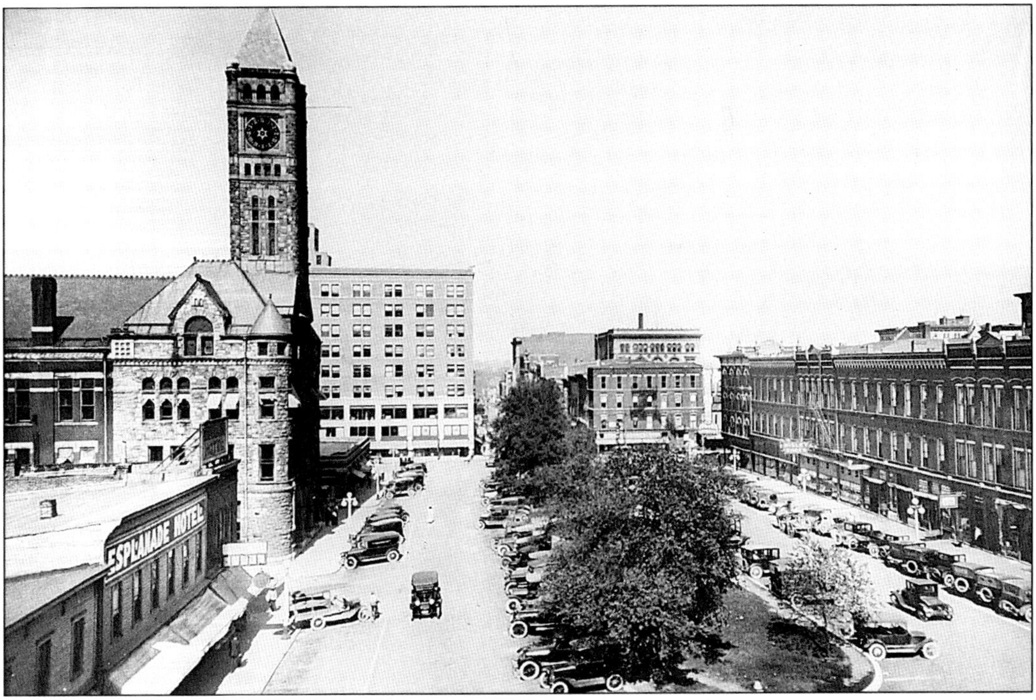

View from Washington Street Looking North at the Esplanade in the Center, Early 1920s. On the right is the Arcade; the old City Hall is on the left. The Esplanade Hotel is pictured on South Market Street.

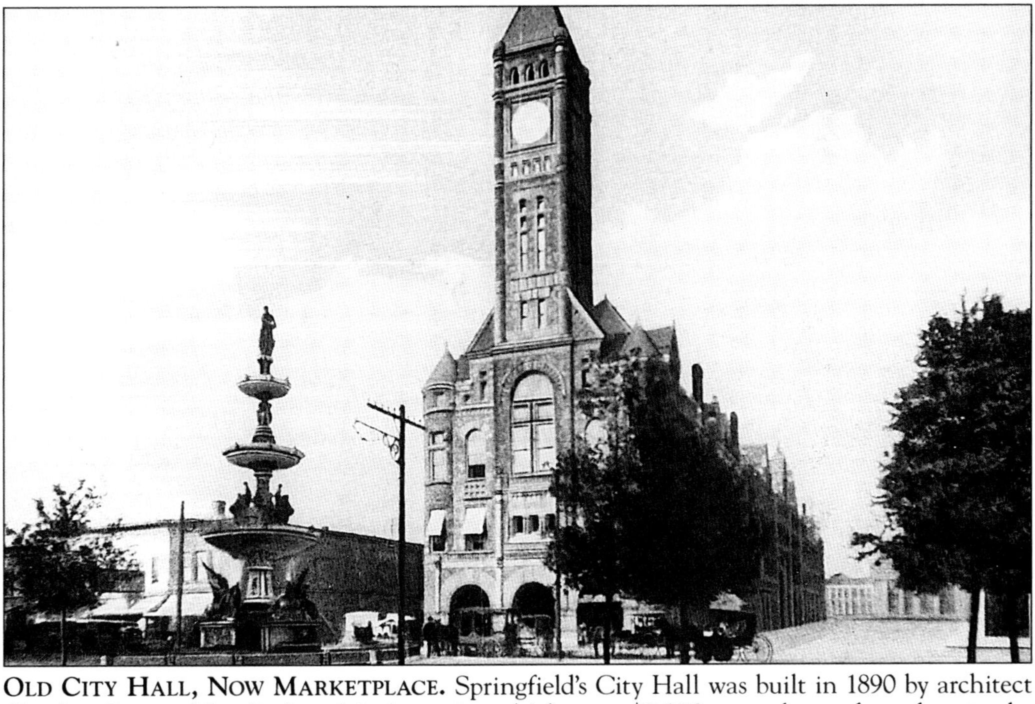

Old City Hall, Now Marketplace. Springfield's City Hall was built in 1890 by architect Charles Cregar. The Esplanade's fountain, which cost $8,000, was donated to the city by Oliver Kelly.

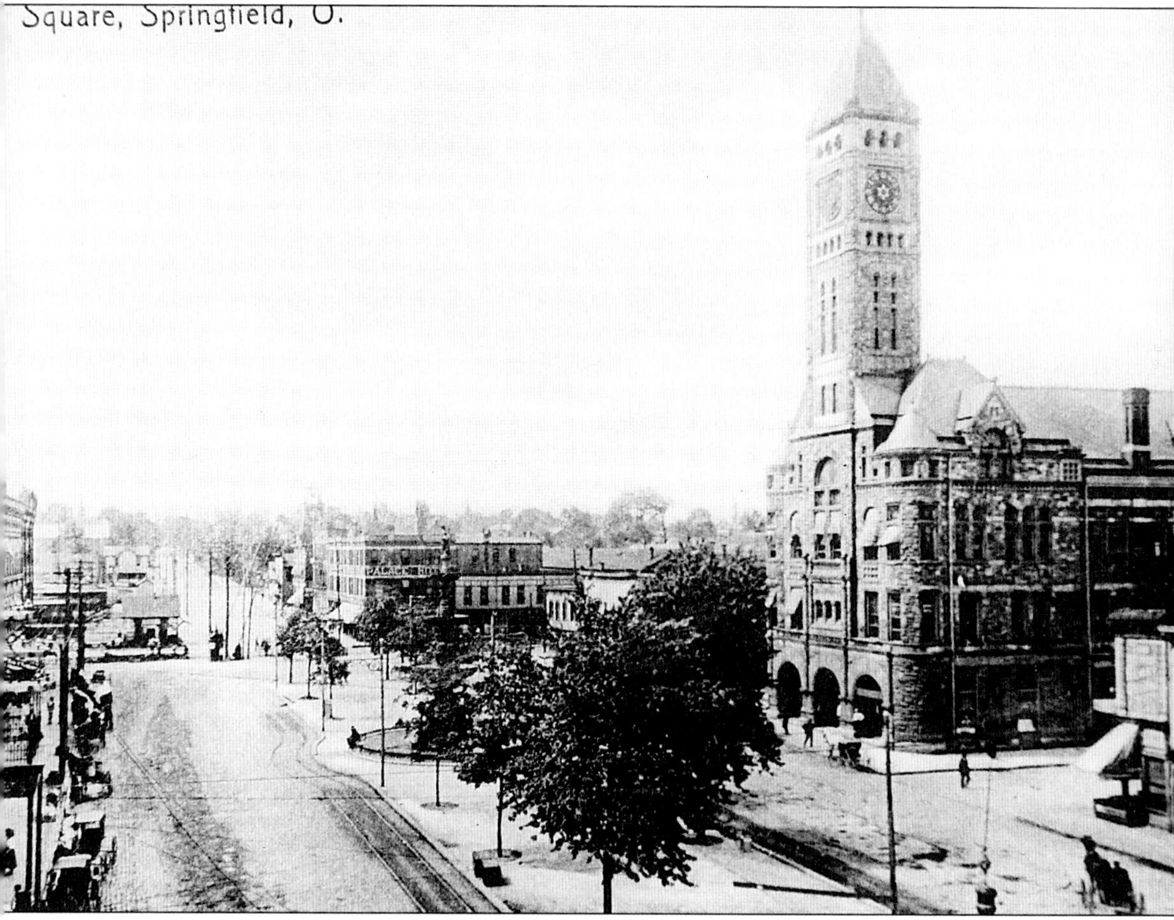

The Esplanade, c. 1910. City Hall appears on the right, and there was a hotel and restaurant where Elderly United is located today.

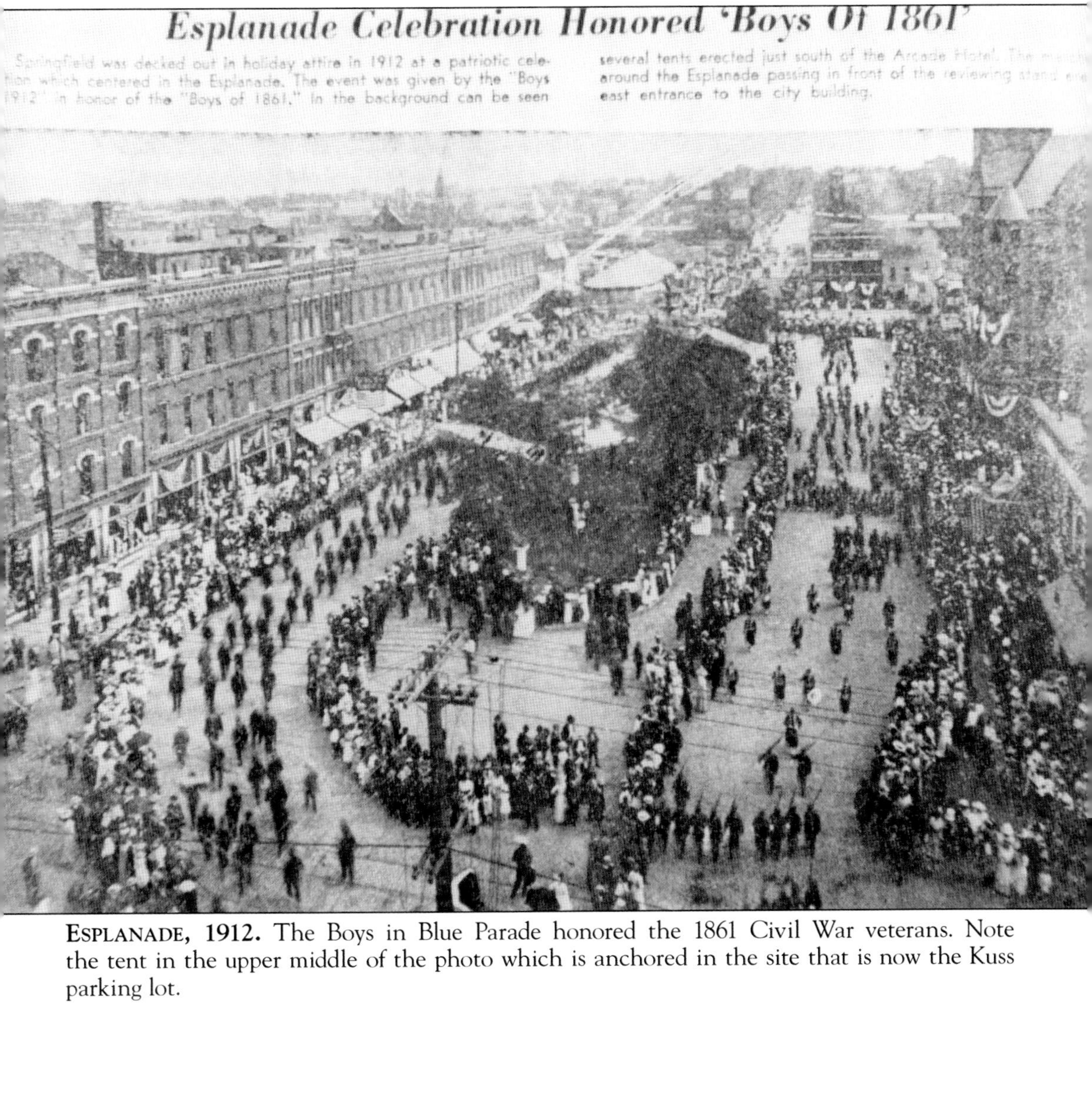

Esplanade Celebration Honored 'Boys Of 1861'

Springfield was decked out in holiday attire in 1912 at a patriotic celebration which centered in the Esplanade. The event was given by the "Boys 1912" in honor of the "Boys of 1861." In the background can be seen several tents erected just south of the Arcade Hotel. The [illegible] around the Esplanade passing in front of the reviewing stand [illegible] east entrance to the city building.

ESPLANADE, 1912. The Boys in Blue Parade honored the 1861 Civil War veterans. Note the tent in the upper middle of the photo which is anchored in the site that is now the Kuss parking lot.

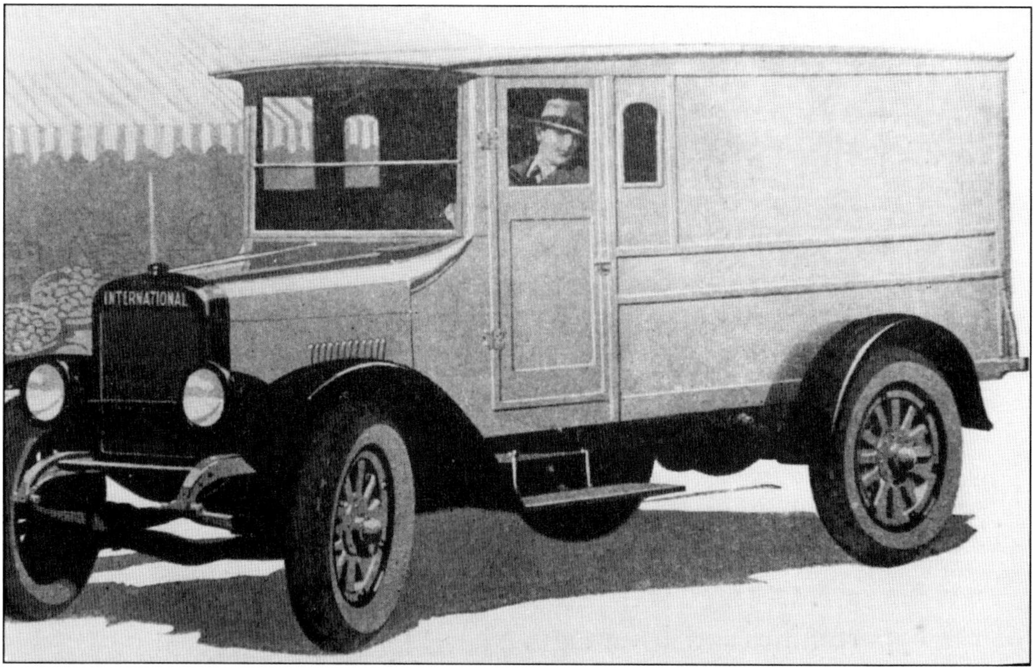

INTERNATIONAL HARVESTER SPEED TRUCK, 1920S.

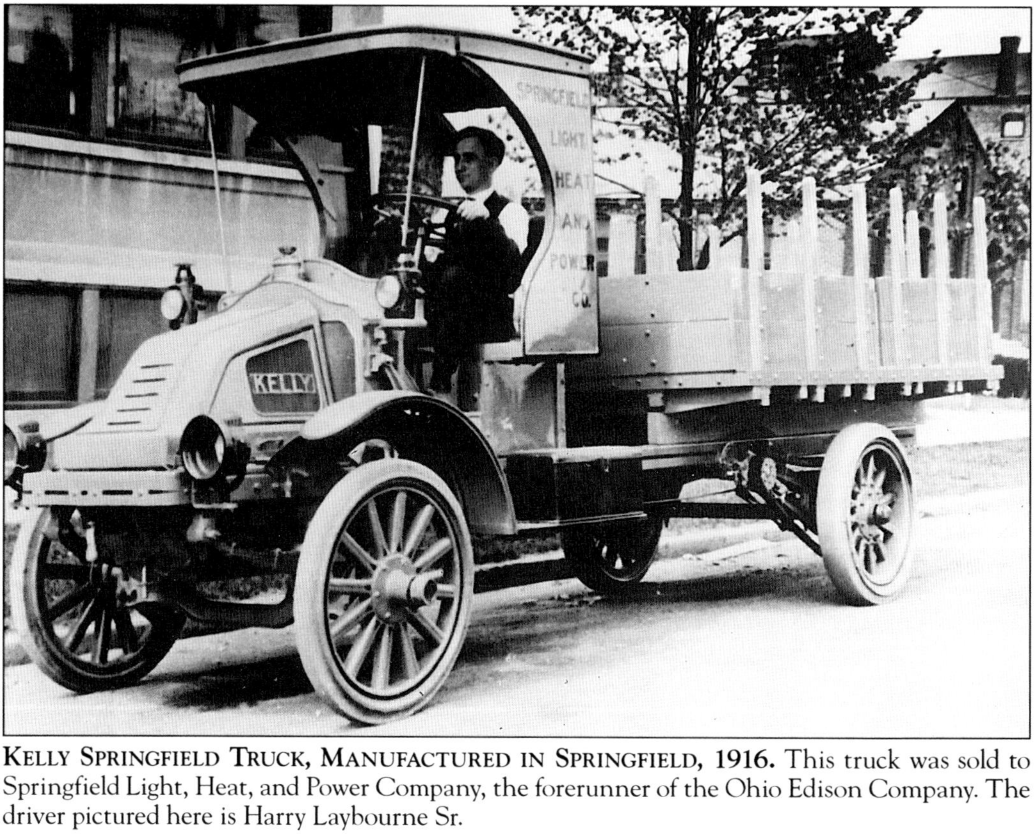

KELLY SPRINGFIELD TRUCK, MANUFACTURED IN SPRINGFIELD, 1916. This truck was sold to Springfield Light, Heat, and Power Company, the forerunner of the Ohio Edison Company. The driver pictured here is Harry Laybourne Sr.

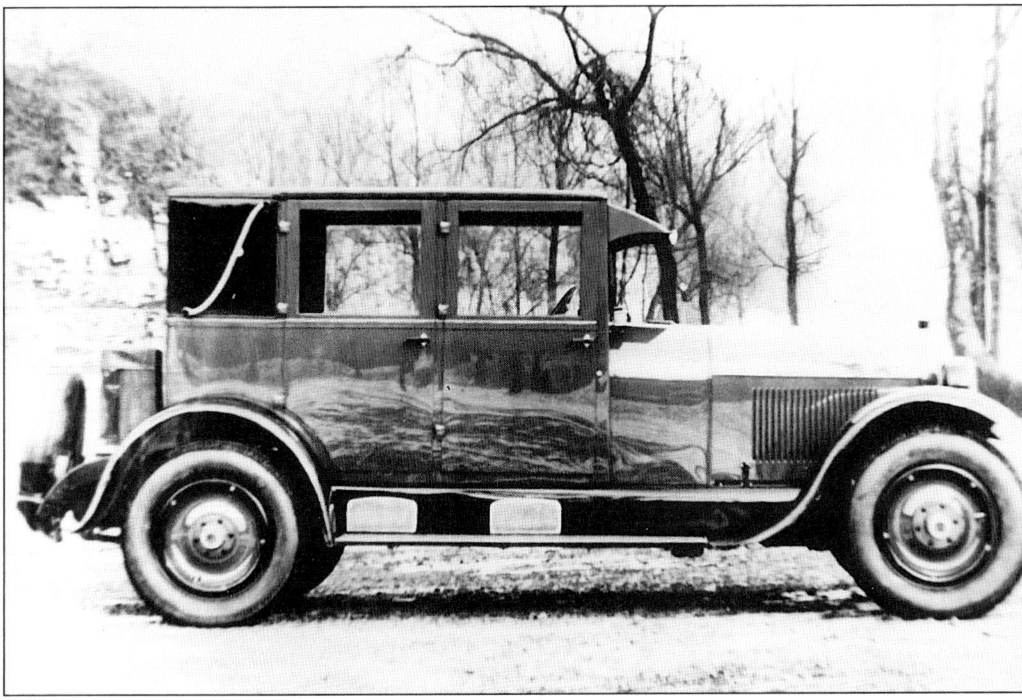

WESTCOTT AUTOMOBILE, 1920. These famous cars were made in Springfield from 1916 to 1923.

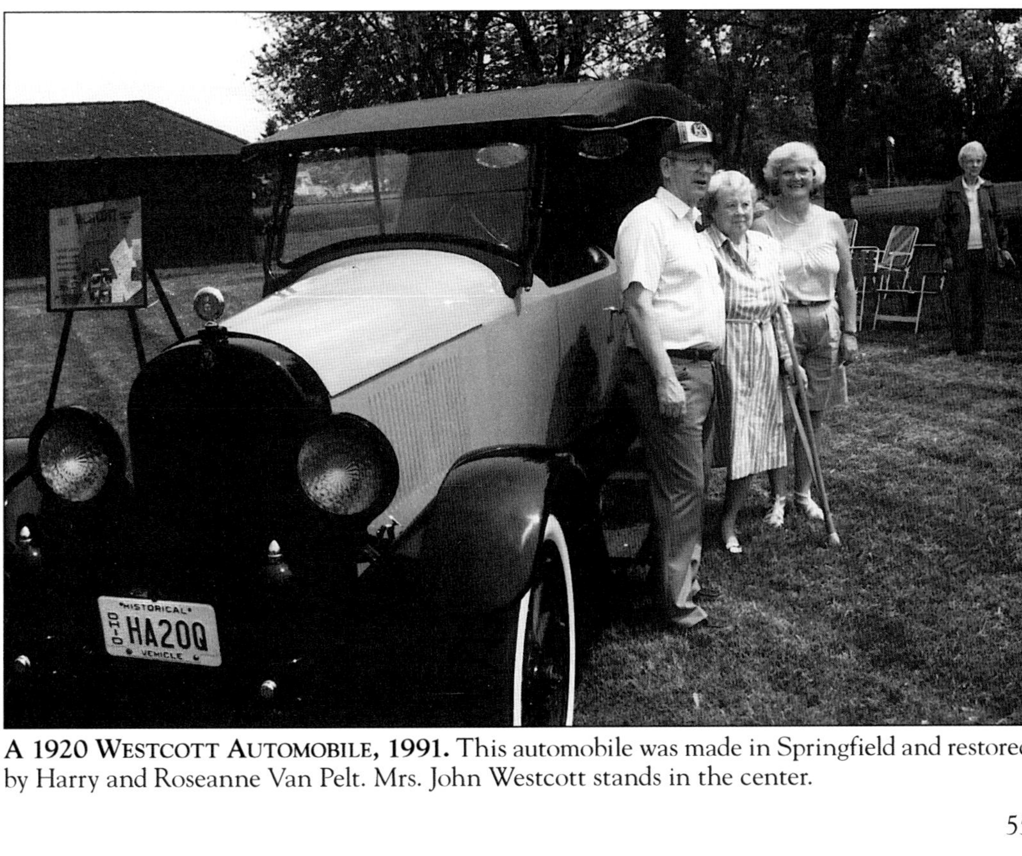

A 1920 WESTCOTT AUTOMOBILE, 1991. This automobile was made in Springfield and restored by Harry and Roseanne Van Pelt. Mrs. John Westcott stands in the center.

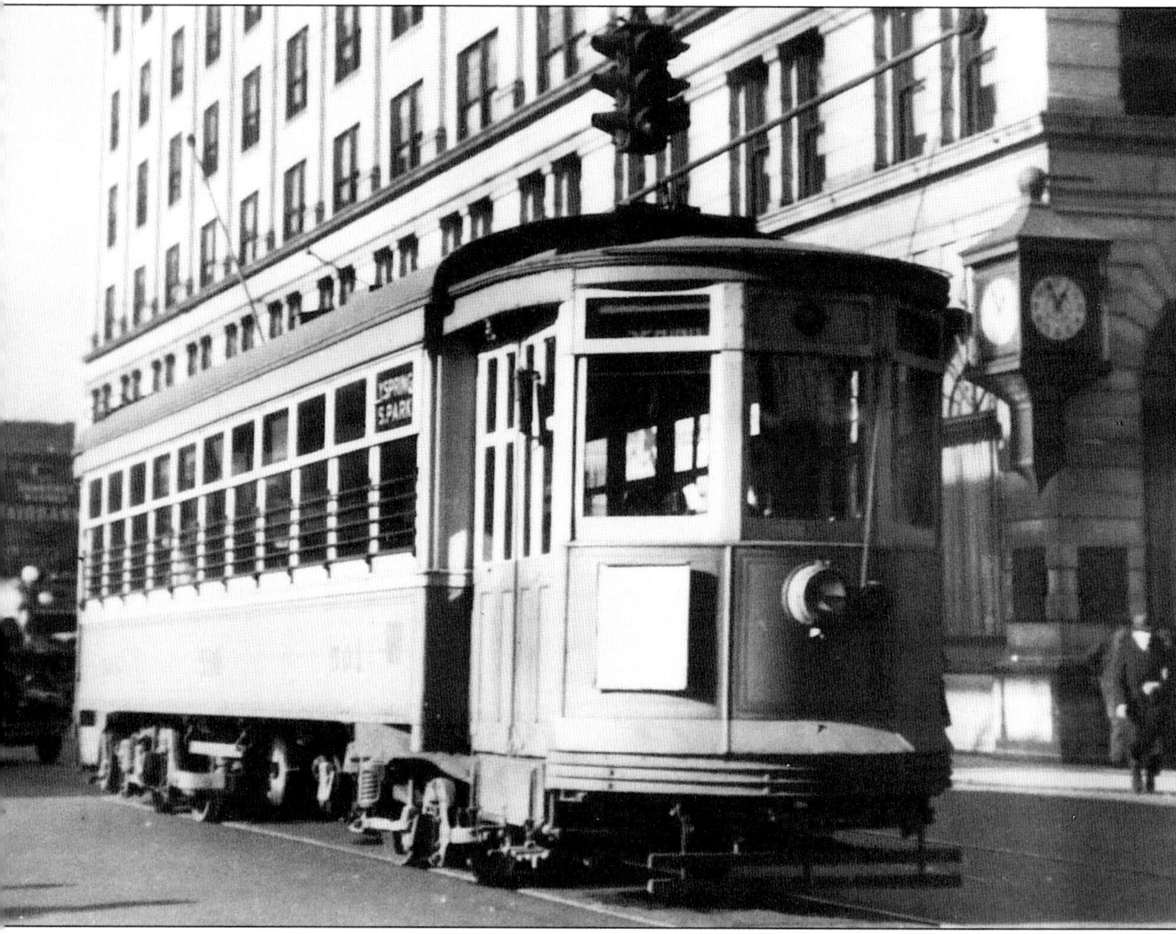

TROLLEY CAR USED IN SPRINGFIELD, EARLY 1930S. The First National Bank is in the background on the corner of Main Street and Fountain Avenue.

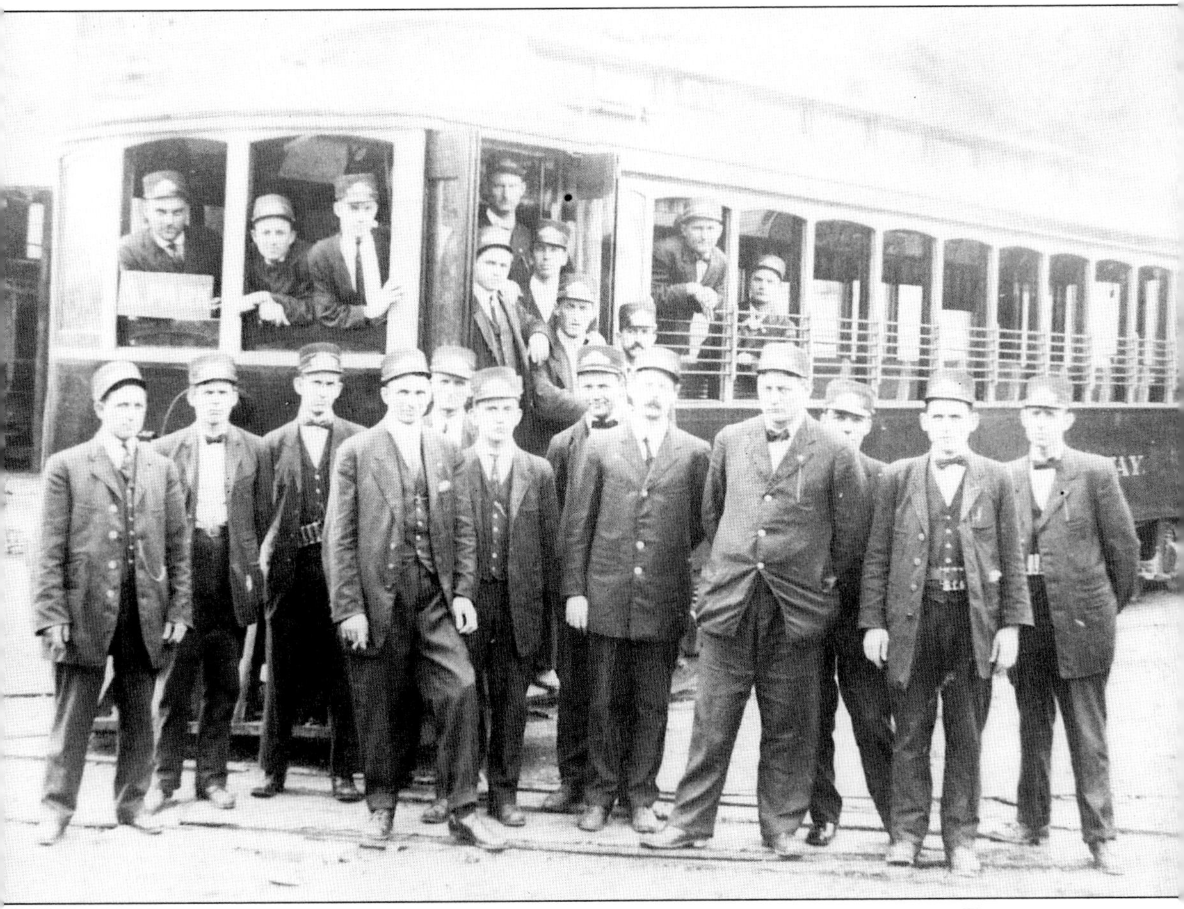

A GATHERING OF TROLLEY CAR CONDUCTORS DEMONSTRATING ONE OF THE TROLLEYS IN USE IN DOWNTOWN SPRINGFIELD, 1920S.

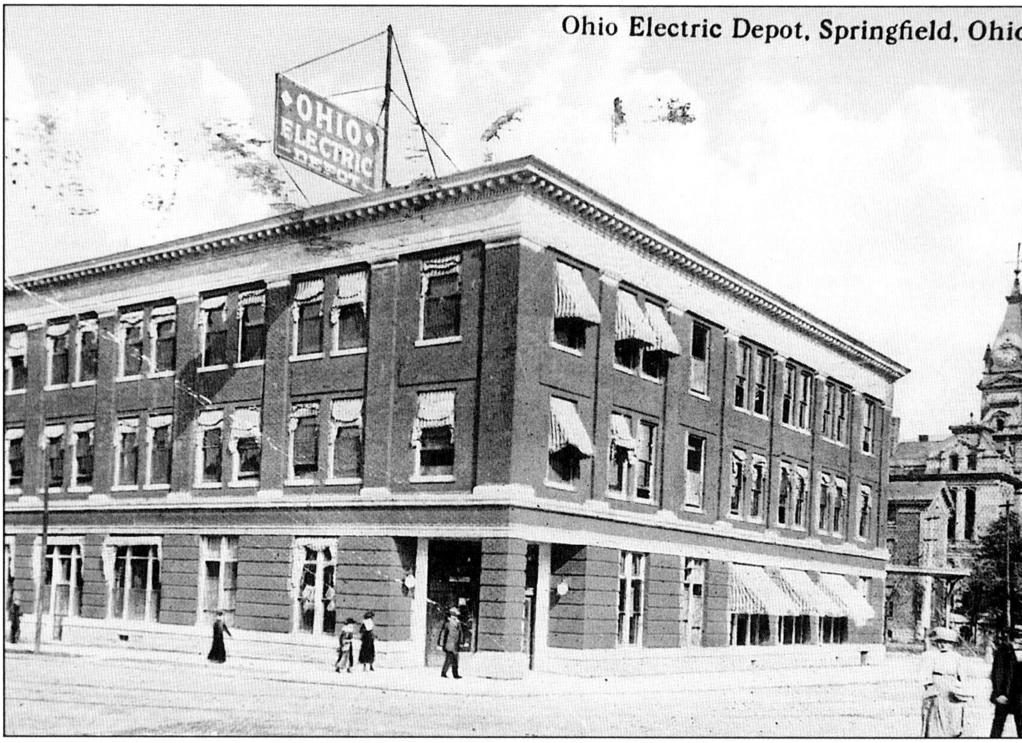

OHIO ELECTRIC DEPOT, LOCATED ON THE NORTHEAST CORNER OF COLUMBIA STREET AND NORTH FOUNTAIN AVENUE, 1915. The old courthouse stands in the background.

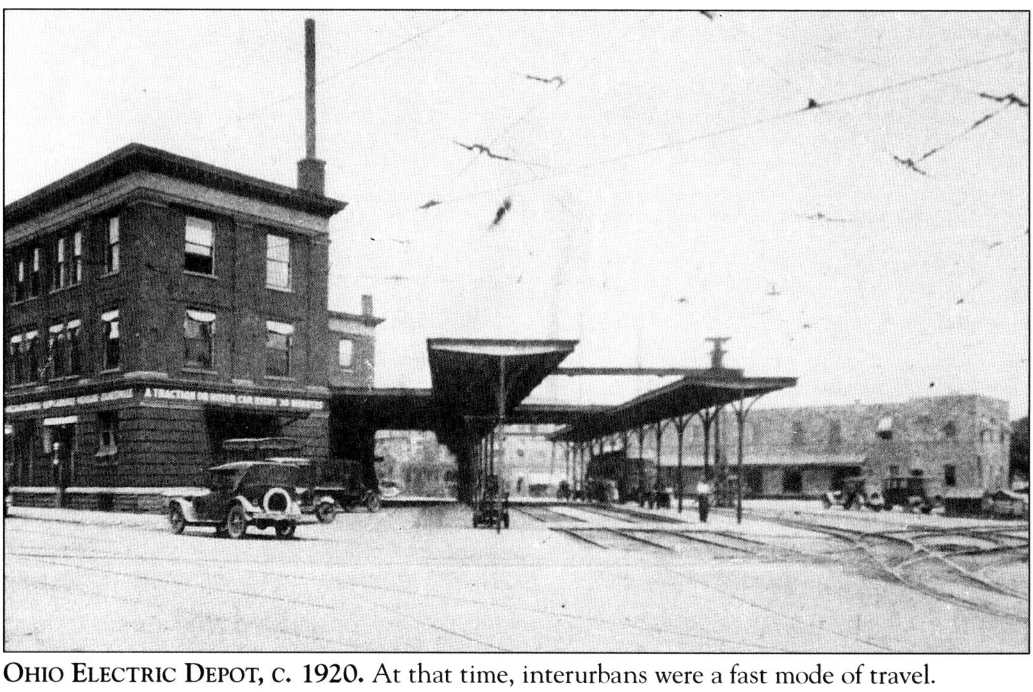

OHIO ELECTRIC DEPOT, C. 1920. At that time, interurbans were a fast mode of travel.

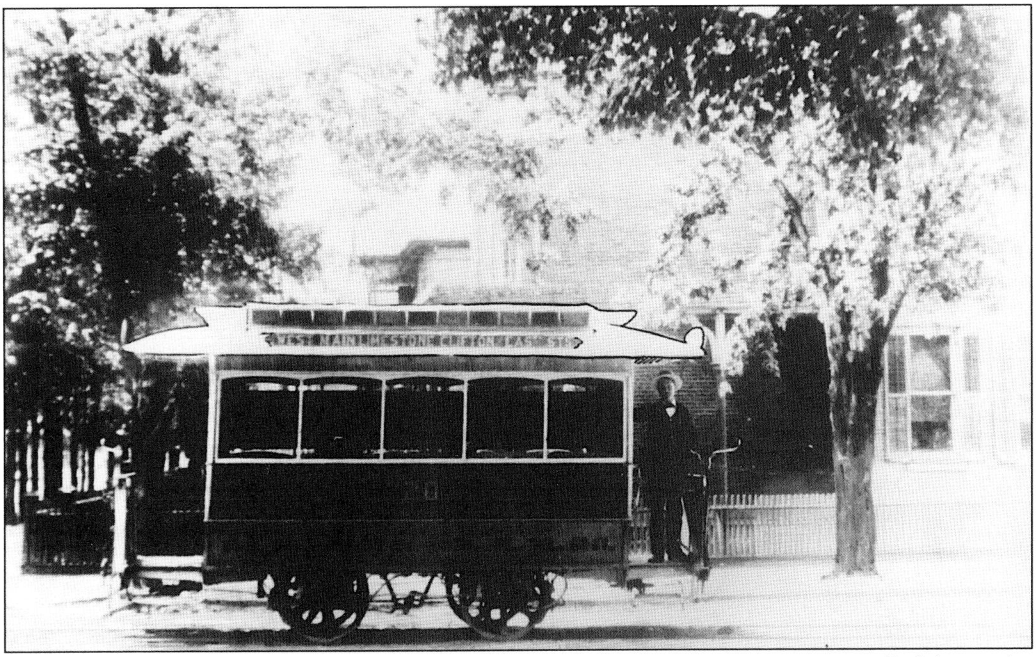

A Turn-of-the-Century Trolley Car. This vehicle could have been pulled by mules or horses.

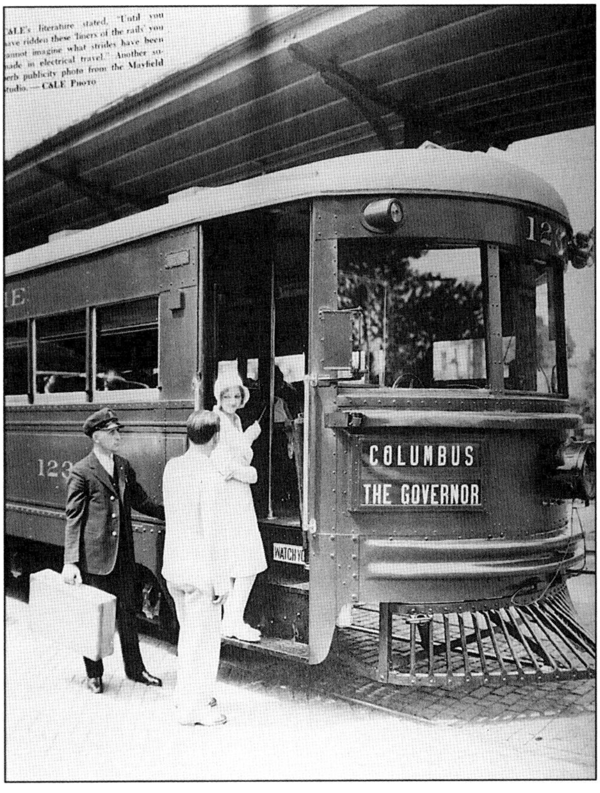

Passengers Boarding the C and LE Traction Car at the Old Ohio Electric Depot.

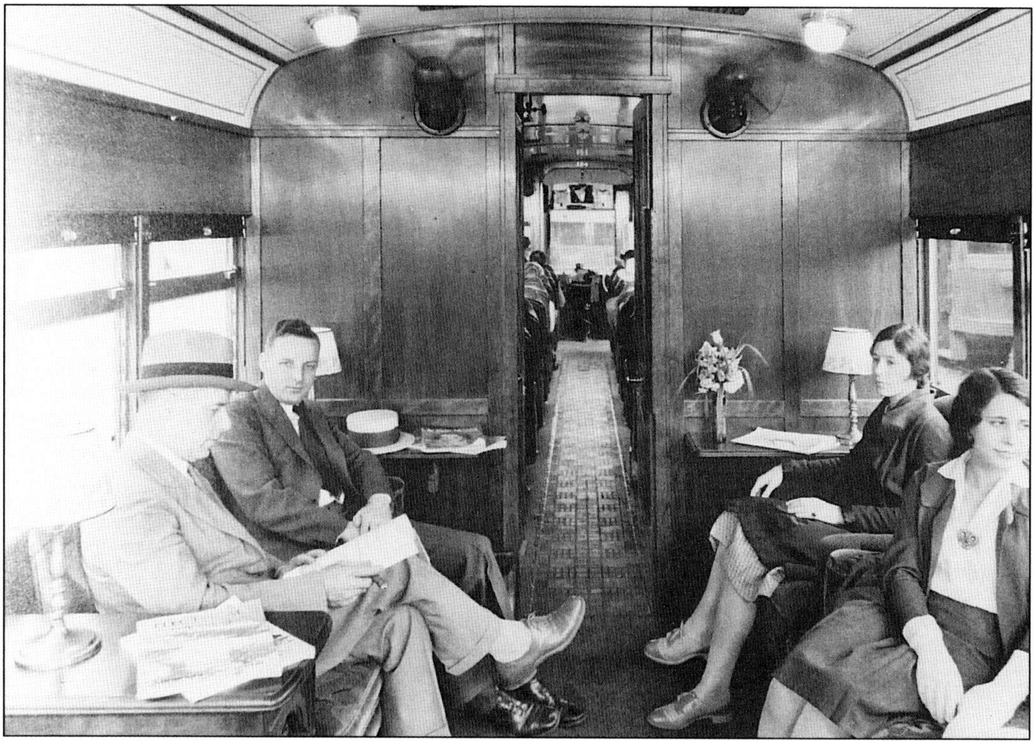

INTERIOR OF THE LOUNGE CAR OF THE FAST INTERURBAN TRACTION CARS, C. 1930S.

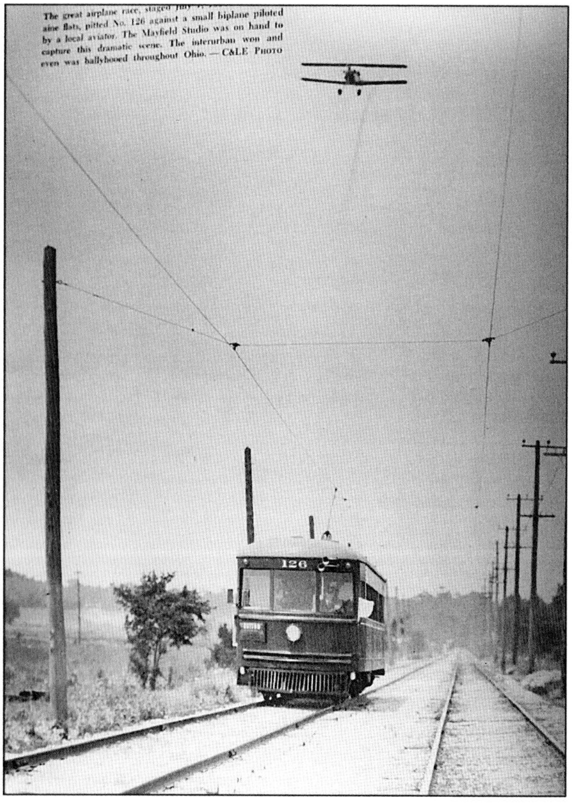

THE GREAT AIRPLANE RACE, JULY 7, 1930. To demonstrate its incredible speed, the C and LE traction car raced a small biplane in the Moraine (Dayton) area. The traction car won.

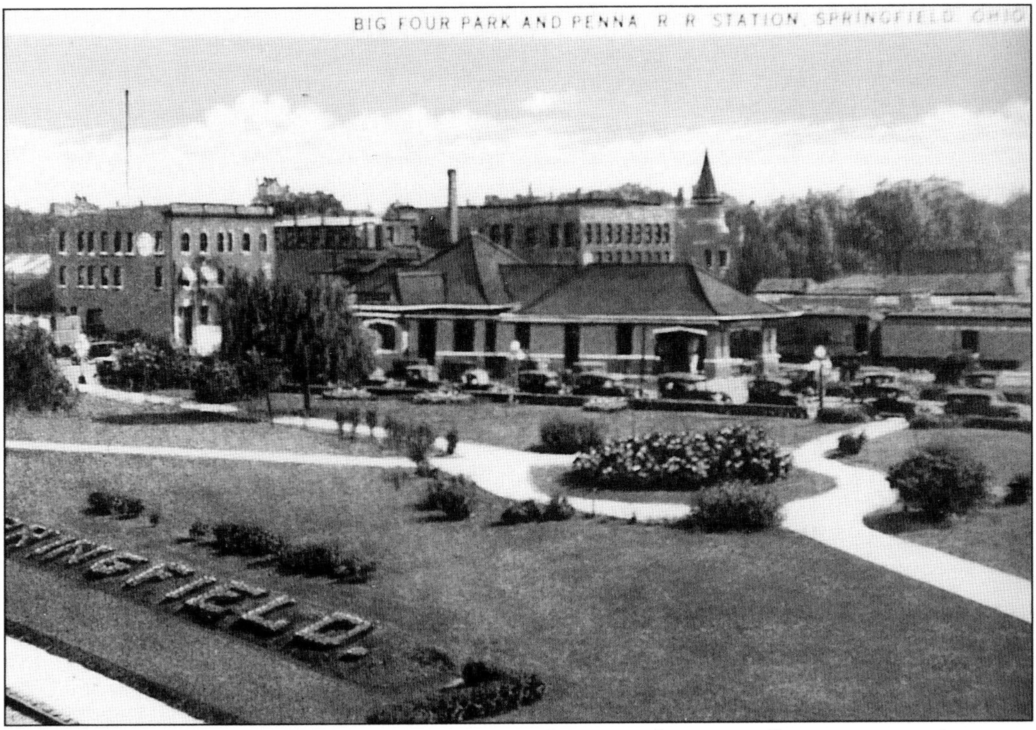

BIG FOUR PARK AND PENNSYLVANIA RAILROAD STATION, LOCATED SOUTH OF THE ARCADE, C. 1920S. This is the modern site of Clark State's Kuss Center.

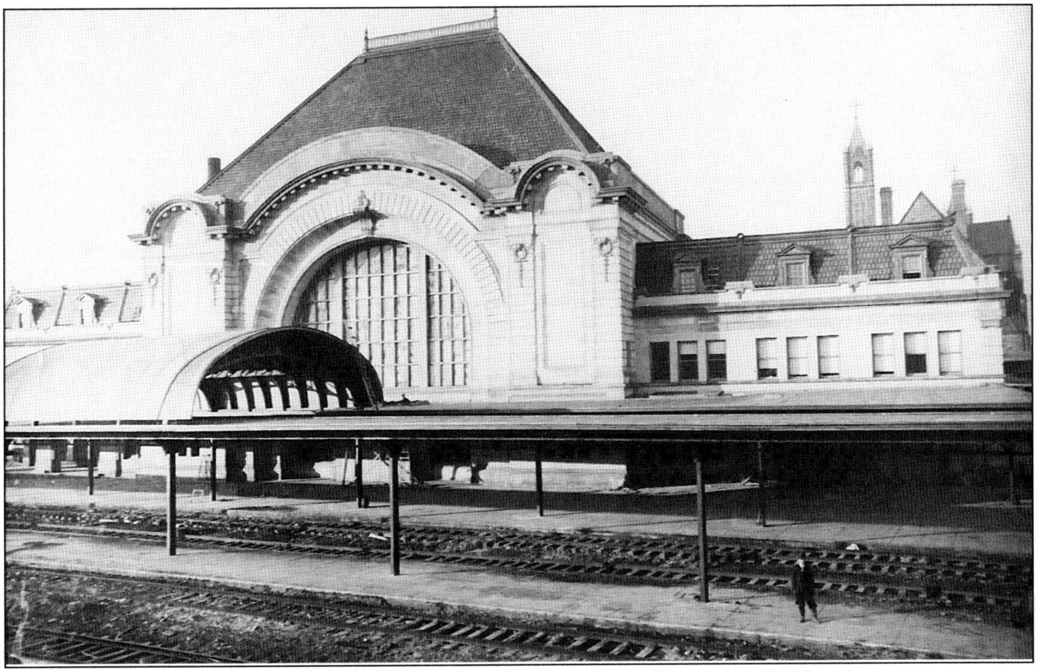

BIG FOUR NEW YORK CENTRAL DEPOT, 1940S. From 1911 to 1969, the depot operated at this location on Washington Street. This view was taken from the south side looking north, showing St. Raphael's Church in the background.

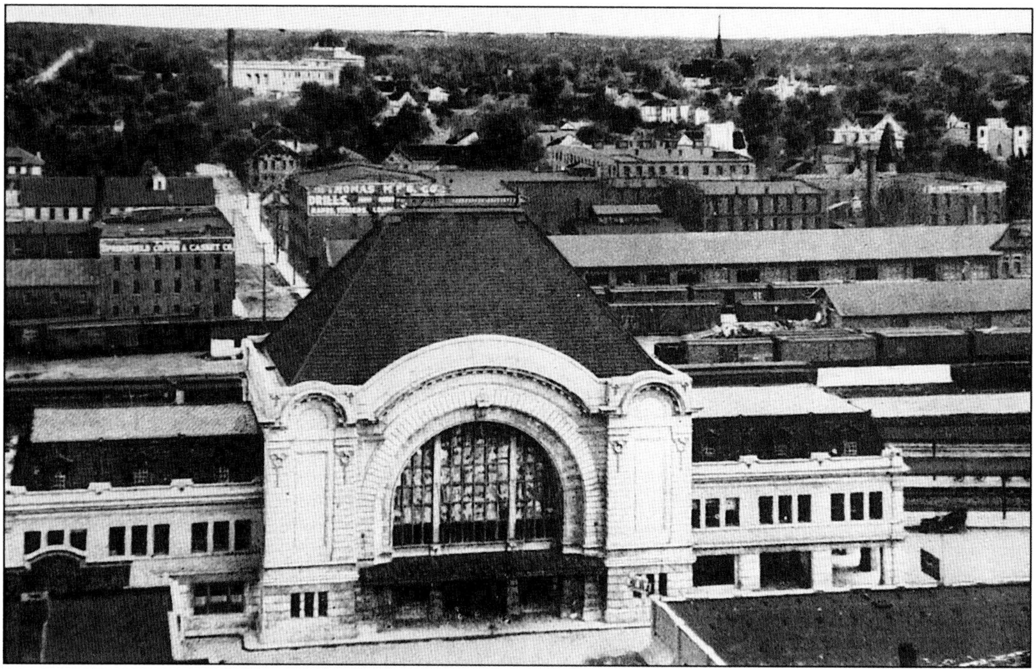

BIG FOUR NEW YORK CENTRAL DEPOT ON WASHINGTON STREET. Forty trains made their way in and out of the depot each day.

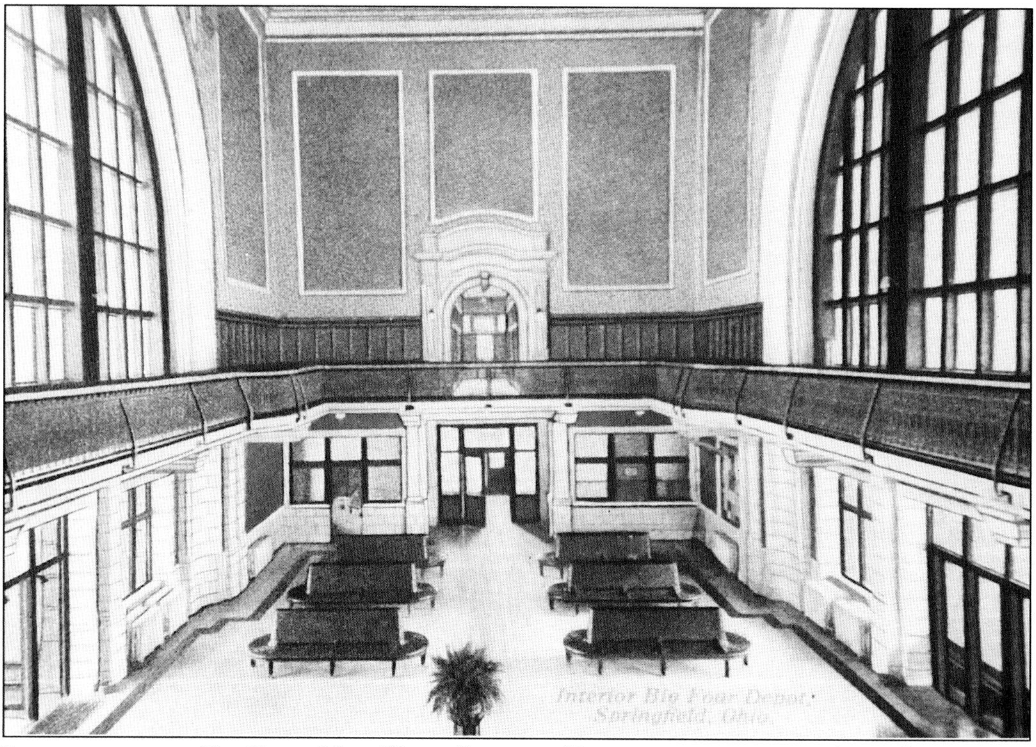

INTERIOR OF THE BIG FOUR NEW YORK CENTRAL DEPOT, C. 1920. Many farewells were said in this lobby during the wars.

Two

HOMES

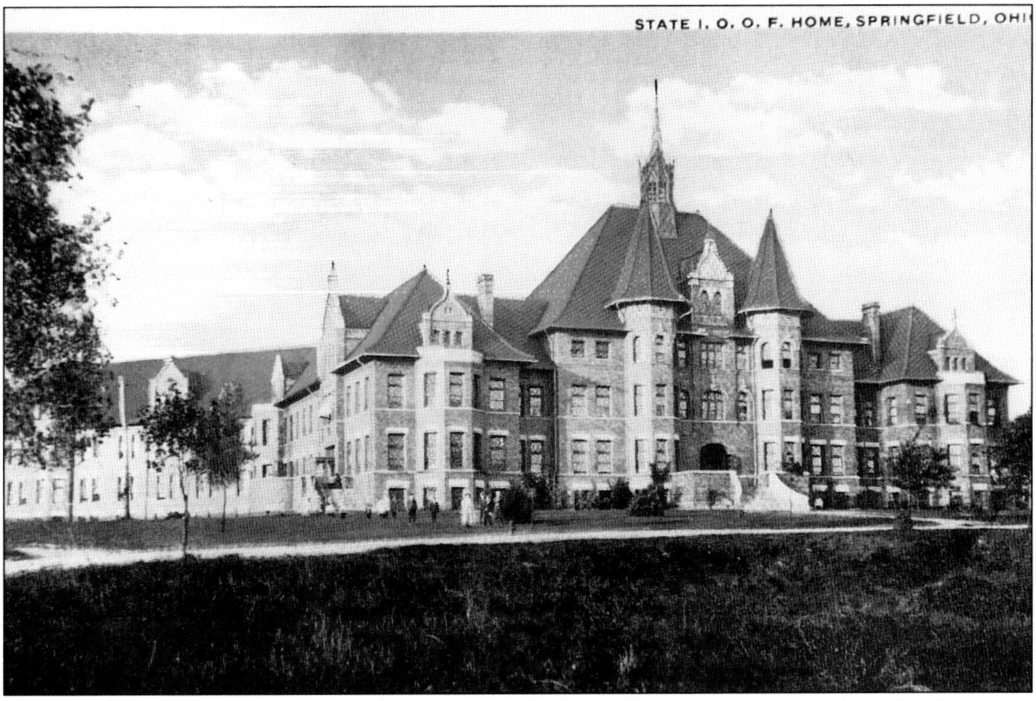

IOOF (INDEPENDENT ORDER OF ODD FELLOWS) HOME, LOCATED AT 404 EAST MCCREIGHT AVENUE. Dedicated on October 27, 1898, it was originally for homeless children and elderly members. Today it is a nursing home.

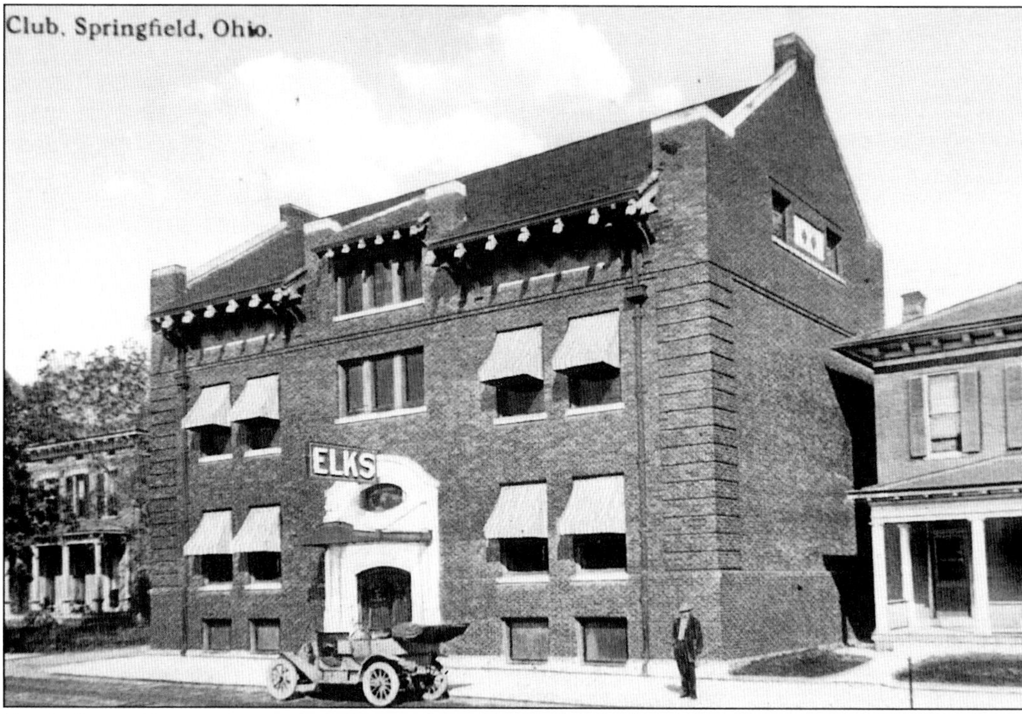

ELK'S CLUB, LOCATED AT 126 WEST HIGH STREET, 1920S.

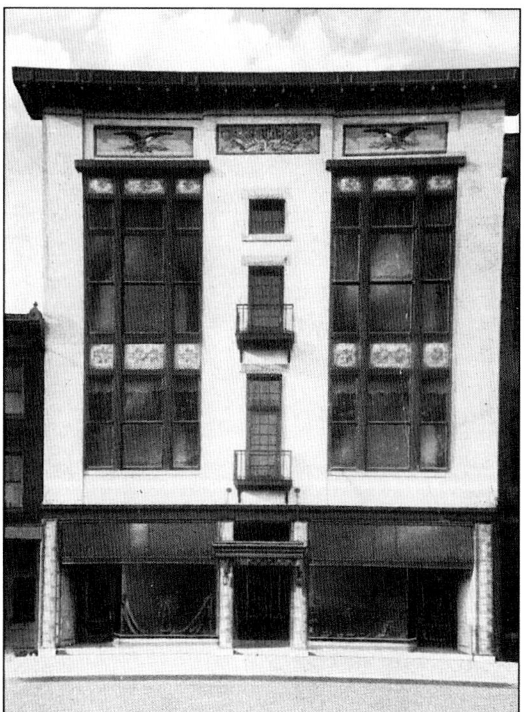

FRATERNAL ORDER OF EAGLES, LOCATED AT 137 1/2 WEST MAIN STREET, 1920S.

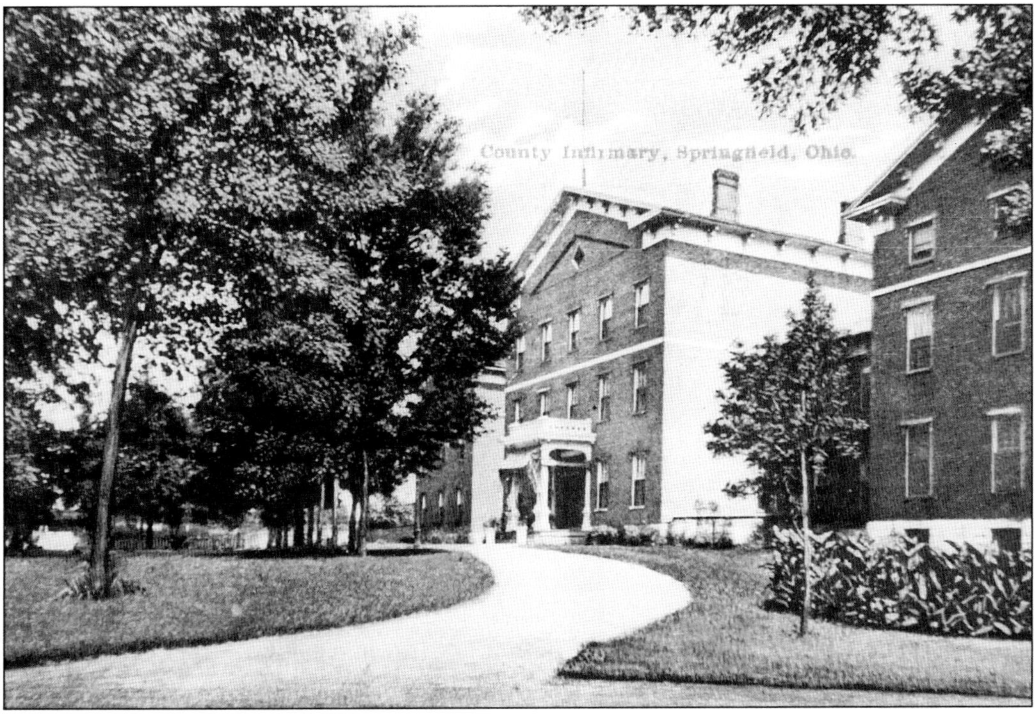

CLARK COUNTY INFIRMARY, LOCATED AT 1575 SNIDER ROAD AT THE INTERSECTION OF LOWER VALLEY PIKE, C. 1920.

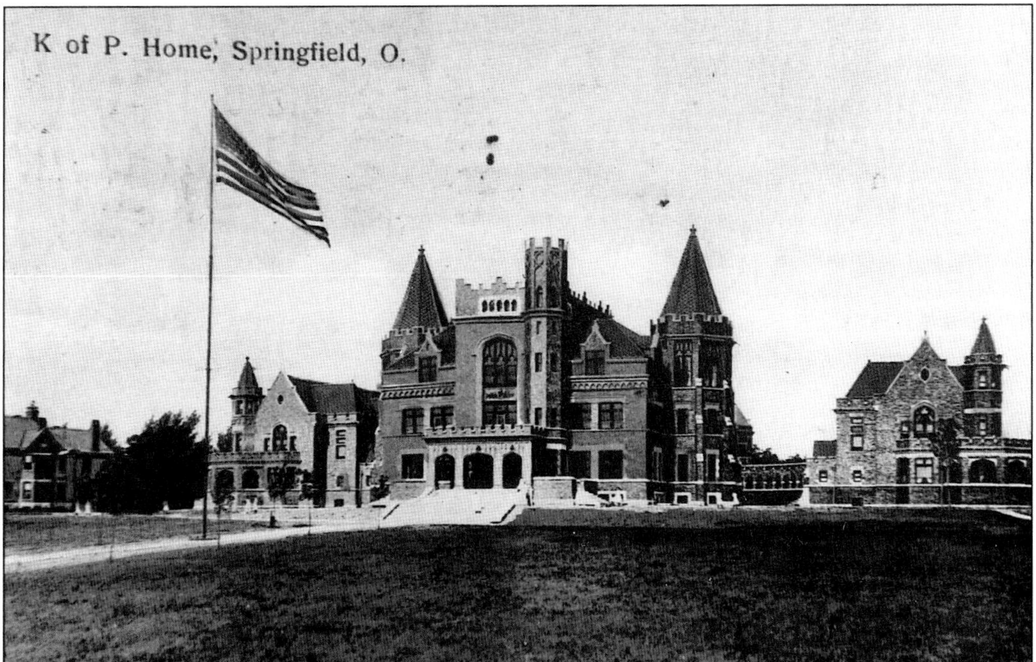

KNIGHTS OF PYTHIAS HOME, LOCATED AT 100 WEST MCCREIGHT AVENUE. Bought from the McCreight family for $25,000, its purpose was to take care of the members' homeless children. Today it is the site of St. John's Center nursing home.

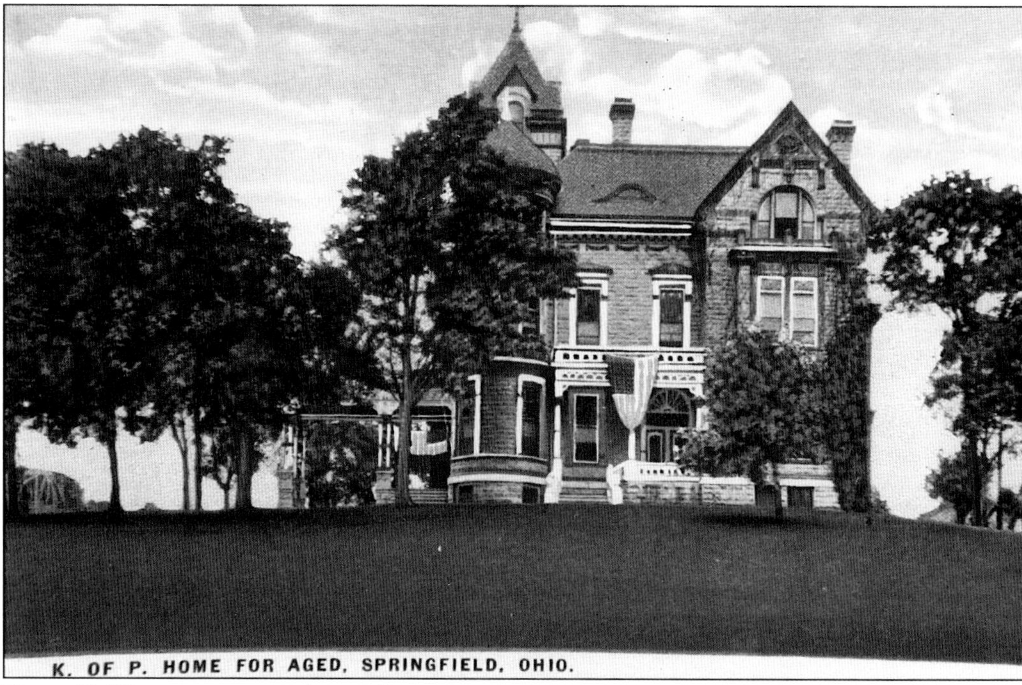

K. OF P. HOME FOR THE AGED, LOCATED AT 901 WEST HIGH STREET, C. 1920S. It was formerly the home of industrialist P.P. Mast.

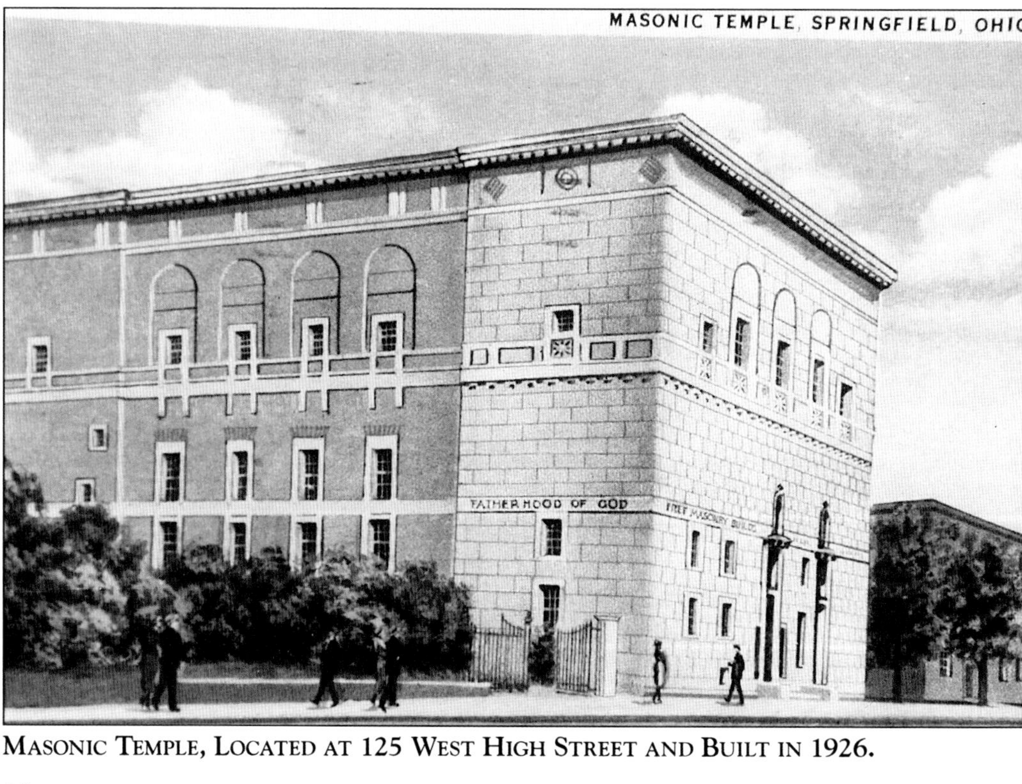

MASONIC TEMPLE, LOCATED AT 125 WEST HIGH STREET AND BUILT IN 1926.

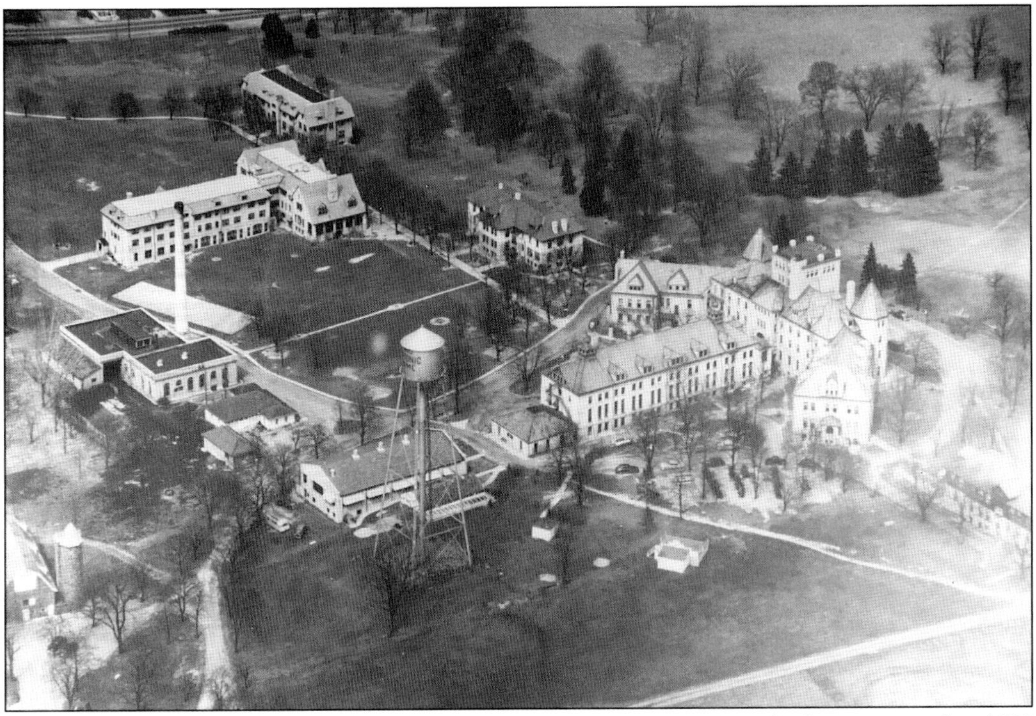

OHIO MASONIC HOME, LOCATED AT 2655 WEST NATIONAL ROAD. The home opened in 1897 as a place to care for the Masonic men and their wives.

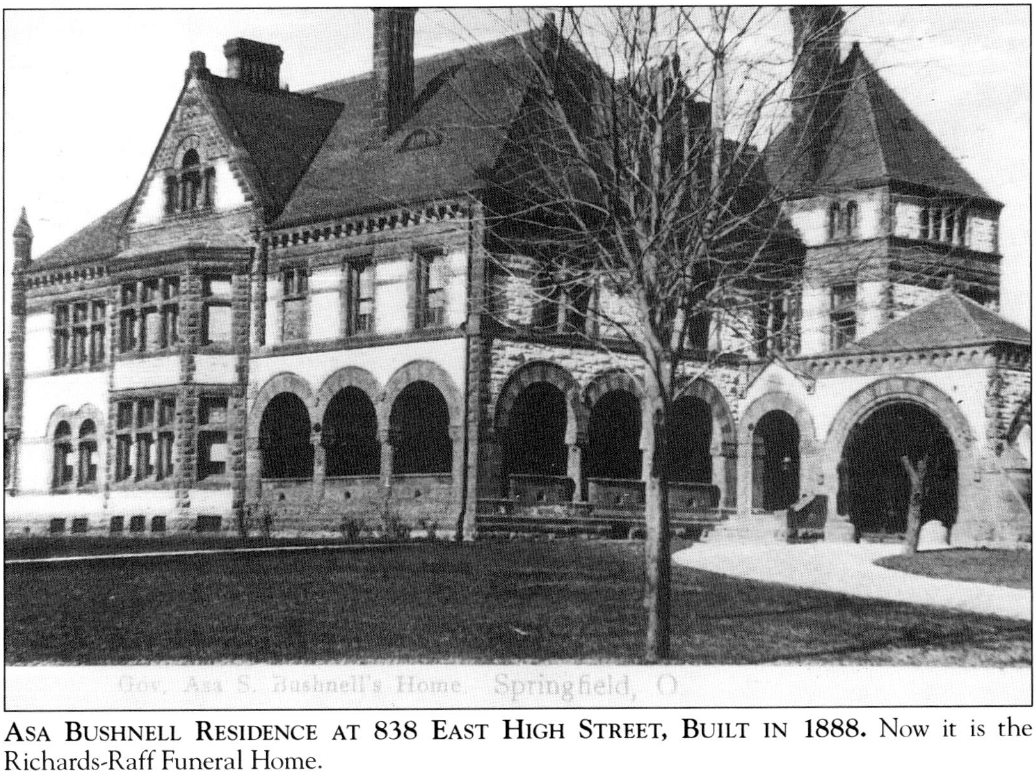

ASA BUSHNELL RESIDENCE AT 838 EAST HIGH STREET, BUILT IN 1888. Now it is the Richards-Raff Funeral Home.

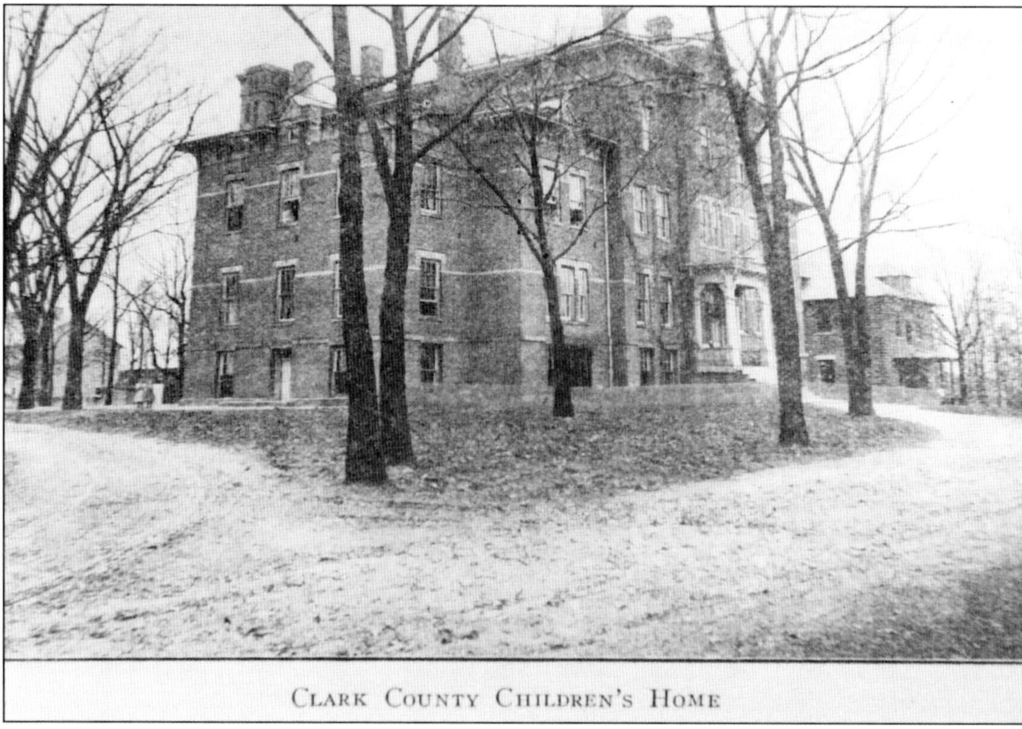

CLARK COUNTY CHILDREN'S HOME, LOCATED AT 525 EAST HOME ROAD, C. 1900S.

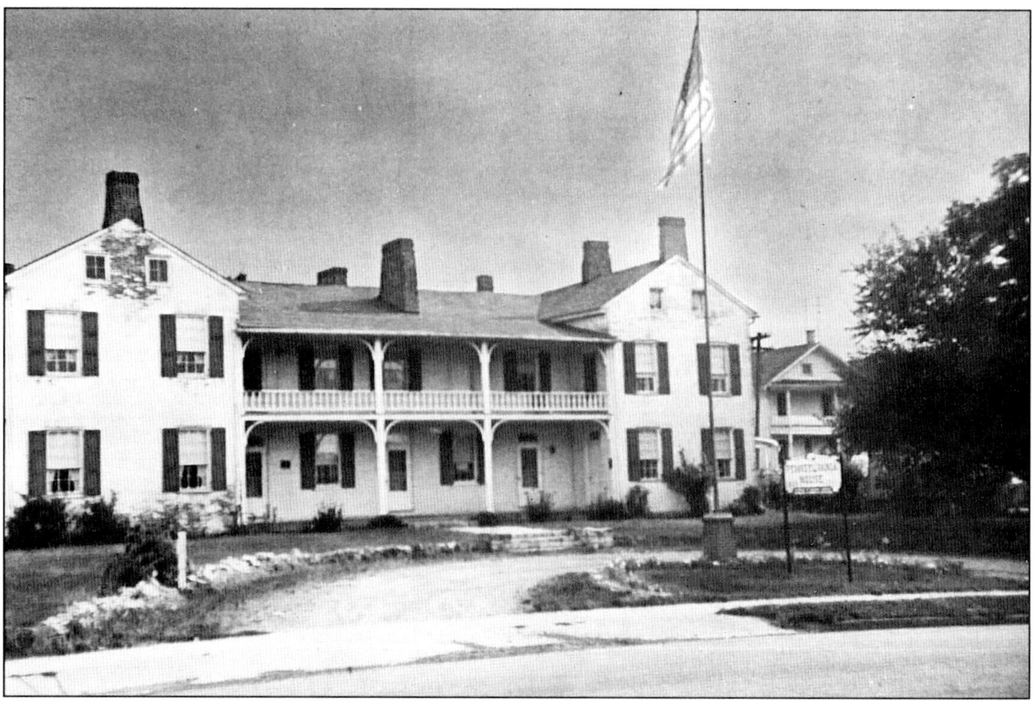

PENNSYLVANIA HOUSE, BUILT IN 1822. Located at 1311 West Main Street, the house is currently maintained by the Daughters of the American Republic.

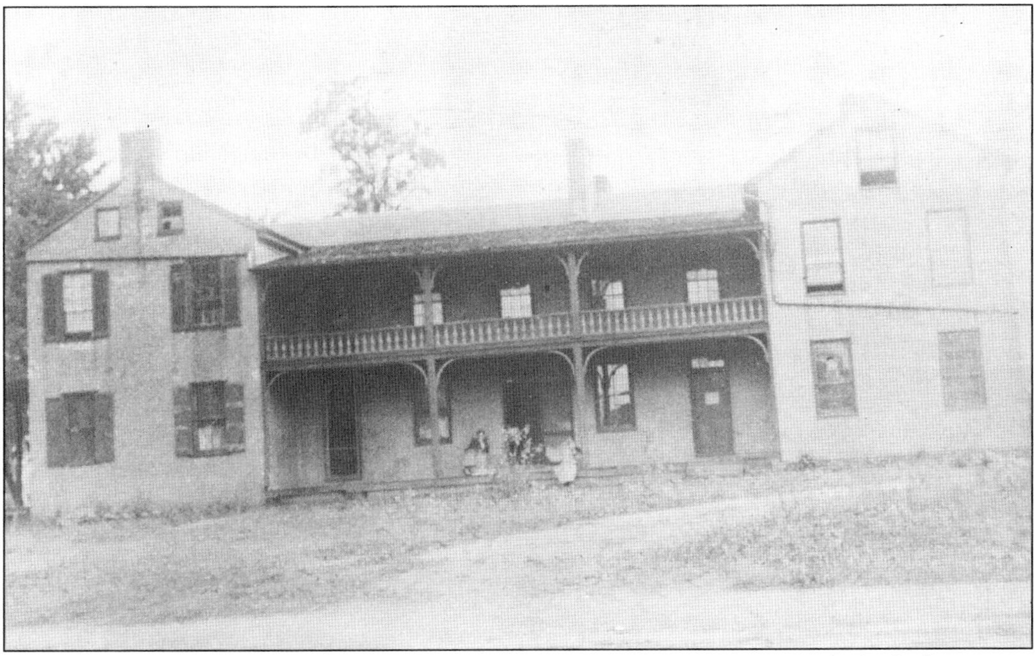

PENNSYLVANIA HOUSE, LATE 1800S. This old photo shows the house as it looked when it was occupied by a family.

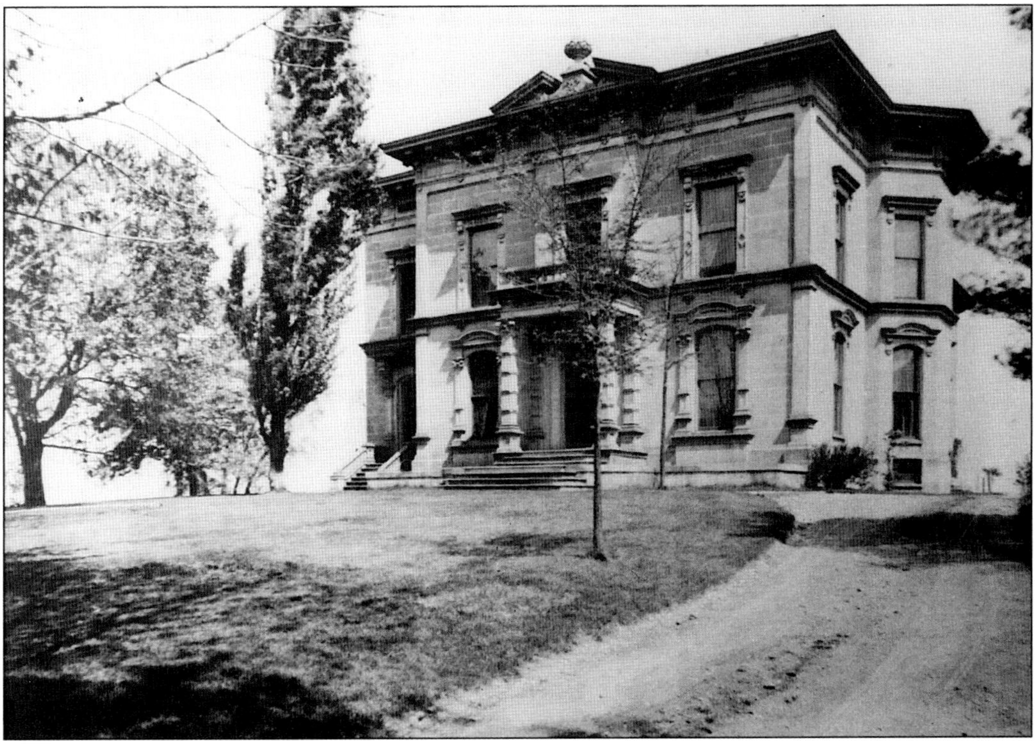

JOHN FOOS RESIDENCE AT 810 EAST HIGH STREET. Formerly this was the home of Miss Margaret Baker, owner of the Champion Company, until it later became the Ker Deen Inn and Drug Castle Offices. Nowadays it stays busy as the John Foos Manor-Bed and Breakfast.

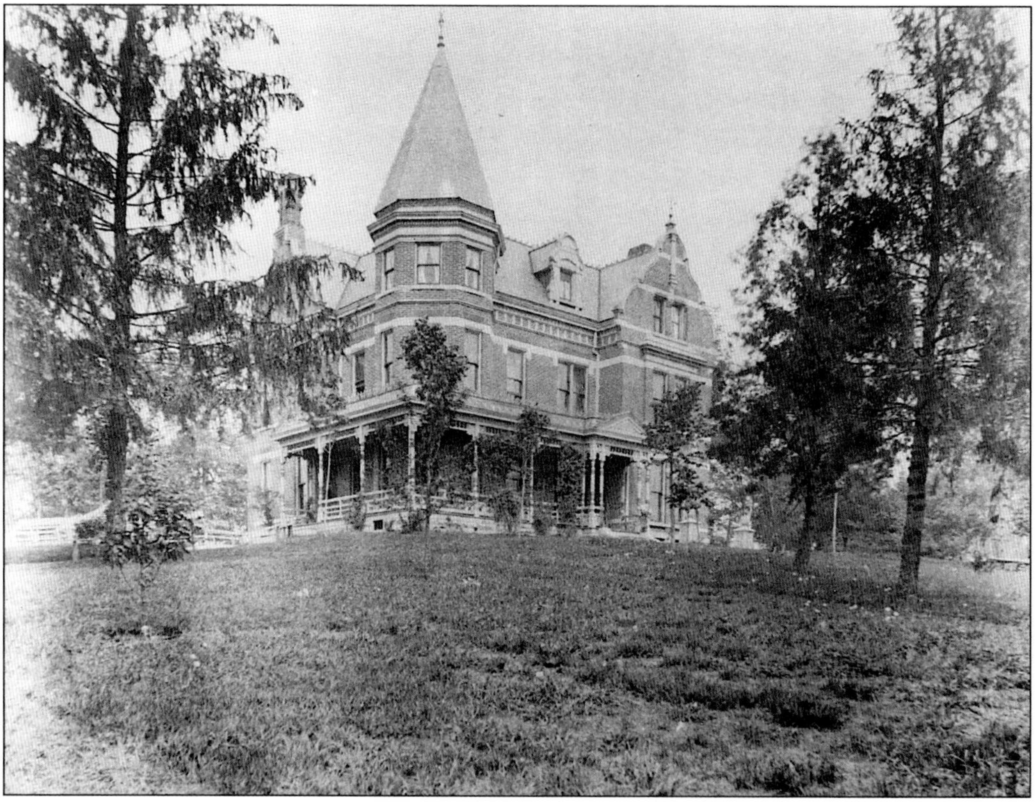

EDWARD WREN RESIDENCE, LOCATED AT 1115 NORTH LIMESTONE STREET, C. 1920S. Previous residents included the Clark County Board of Education and the Deganhart Funeral Home.

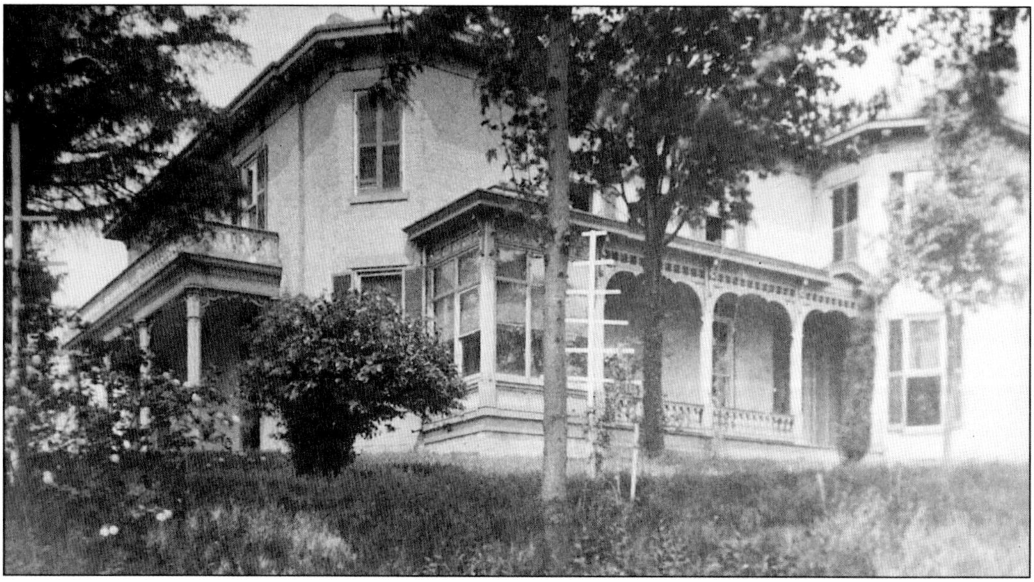

ROSS MITCHELL RESIDENCE, LOCATED AT 1515 NORTH BELMONT AVENUE, 1910S. Mr. Mitchell was one of the well-known industrialists in Springfield.

Three

PARKS AND SCHOOLS

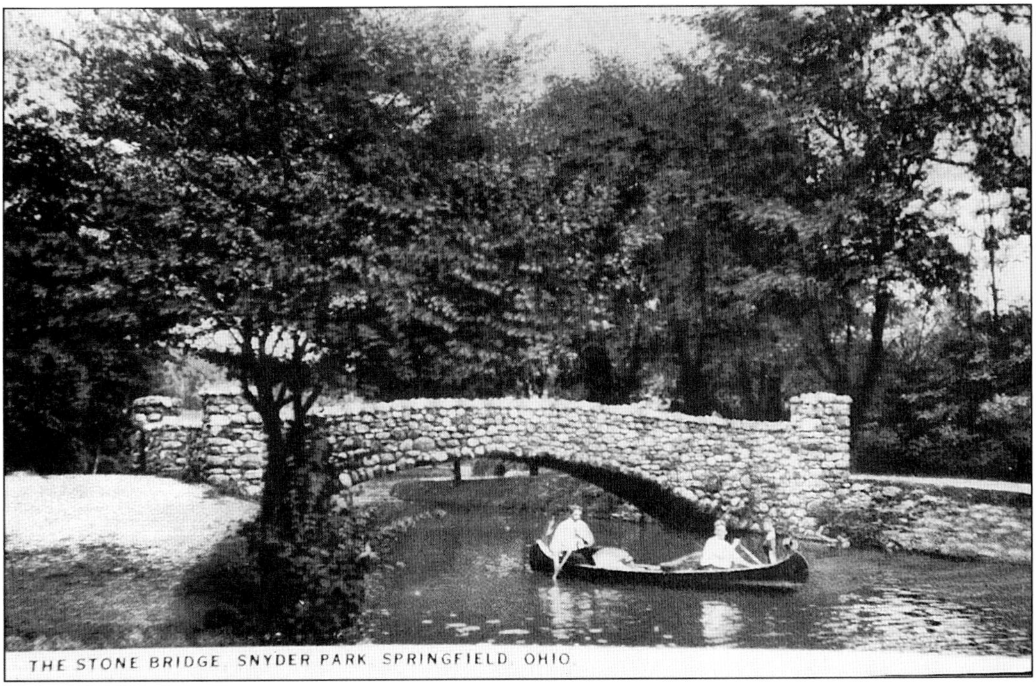

STONE BRIDGE IN SNYDER PARK, C. 1920. Fred Burmeister and his brother are the two men pictured in the canoe.

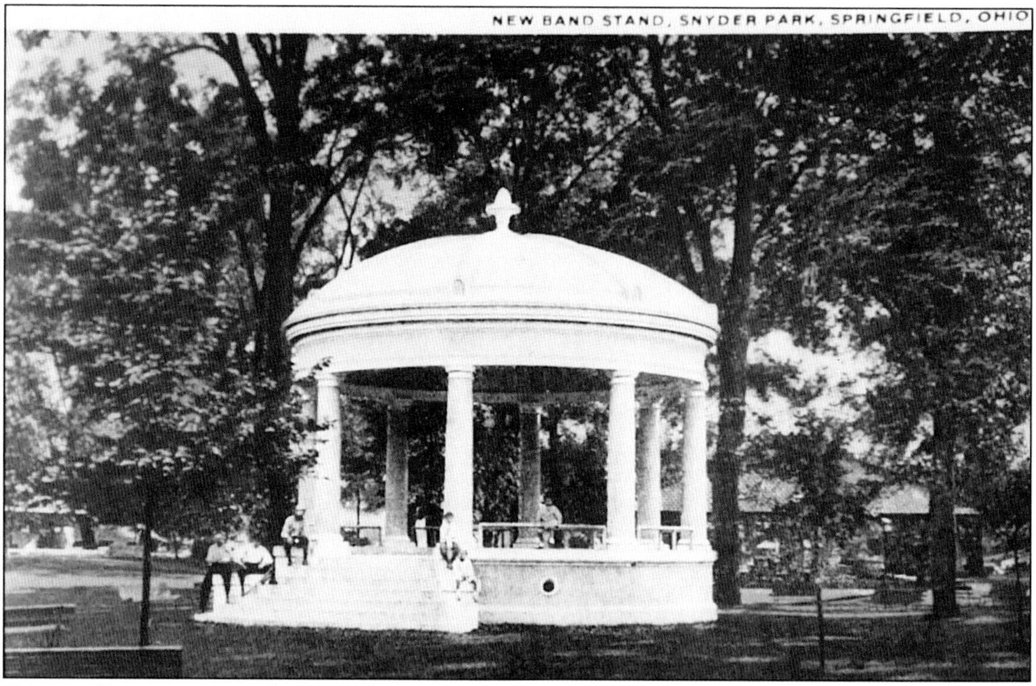

SNYDER PARK, 1920S. This view shows the famous band shell by the main shelter house located near the boathouse. It was designed by local architect Robert Gotwald and was removed in the 1930s, probably due to deterioration.

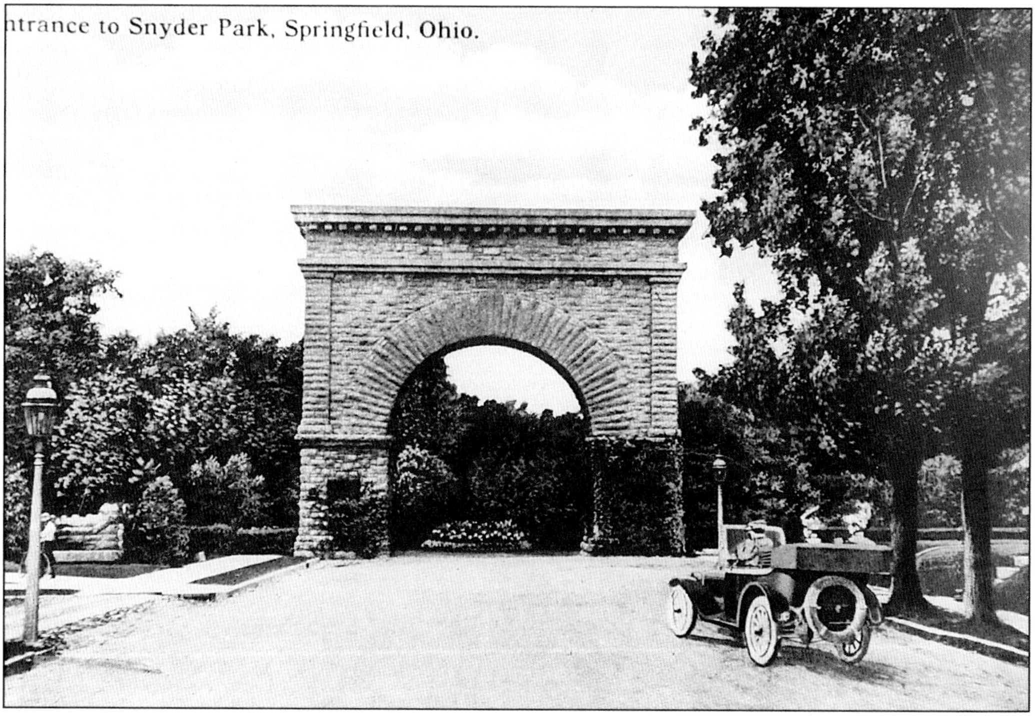

ARCH ENTRANCE TO SNYDER PARK, 1920S. This arch was funded by the local people's contributions.

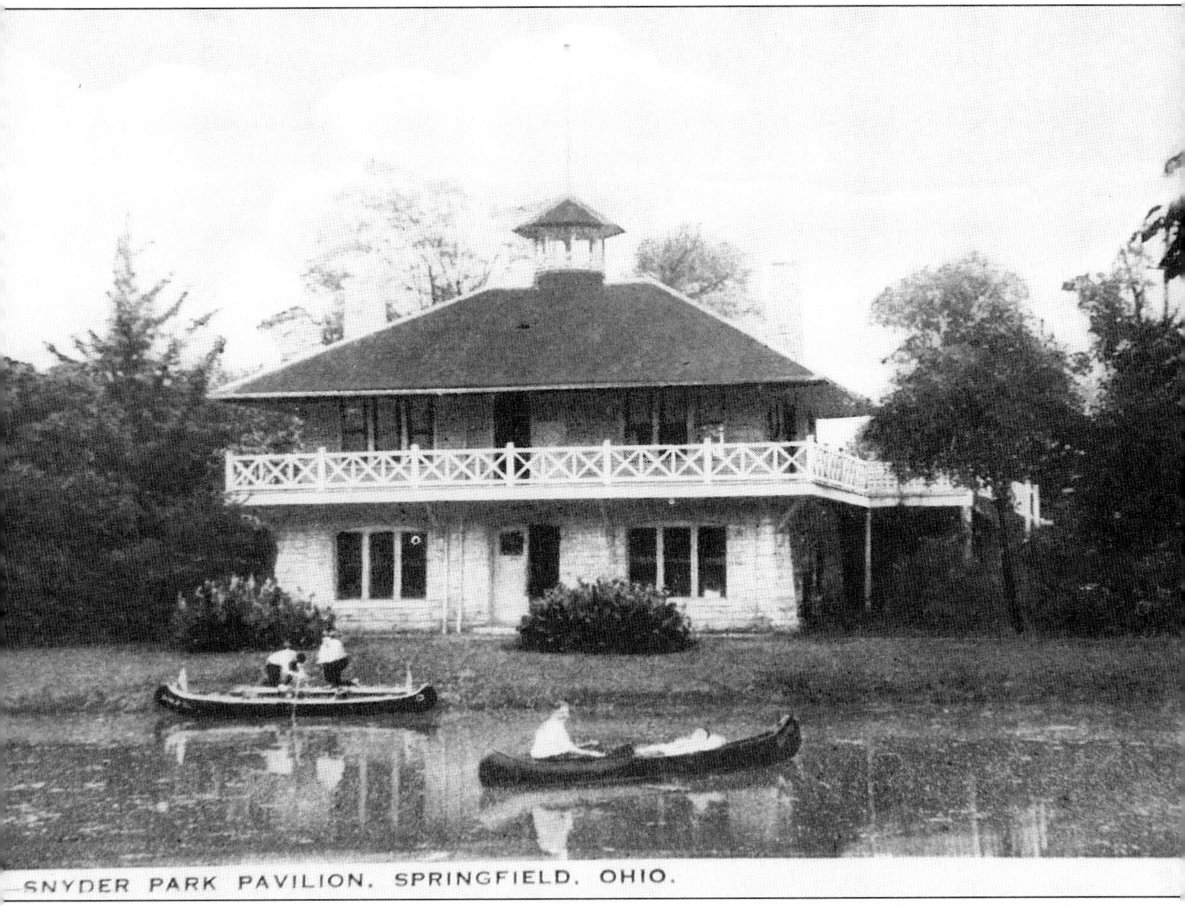

SNYDER PARK REST SHELTER, 1920S. This structure provided shelter while people waited to use the trolley car. Today it is a warehouse for the park.

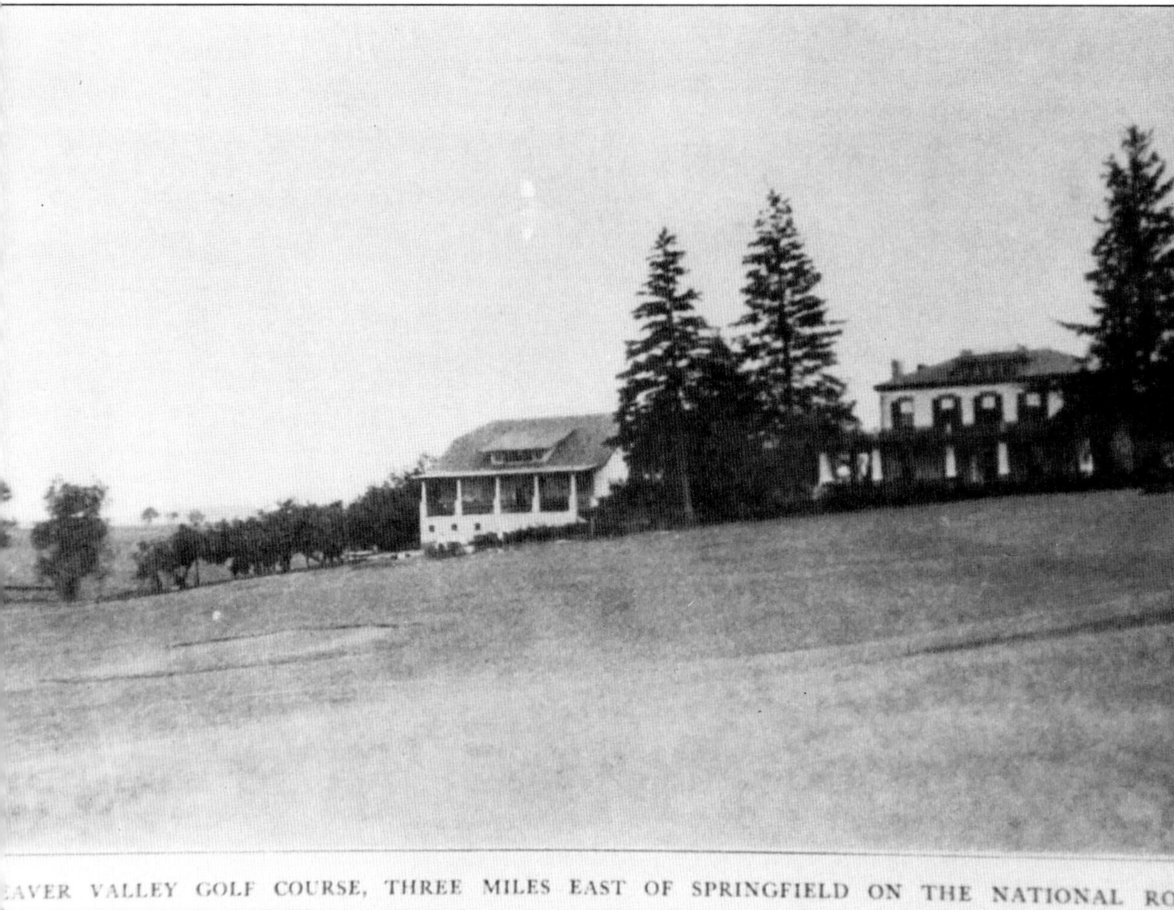

Beaver Valley Golf Course, 1920s. This golf course, located 3 miles east of Springfield on Route 40 near Harmony, went out of business during the 1929 depression.

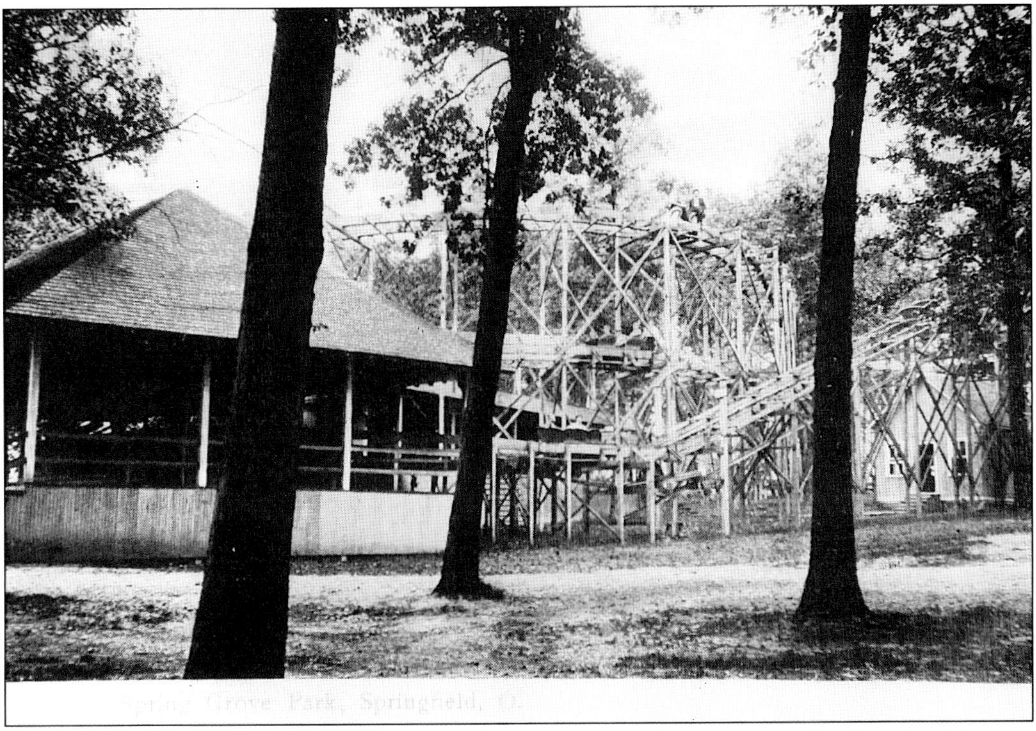

AVALON PARK, 1915. The roller coaster and merry-go-round were among the favorite rides.

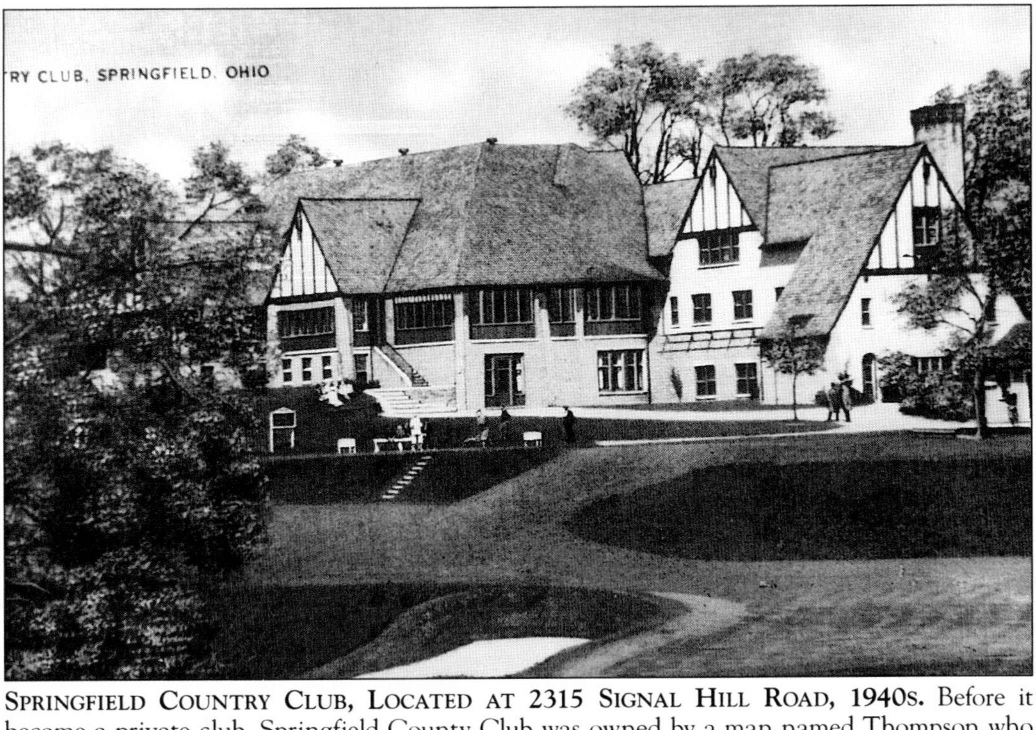

SPRINGFIELD COUNTRY CLUB, LOCATED AT 2315 SIGNAL HILL ROAD, 1940S. Before it became a private club, Springfield County Club was owned by a man named Thompson who used the land to raise Shetland ponies.

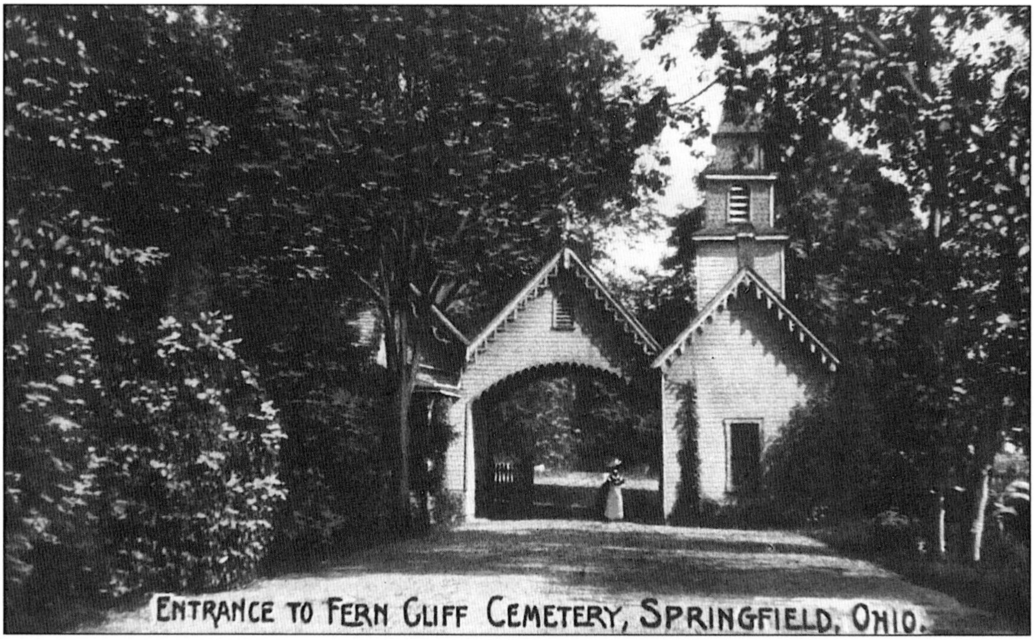

FERNCLIFF CEMETERY, OLD ENTRANCE ON PLUM STREET, 1915.

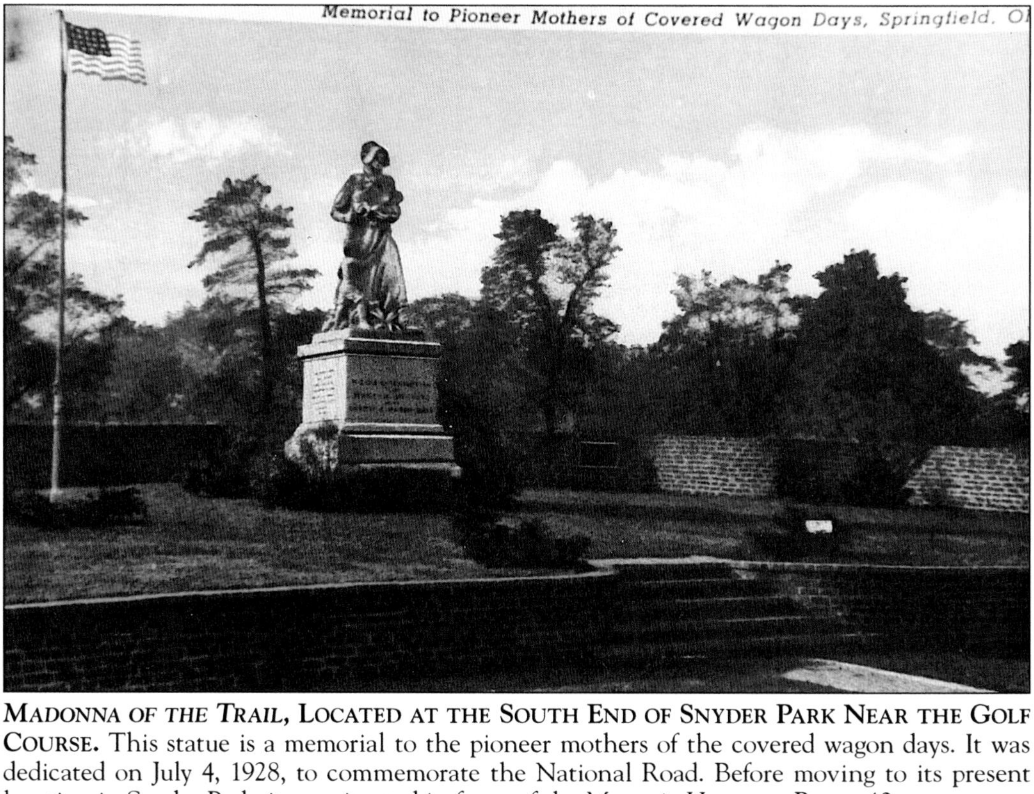

MADONNA OF *THE TRAIL*, LOCATED AT THE SOUTH END OF SNYDER PARK NEAR THE GOLF COURSE. This statue is a memorial to the pioneer mothers of the covered wagon days. It was dedicated on July 4, 1928, to commemorate the National Road. Before moving to its present location in Snyder Park, it was situated in front of the Masonic Home on Route 40 west.

GEORGE ROGERS CLARK MEMORIAL AT THE GEORGE ROGERS CLARK PARK, 1930S. The park was created in 1930 by the State and contained over 200 acres.

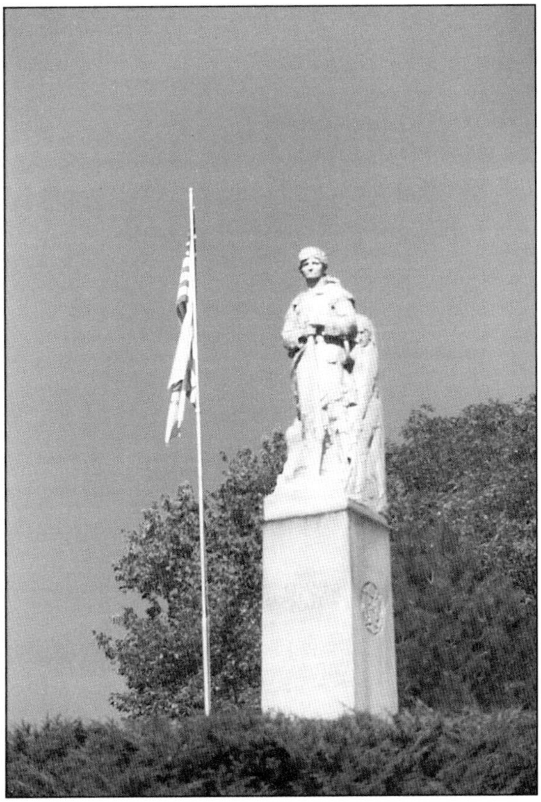

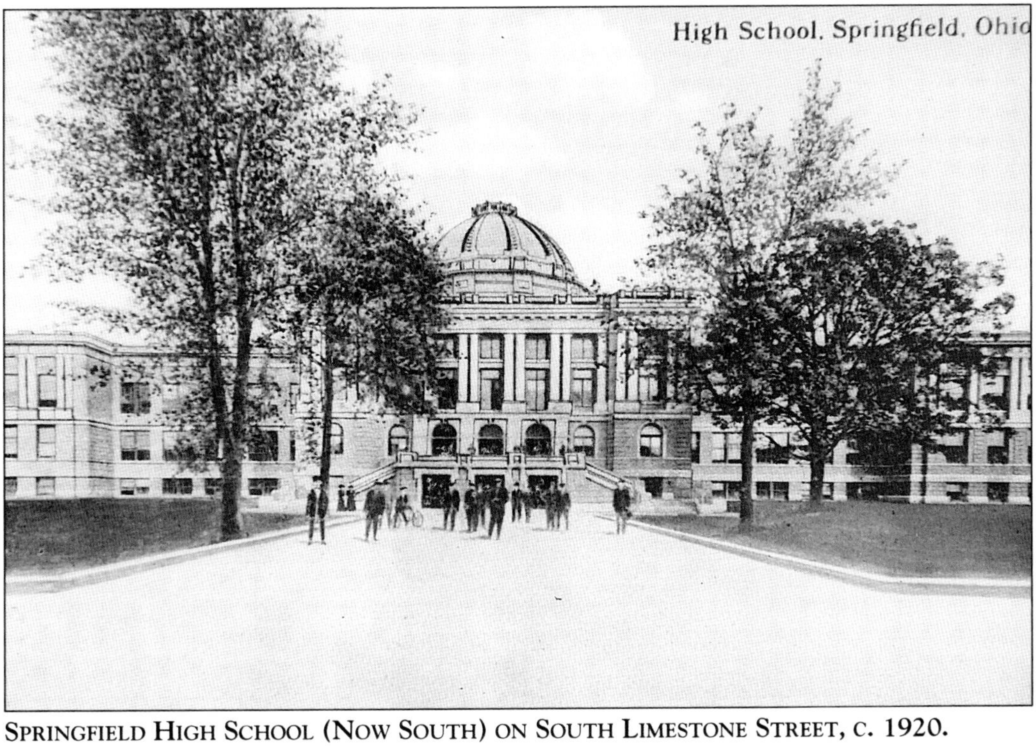

SPRINGFIELD HIGH SCHOOL (NOW SOUTH) ON SOUTH LIMESTONE STREET, C. 1920.

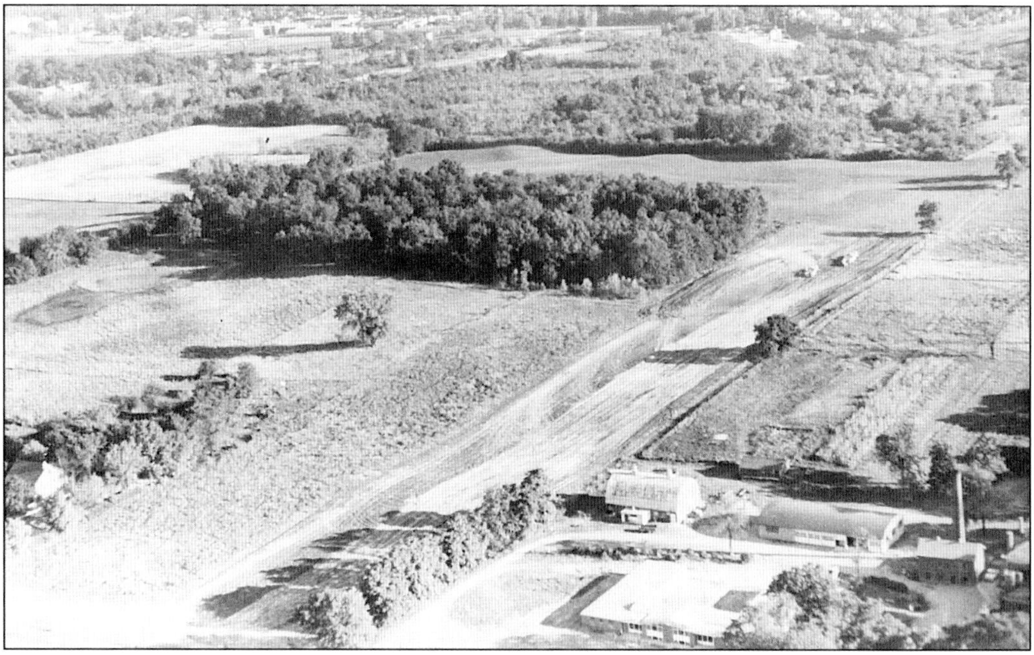

Aerial View from East Home Road Looking South at the New Entrance for North High School, 1958. On the lower right is the Clark County Children's Home.

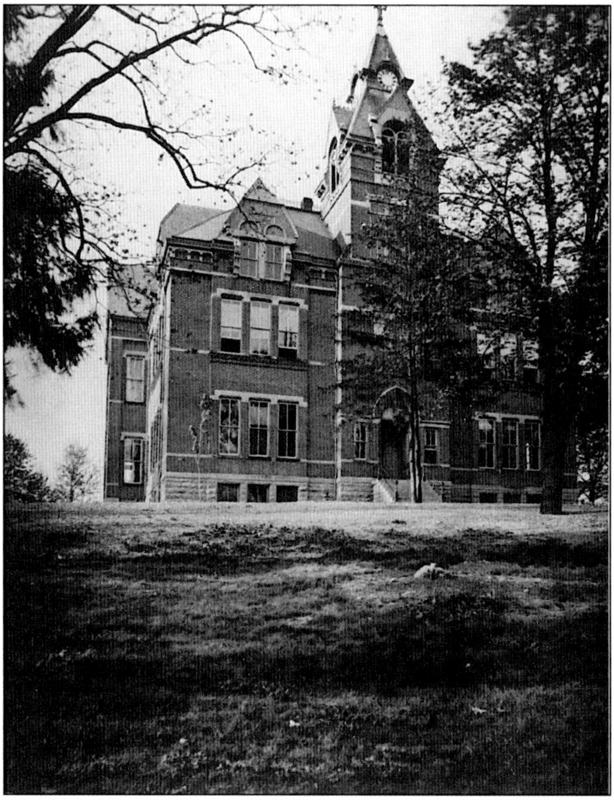

Northern School, Located on College Avenue between North Limestone and North Fountain Avenue on the South Side of the Street, 1910s. In 1801, this was the site of James Demint's first cabin. Today it is the home of the Springfield Board of Education.

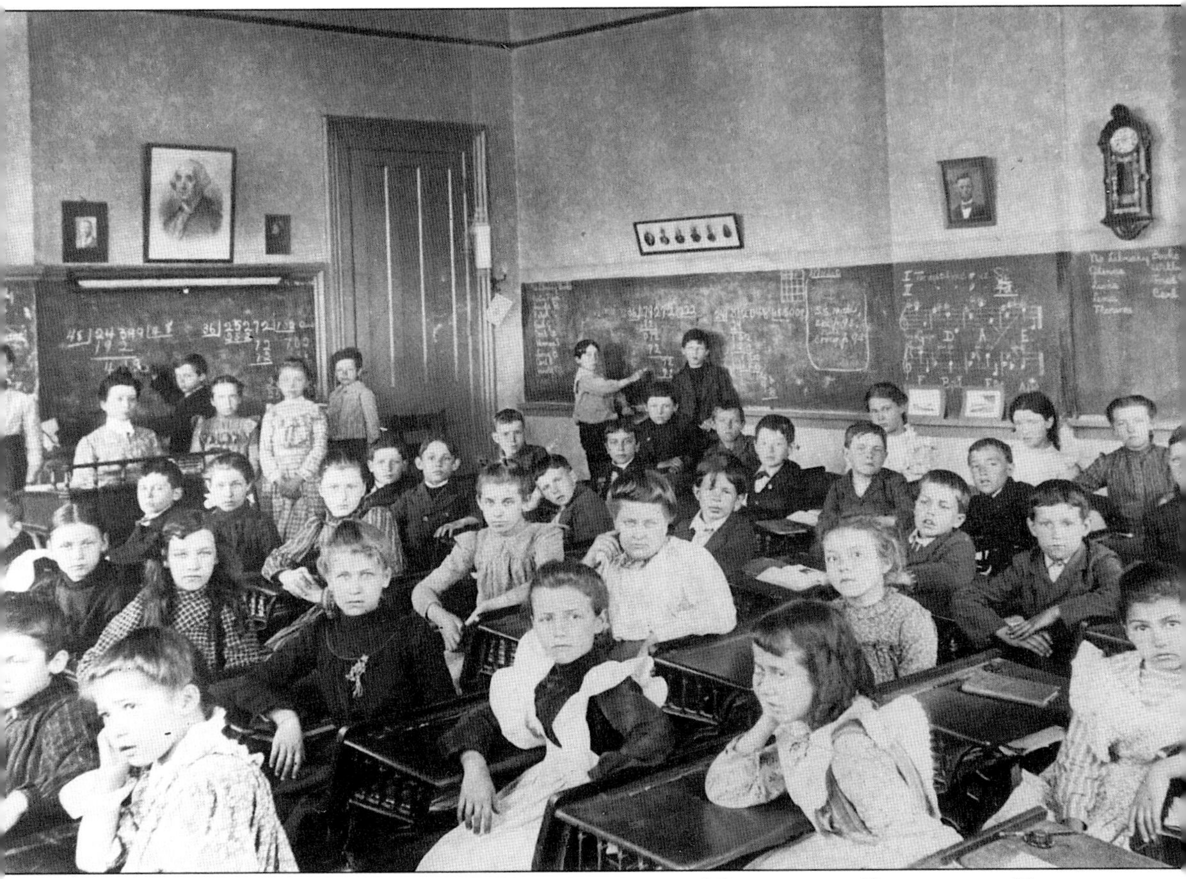

WESTERN ELEMENTARY SCHOOL, LOCATED AT THE NORTHEAST CORNER OF YELLOW SPRINGS STREET AND WEST MAIN STREET, 1900. This school was destroyed by fire on January 4, 1954.

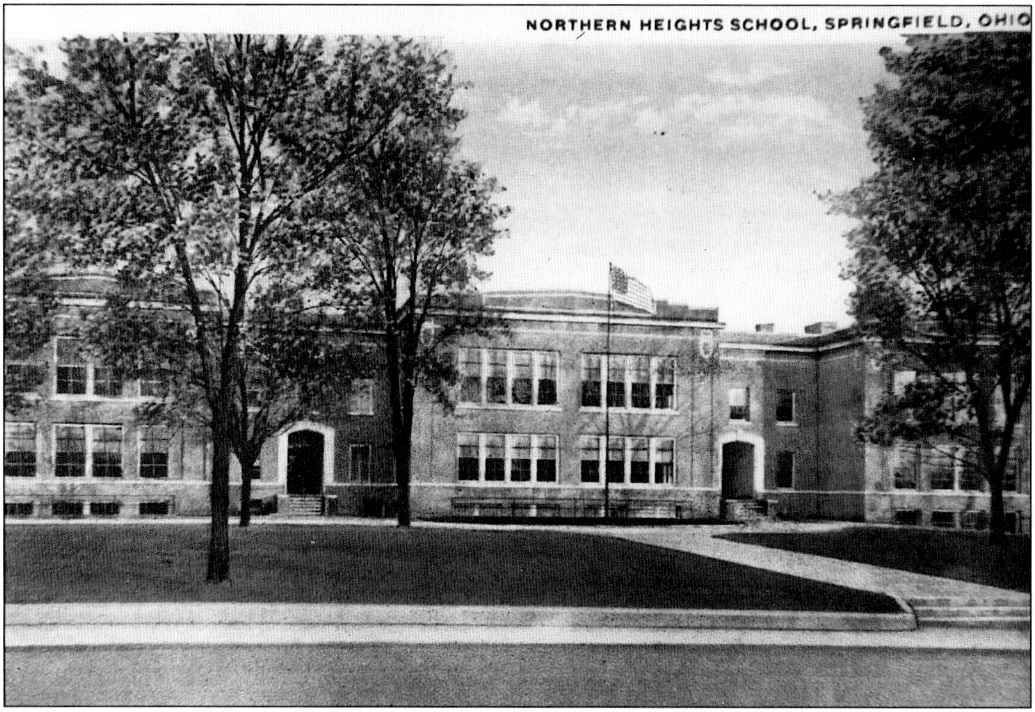

McGuffey School (Formerly Northern Heights), Located at the Northeast Corner of Winton and East Northern Avenue. Originally, it was built as a poor house for use by older citizens.

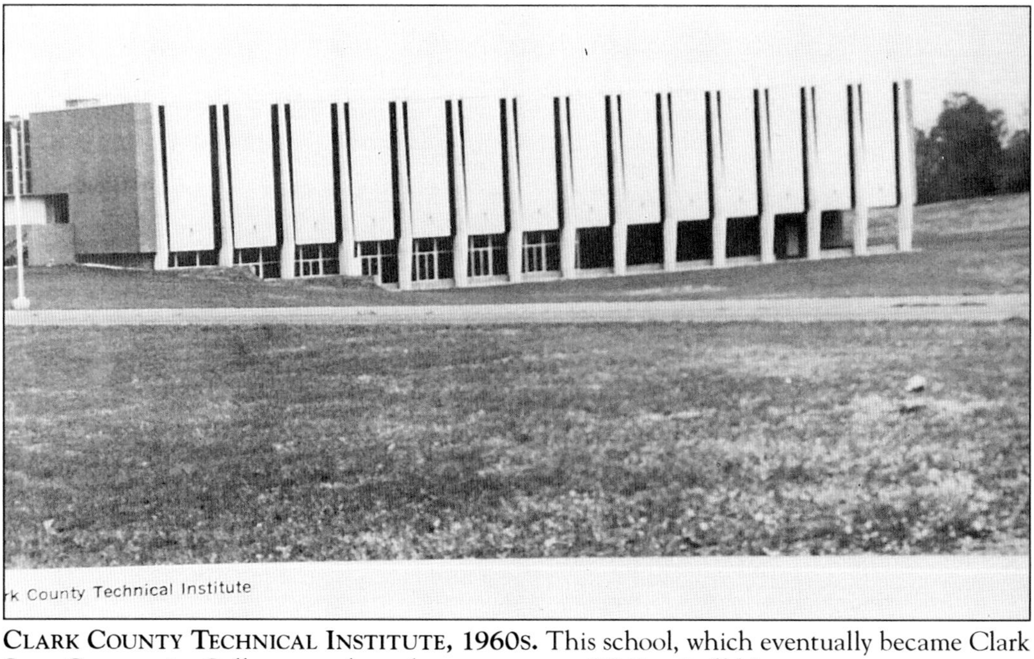

Clark County Technical Institute, 1960s. This school, which eventually became Clark State Community College, now has a large campus at 570 East Leffel Lane.

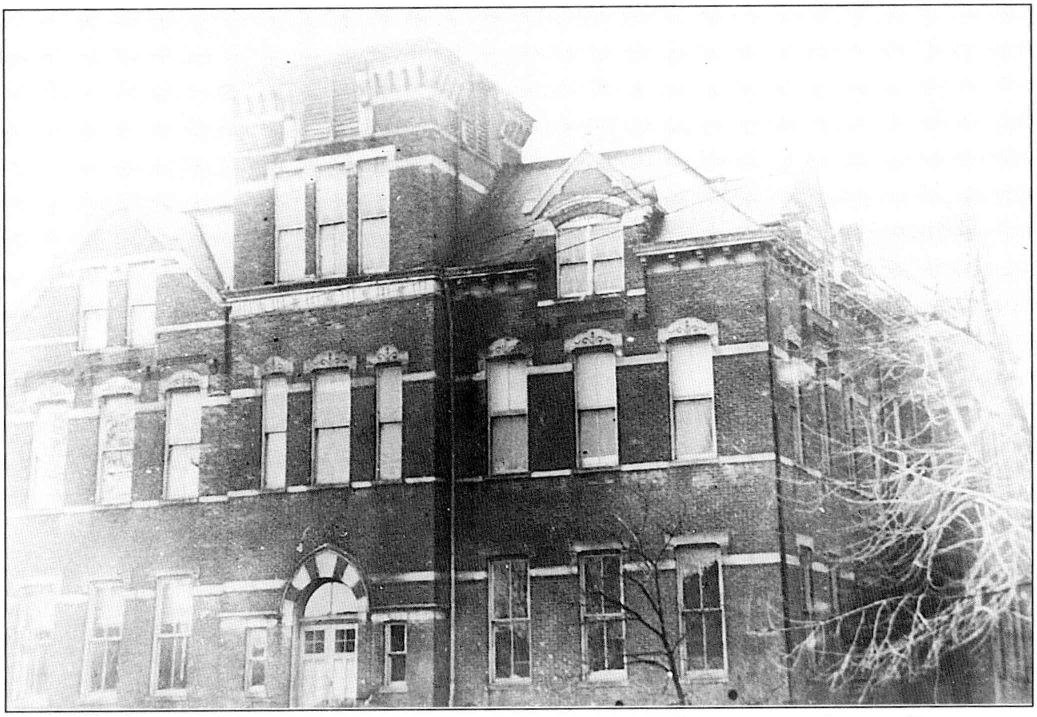

OLD EMERSON SCHOOL, LOCATED ON THE SOUTHEAST CORNER OF SELMA ROAD AND TIBBETTS, 1920S.

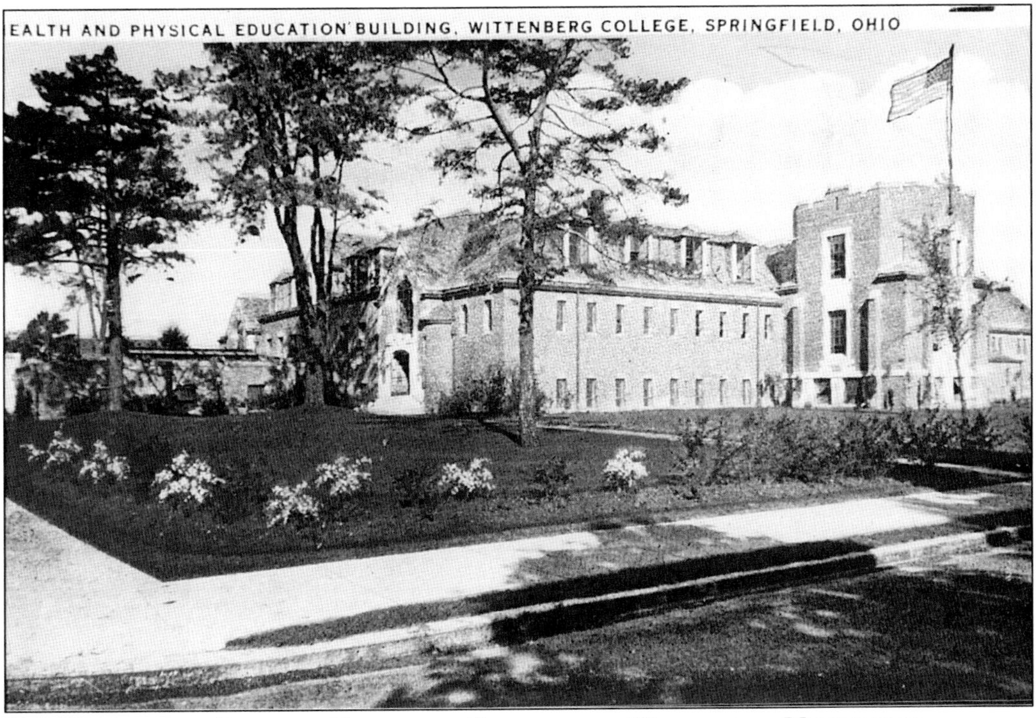

THE HEALTH AND PHYSICAL EDUCATION BUILDING AT WITTENBERG UNIVERSITY.

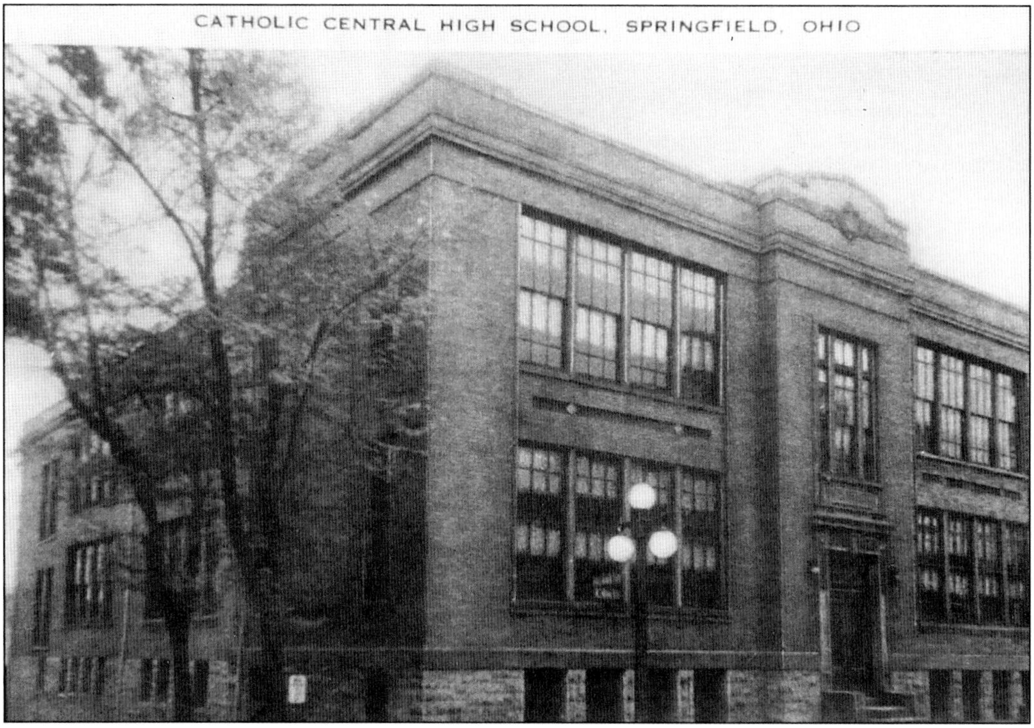

CATHOLIC CENTRAL HIGH SCHOOL, LOCATED AT 237 EAST HIGH STREET, 1940S.

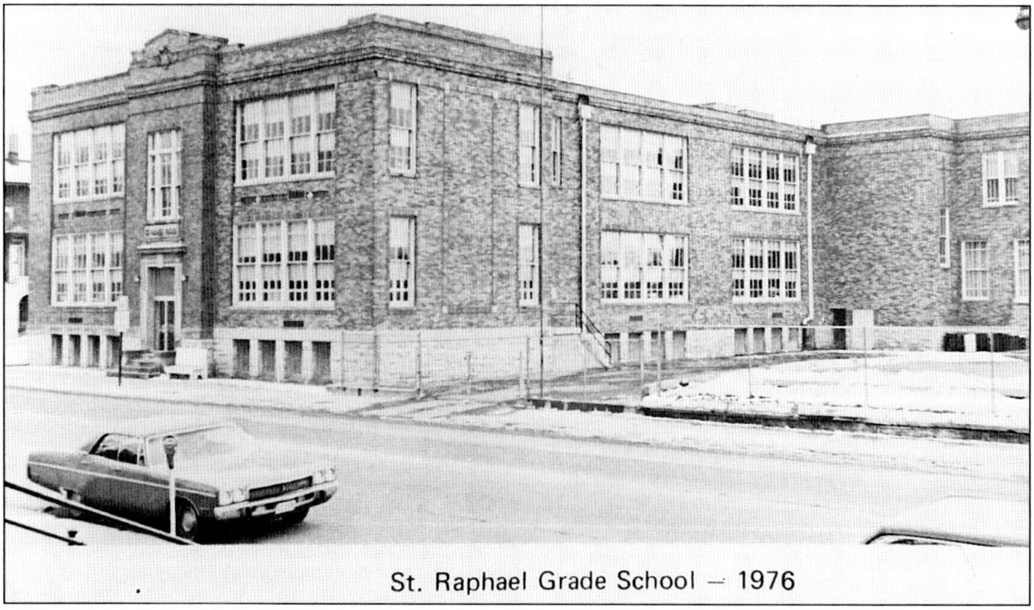

STREET RAPHAEL GRADE SCHOOL ON EAST HIGH STREET NEAR THE CHURCH, 1976.

Four

MUNICIPAL BUILDINGS

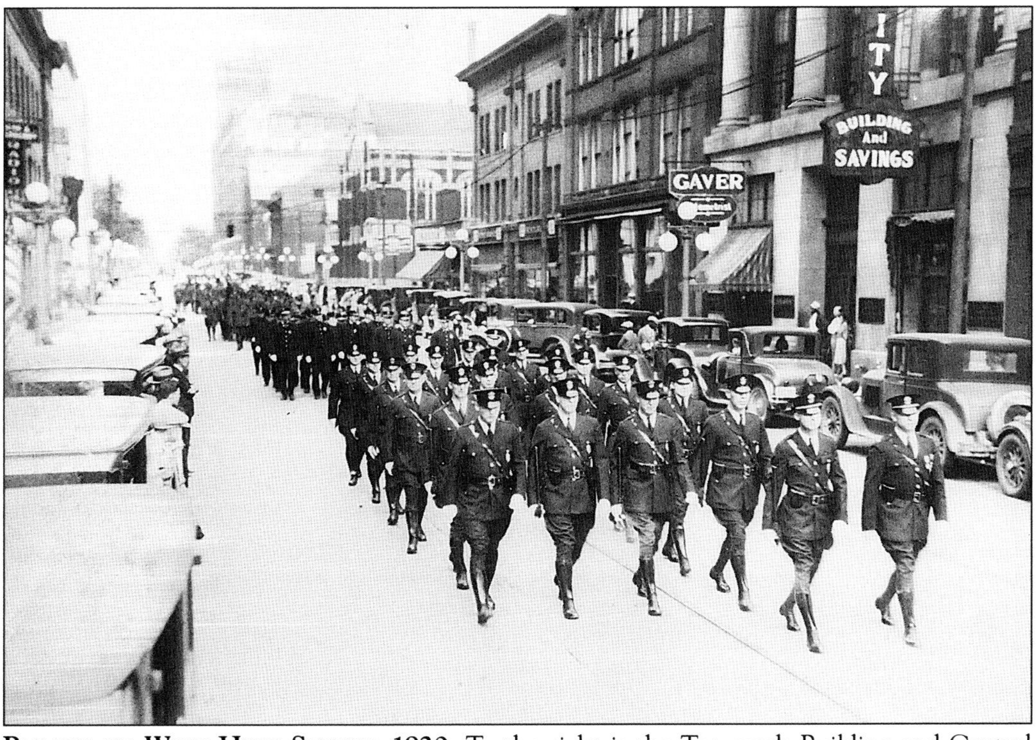

PARADE ON WEST HIGH STREET, 1920. To the right is the Tecumseh Building and Central Methodist Church.

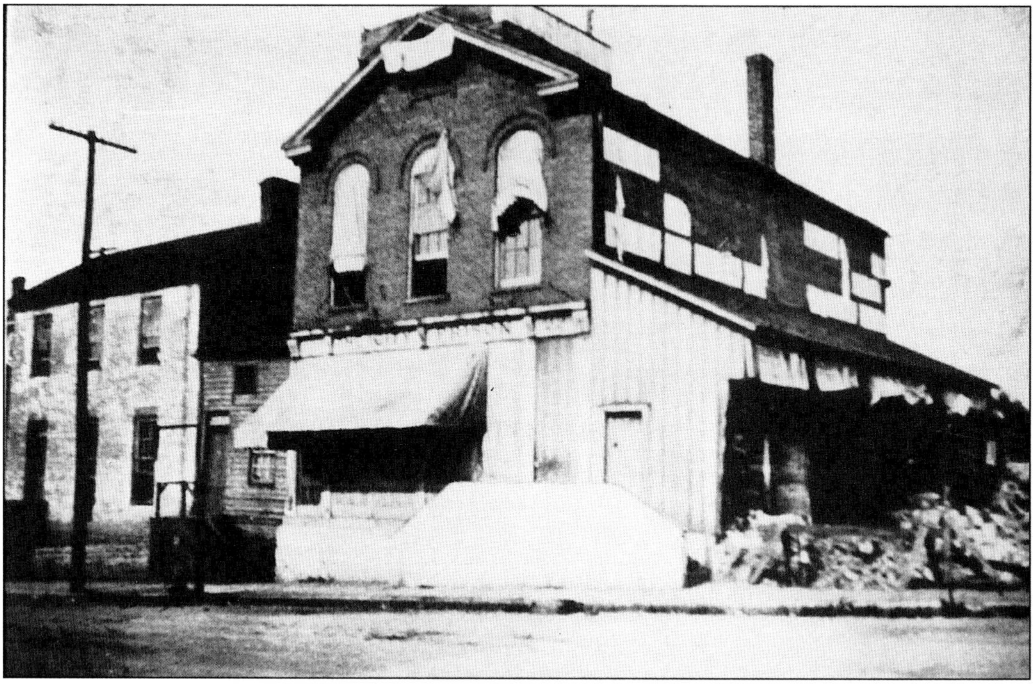

The Old City Jail, Located on the East Side of Spring Street between Main and High Street, c. 1890. In the 1890s, this jailhouse was replaced by the jail where Fire Engine House #1 is located today on North Fountain Avenue.

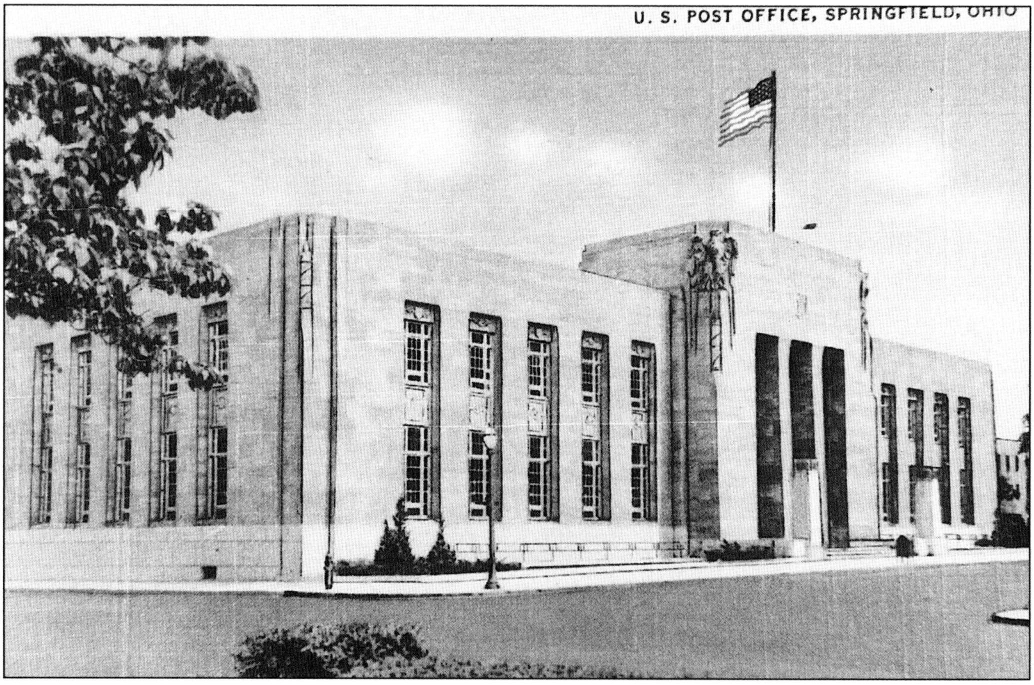

Today's Post Office, Located on the Southeast Corner of East North Street and North Limestone Street, c. 1950. This building was constructed in 1934 at a cost of $750,000.

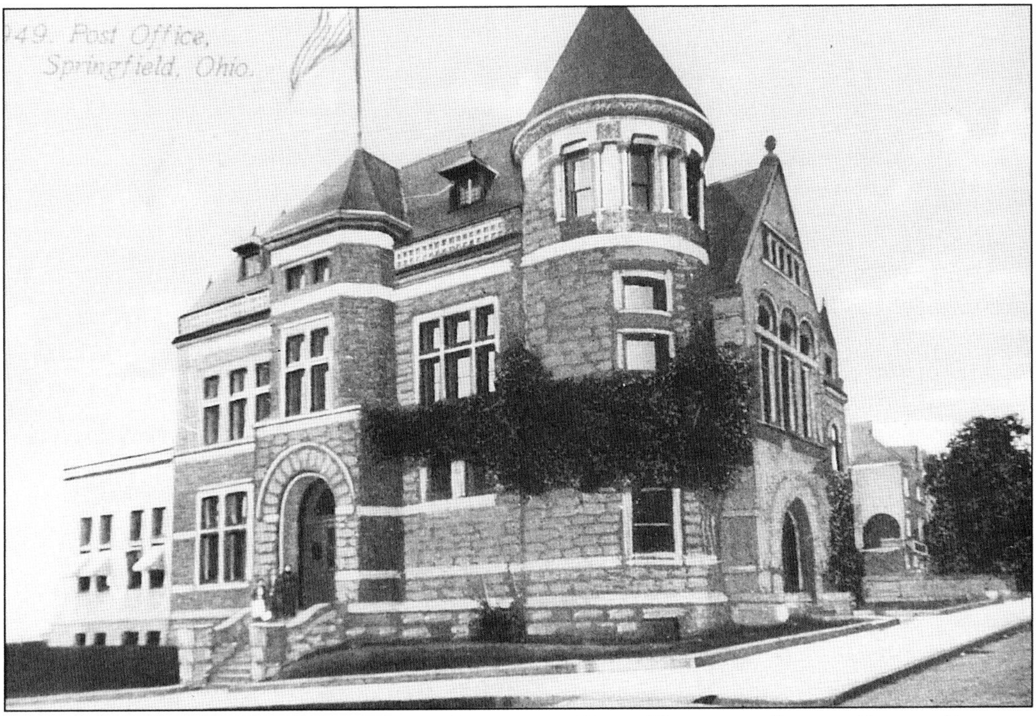

THE POST OFFICE ON THE NORTHEAST CORNER OF EAST HIGH AND SOUTH SPRING STREET, C. 1913.

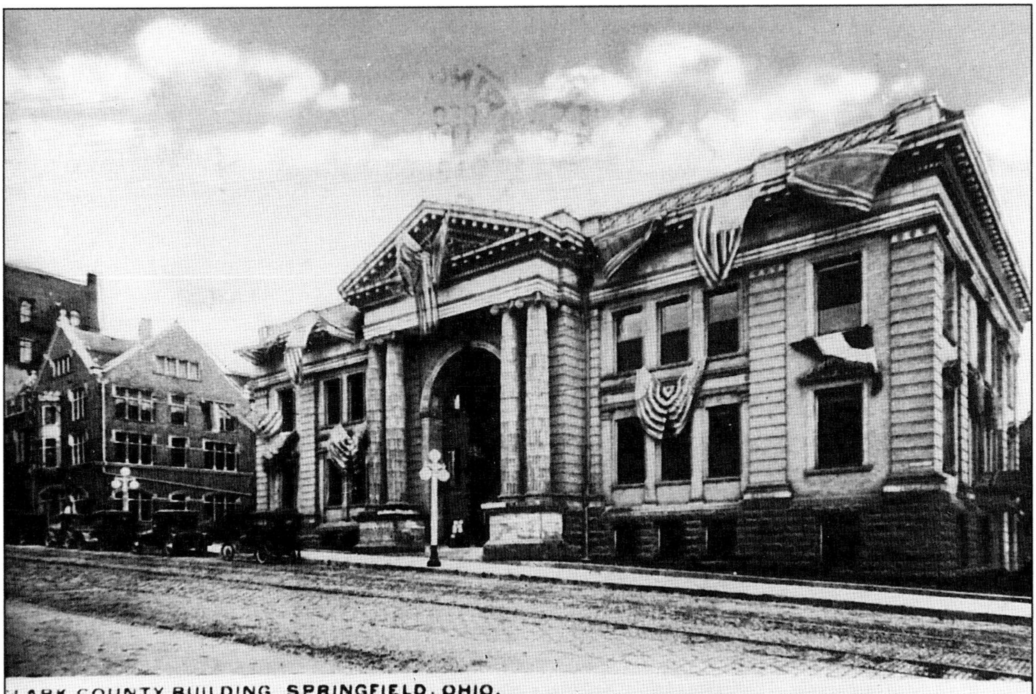

THE CLARK COUNTY BUILDING ON THE SOUTHWEST CORNER OF NORTH LIMESTONE AND EAST COLUMBIA STREET, 1920S.

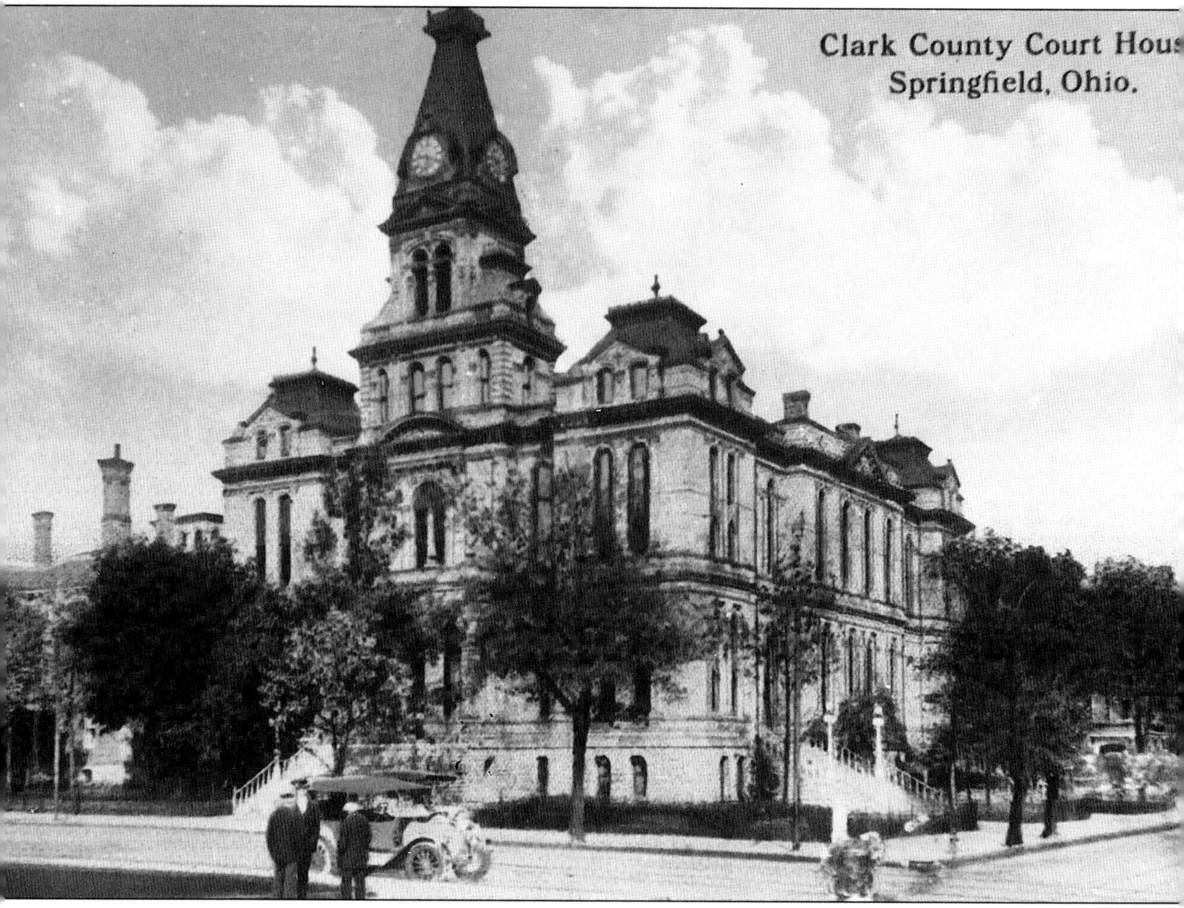

THE OLD CLARK COUNTY COURTHOUSE, LOCATED ON THE NORTHWEST CORNER OF EAST COLUMBIA AND NORTH LIMESTONE STREET, EARLY 1910S. This photo, taken before the fire, shows how the structure originally looked.

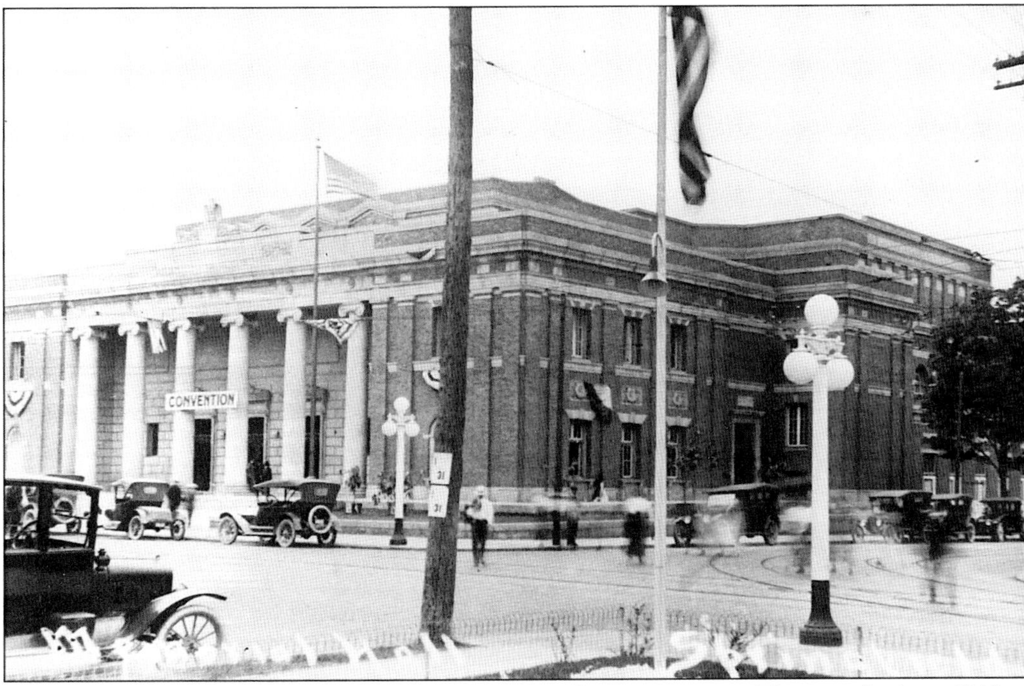

MEMORIAL HALL, LOCATED AT 300 WEST MAIN STREET, 1920S. This was built in 1915 in honor of all veterans.

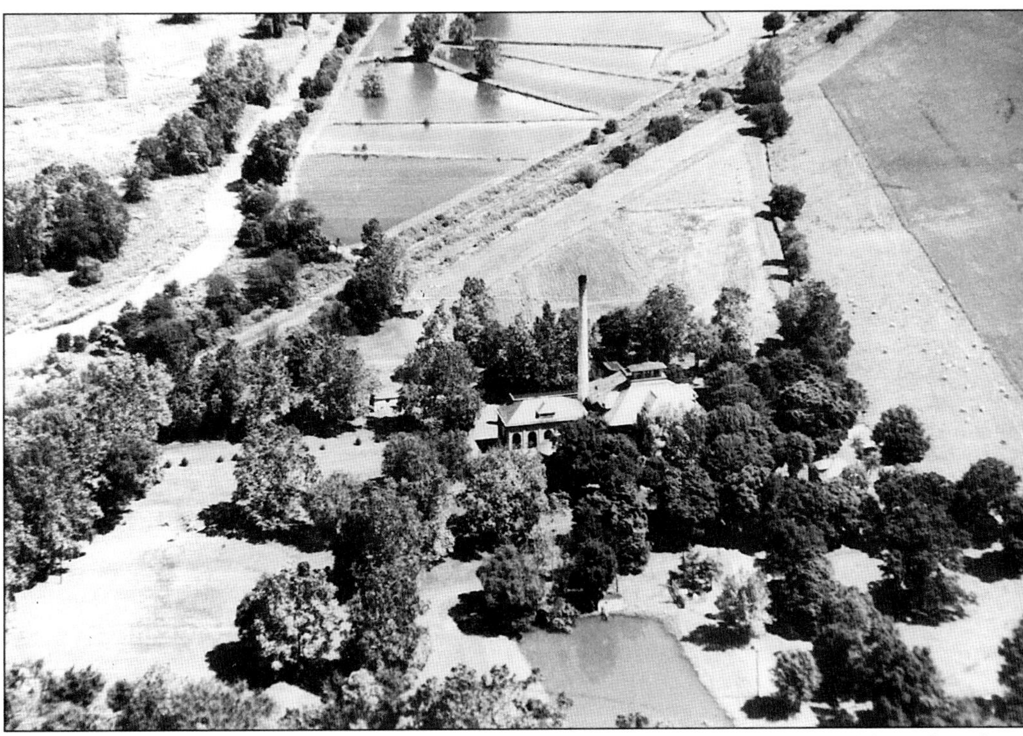

THE SECOND WATERWORKS, BUILT IN 1895. It occupied 67 acres in the old Reid Park off Columbus Road.

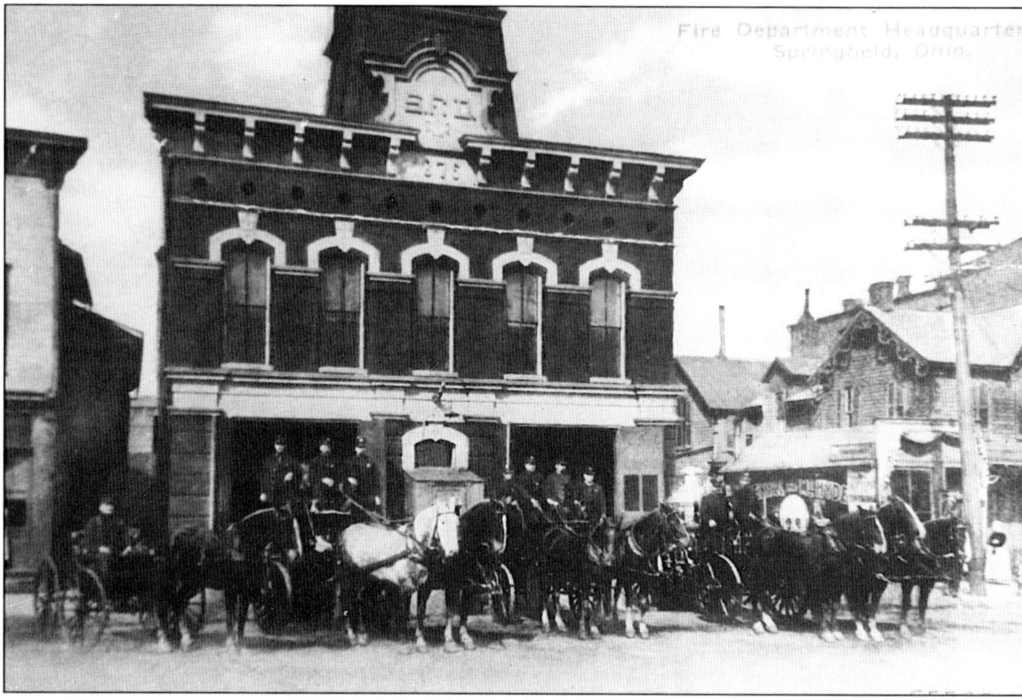

FIRE HOUSE #1 IN THE 200 BLOCK ON SOUTH FOUNTAIN AVENUE, LATE 1890S.

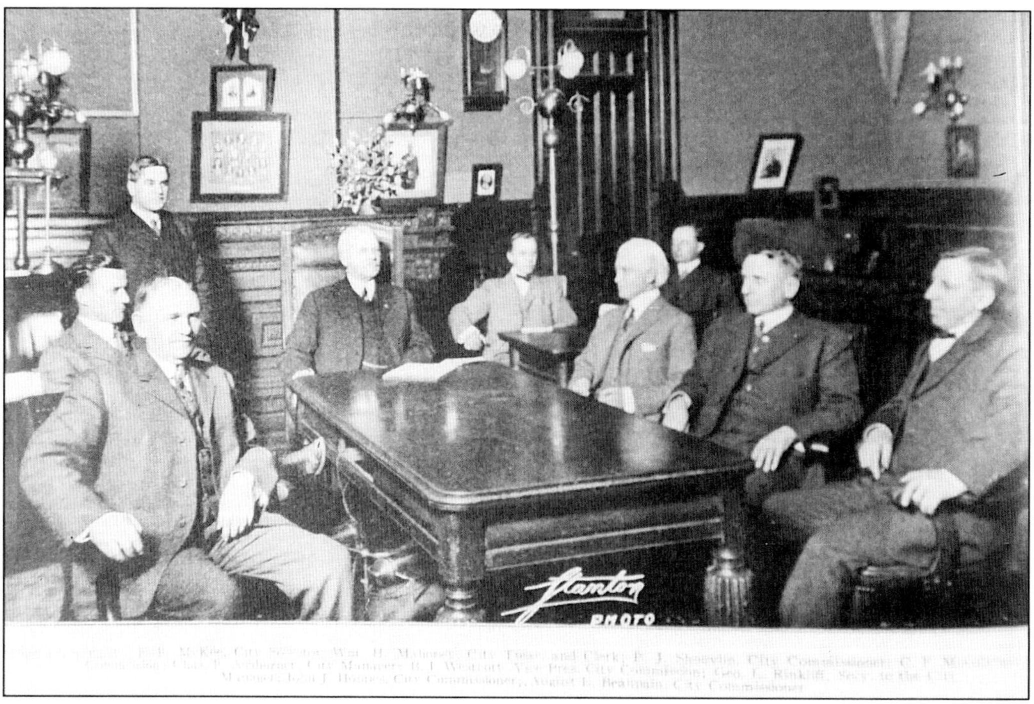

MEETING OF THE CITY OFFICIALS AND COMMISSIONERS, EARLY 1900S. P.J. Shoulvin and B.J. Westcott were two of the city commissioners.

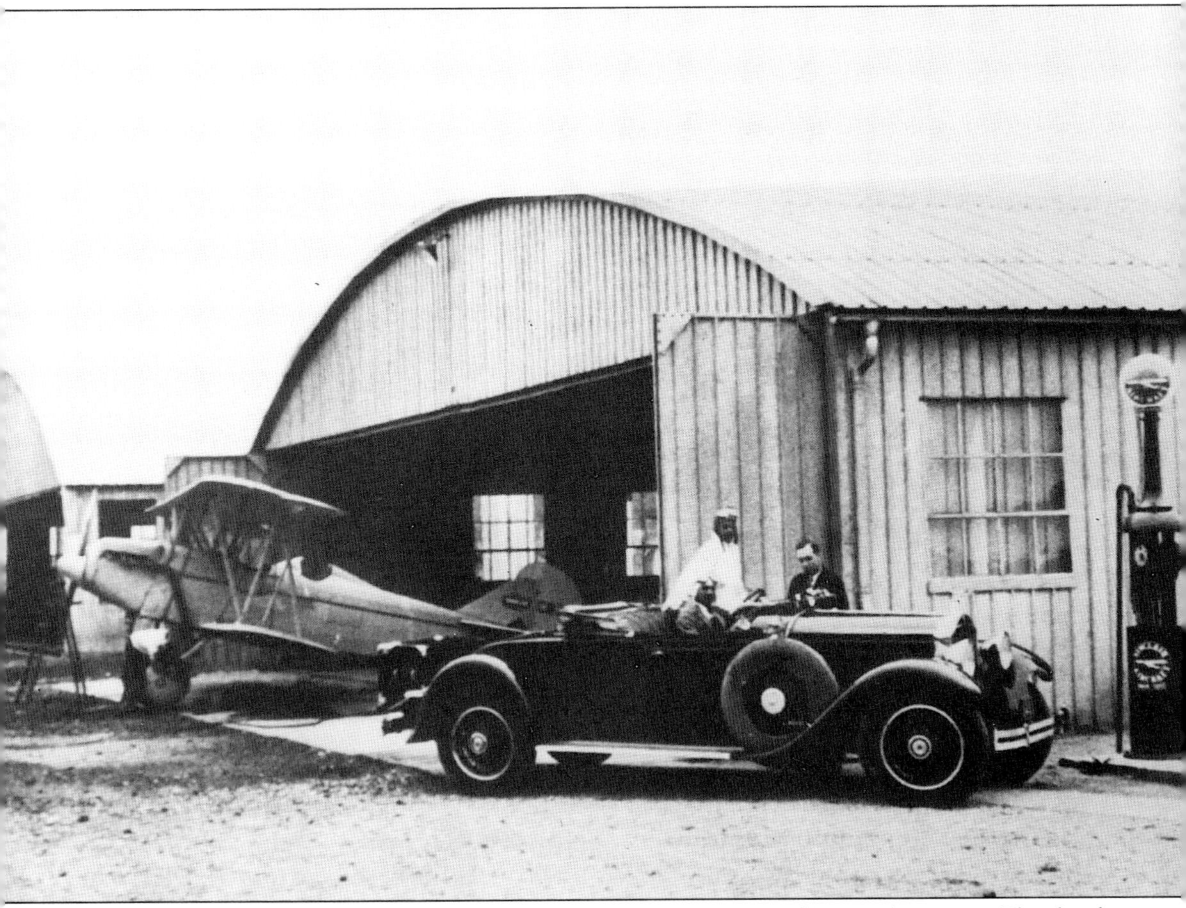

THE OLD SPRINGFIELD AIRPORT, LOCATED ON ROUTE 41 EAST (OLD 70), 1920S. This land is now the grounds for the Clark County Fair and other shows. Wouldn't the automobile, plane, and gas pump be valuable collector's items today?

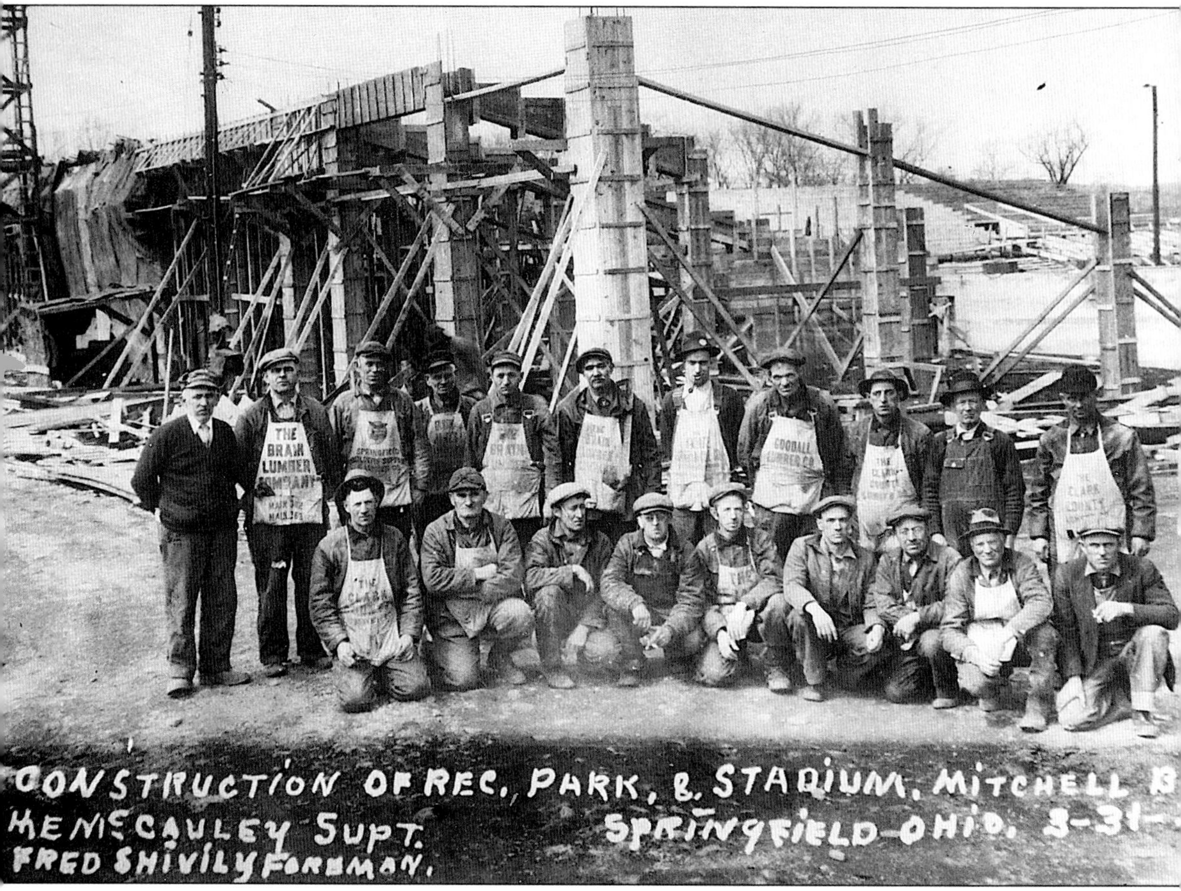

MUNICIPAL STADIUM ON MITCHELL BOULEVARD, UNDER CONSTRUCTION IN 1937 BY THE WPA.

Five

CHURCHES

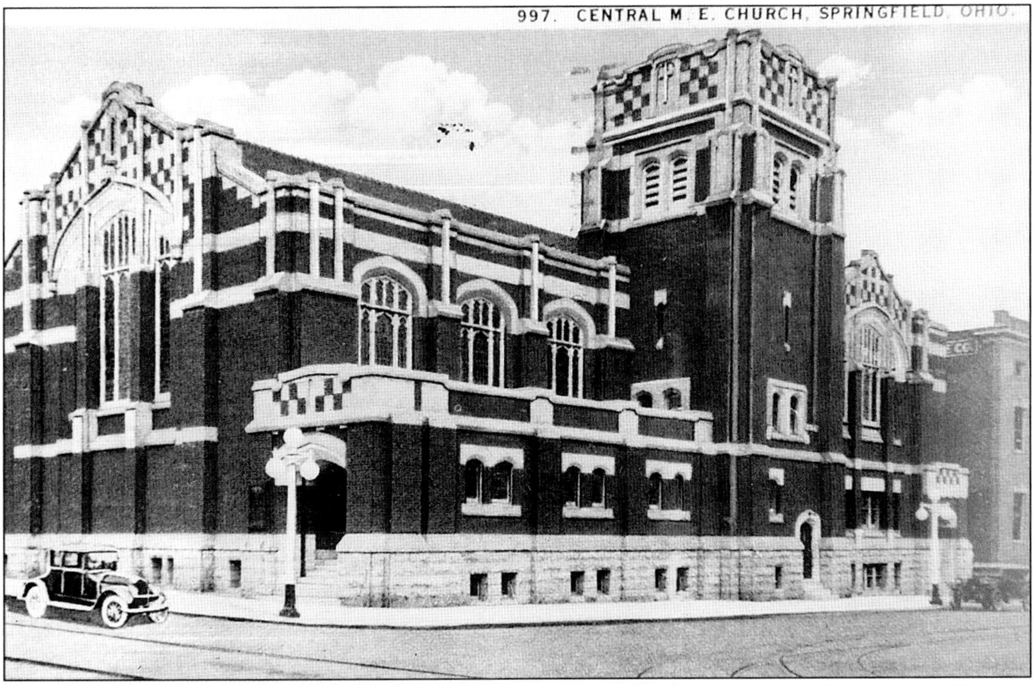

CENTRAL UNITED METHODIST CHURCH, LOCATED ON THE NORTHWEST CORNER OF SOUTH CENTER STREET AND WEST HIGH STREET, C. 1924. Organized in 1805, the Methodist church was the oldest denomination in Springfield. This building is the fourth structure and was built in 1914.

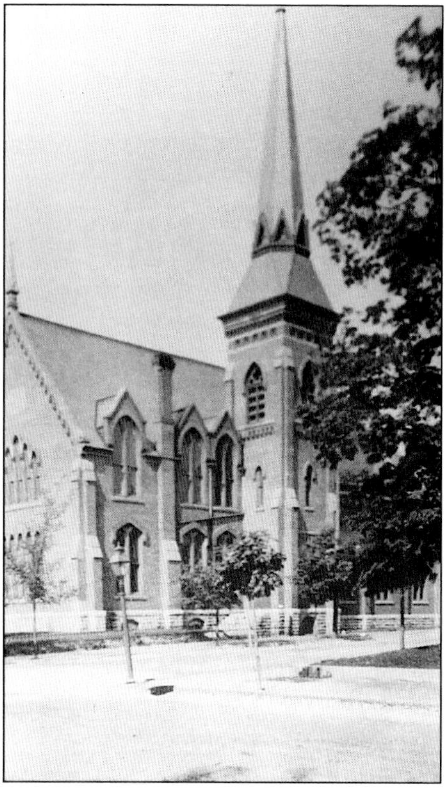

FIRST BAPTIST CHURCH ON THE NORTHEAST CORNER OF MILLER STREET AND SOUTH FOUNTAIN AVENUE, 1910S.

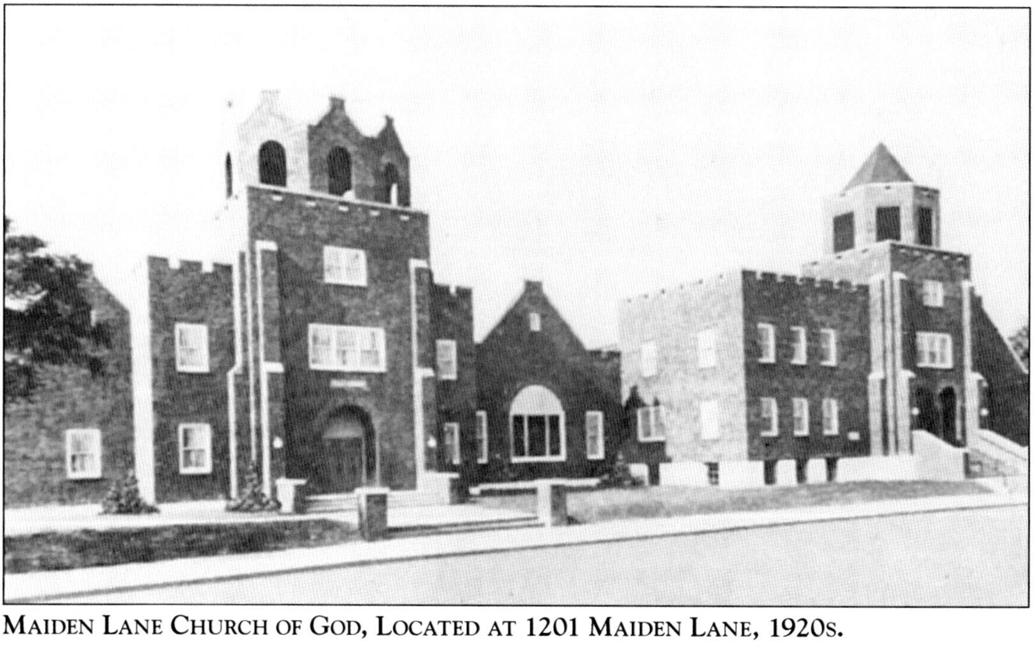

MAIDEN LANE CHURCH OF GOD, LOCATED AT 1201 MAIDEN LANE, 1920S.

ST. RAPHAEL'S CATHOLIC CHURCH, LOCATED AT 225 EAST HIGH STREET. This church was built in 1898 to replace the first church, which was built about 1849. As one of the most beautiful structures in Springfield, it was designed by local architect Charles Cregar and built at a cost of $75,000.

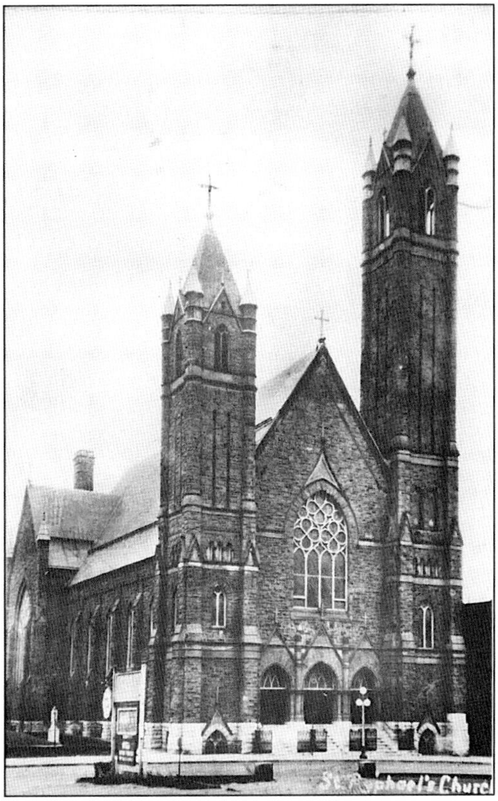

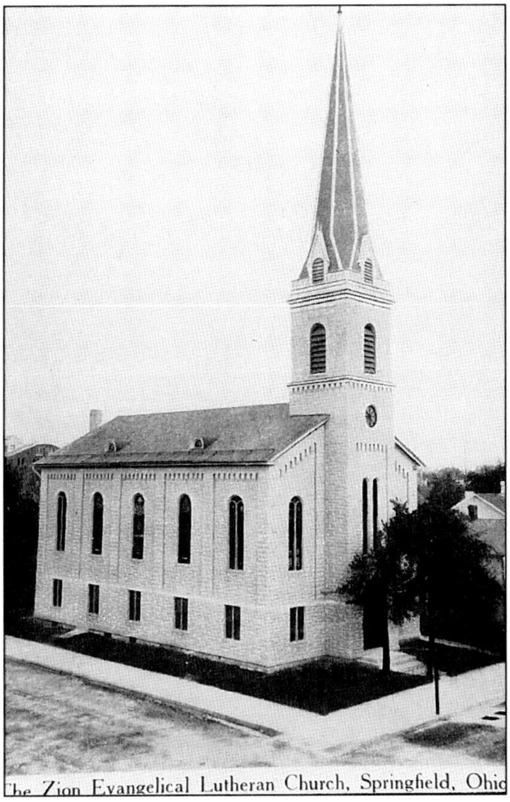

ZION LUTHERAN CHURCH ON THE SOUTHEAST CORNER OF NORTH PLUM AND WEST COLUMBIA STREET, 1940S. This church was built in the early 1900s as a spin-off of St. John's Lutheran Church, which was built in 1895 and located just two blocks to the west.

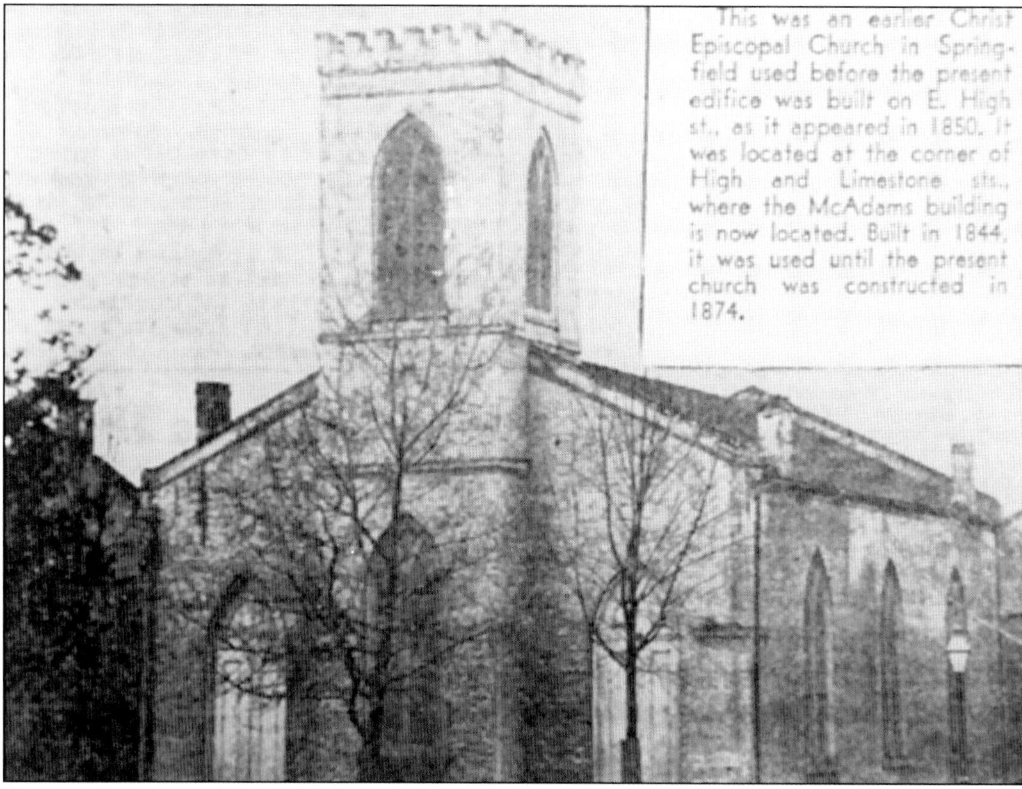

Christ Episcopal Church at Its First Location on the Southwest Corner of South Limestone Street and West High Street, Built in 1844.

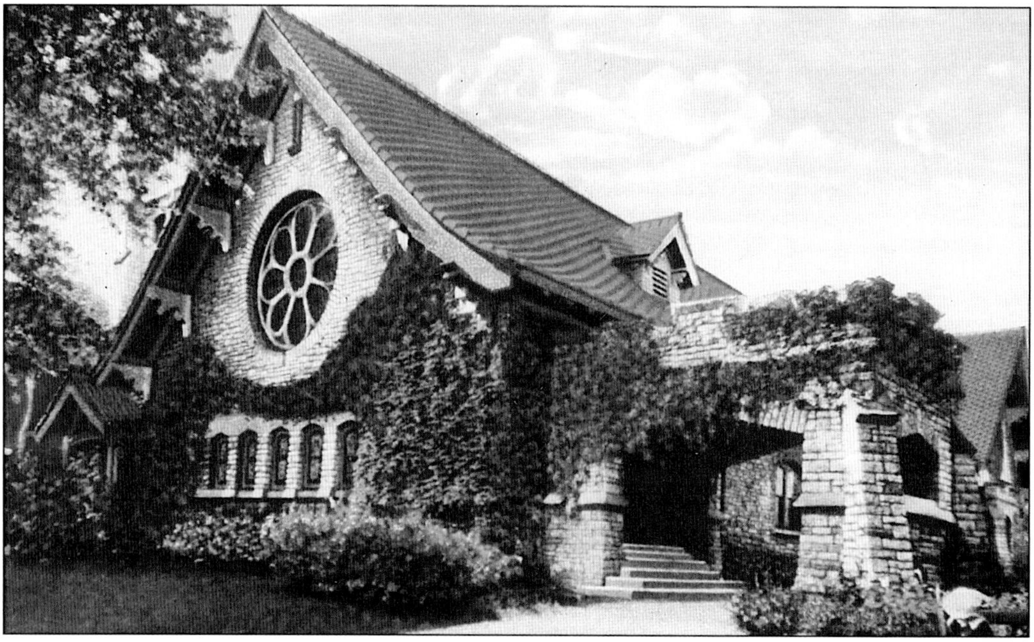

High Street United Methodist Church, Built in 1904 at 230 East High Street, 1930s.

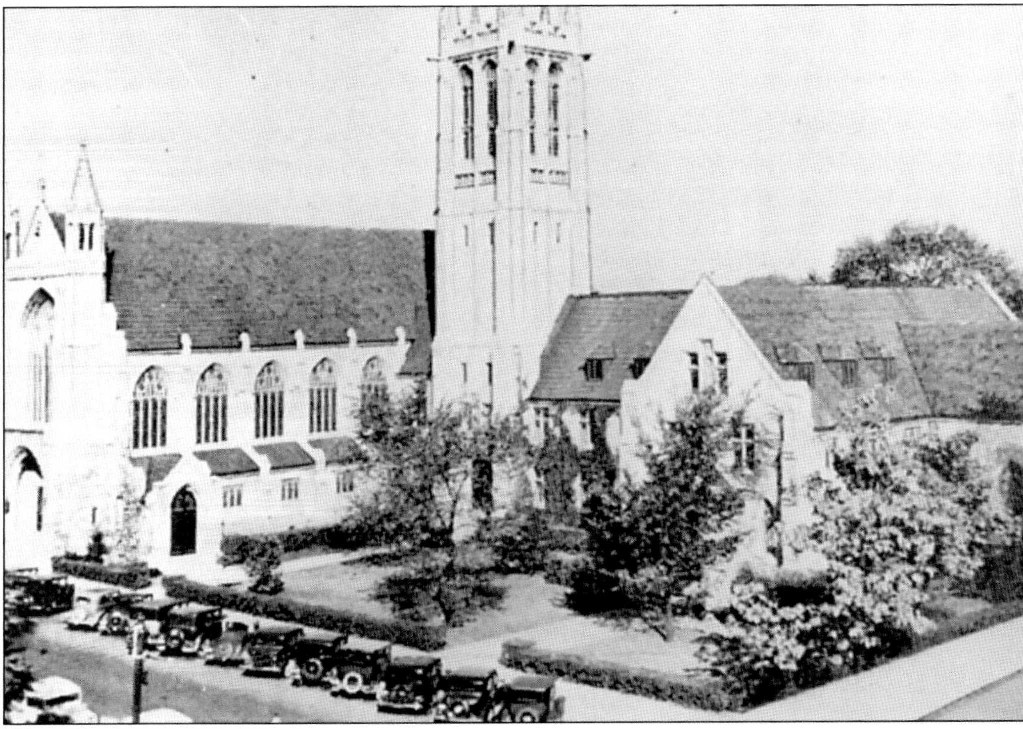

COVENANT PRESBYTERIAN CHURCH ON THE NORTHWEST CORNER OF NORTH STREET AND NORTH LIMESTONE STREET, BUILT IN 1927.

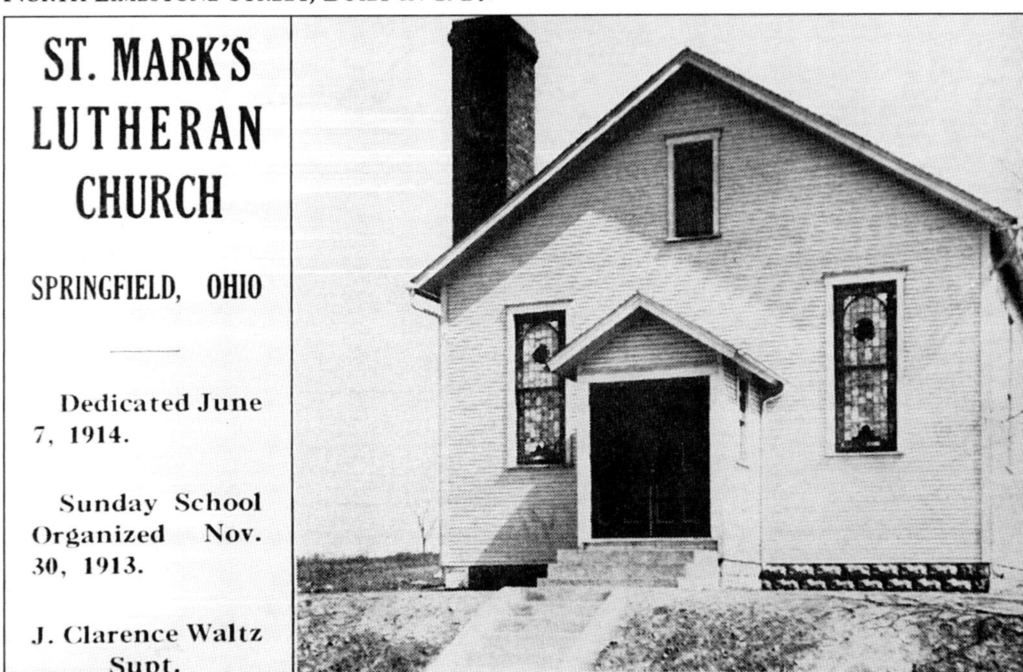

ST. MARK'S LUTHERAN CHURCH, LOCATED IN THE 900 BLOCK OF BECHTLE AVENUE, C. 1914. Later, it became a Baptist church.

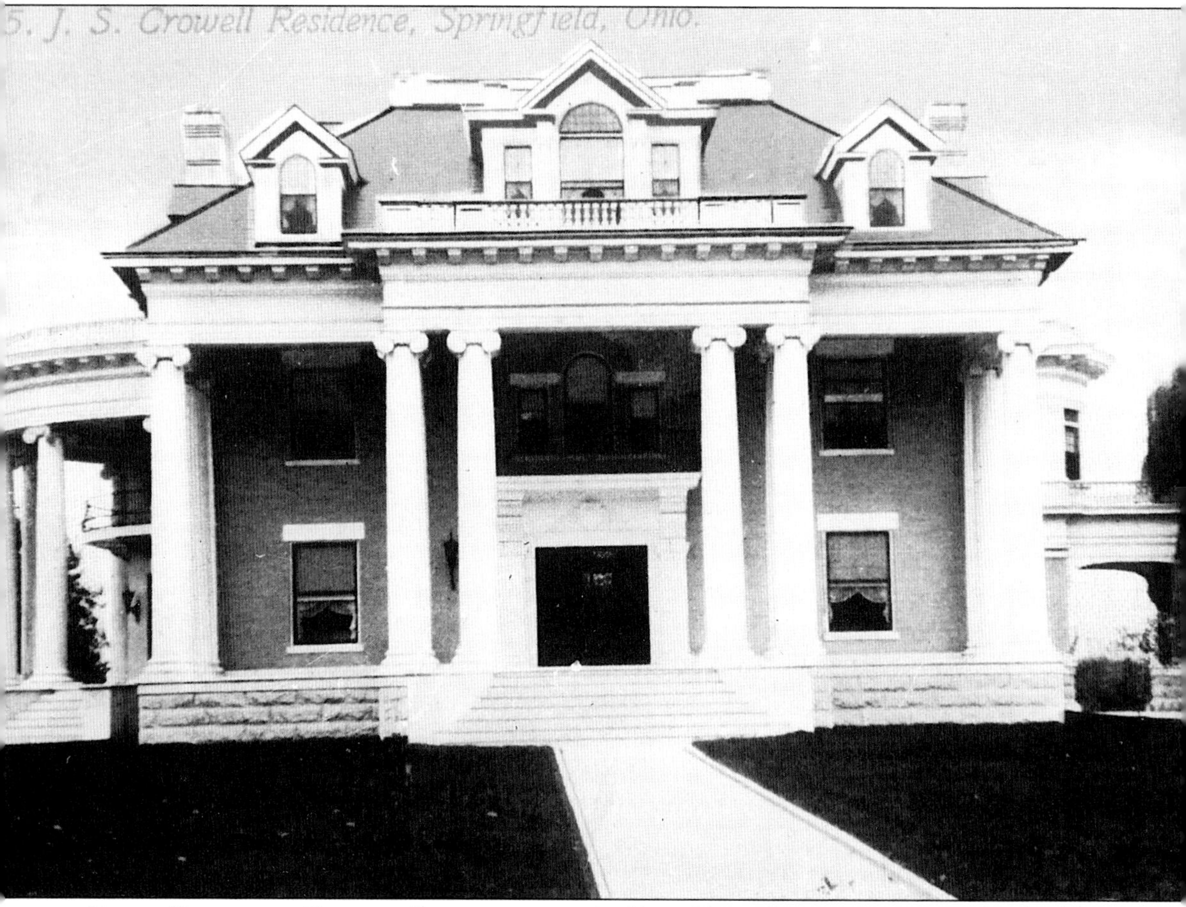

GREEK ORTHODOX CHURCH, LOCATED AT 1127 EAST HIGH STREET, C. 1920. This building had many previous owners, including J.S. Crowell, of the publishing company, and Dr. Martin, another well-known Springfield resident.

Six

Businesses

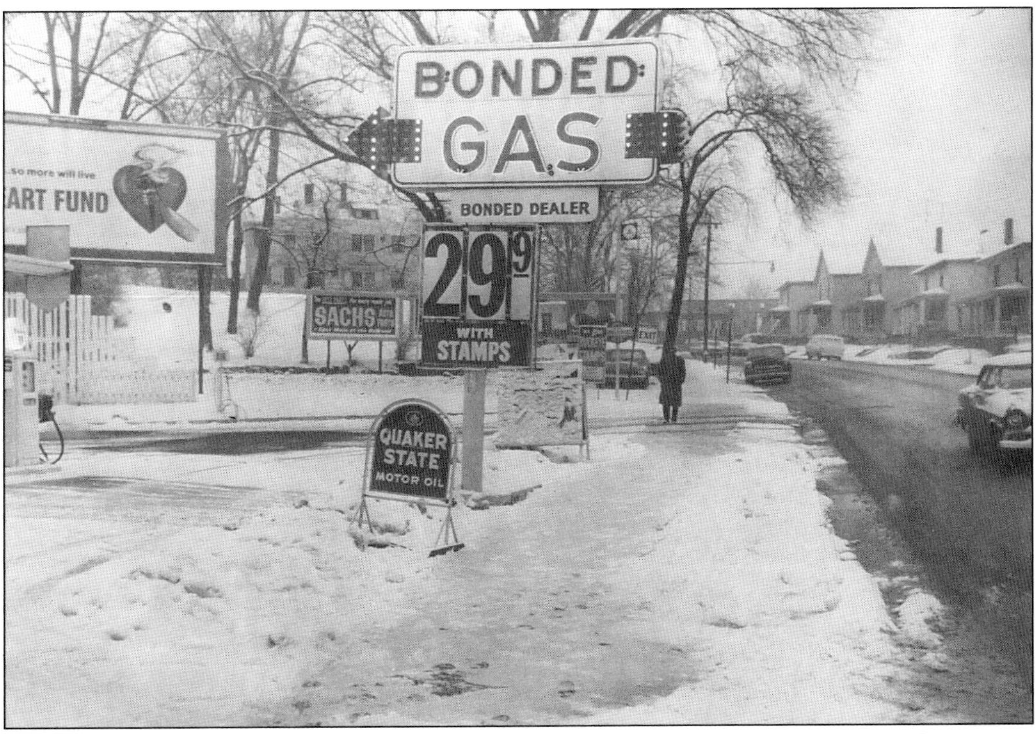

Bonded Gas Station on North Limestone Street across from Wobbe's Dry Cleaners, 1960s. Today this location is the parking lot for Norwest Mortgage.

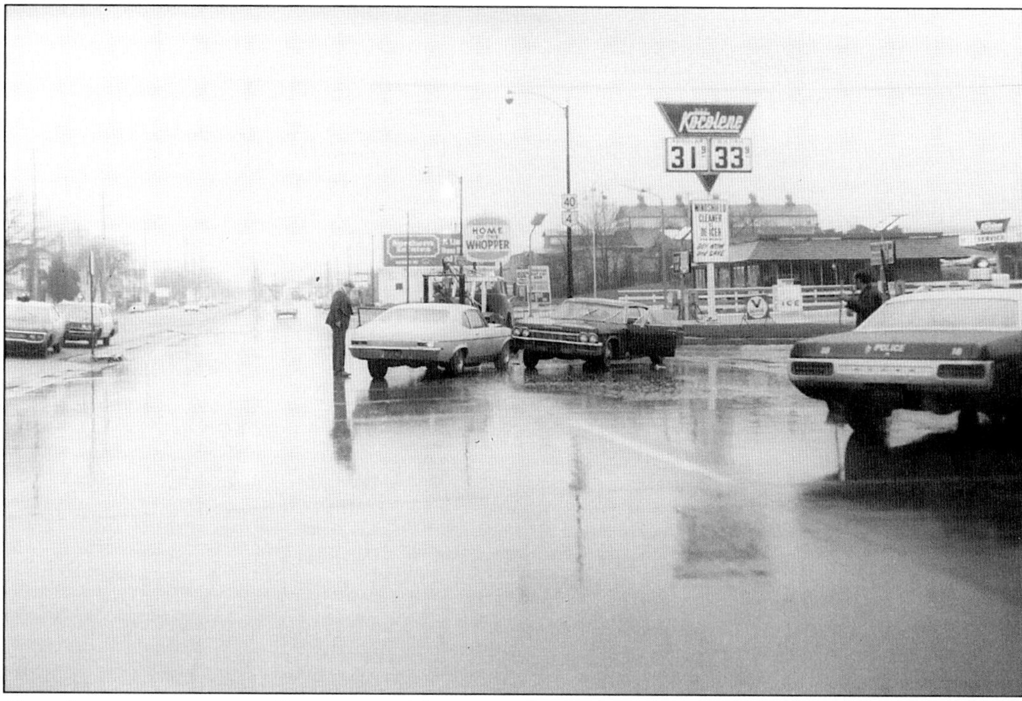

Car Accident on the Corner of Zischler Street and West North Street, c. 1960. This photo shows the low price for Kocolene gas.

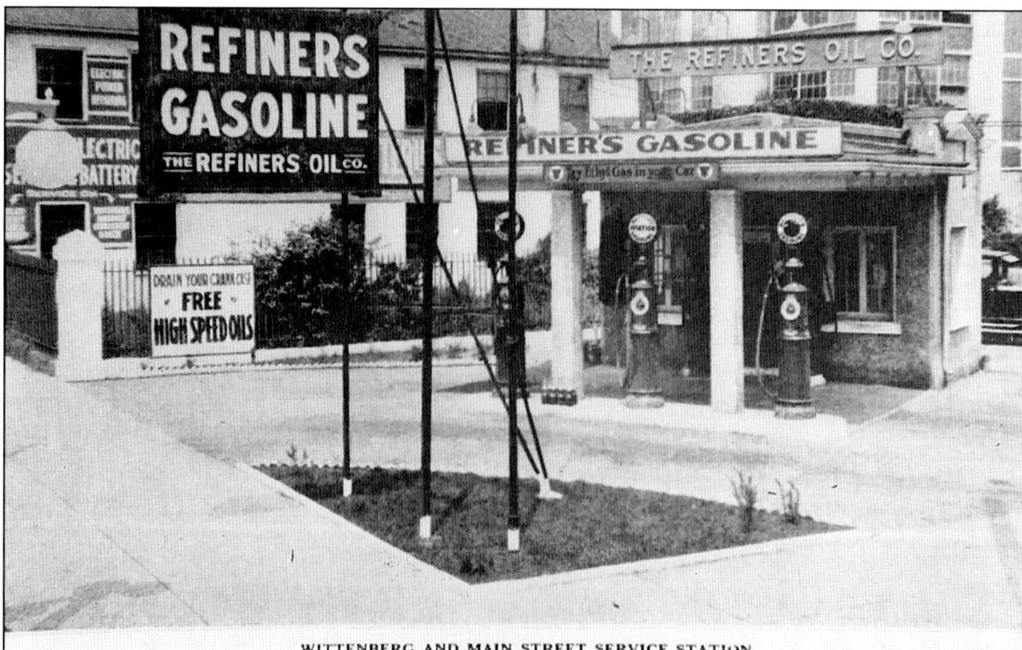

Refiner's Oil Company, Located on the Northwest Corner of West Main and Wittenberg, 1920s. This was a typical gas station of that era.

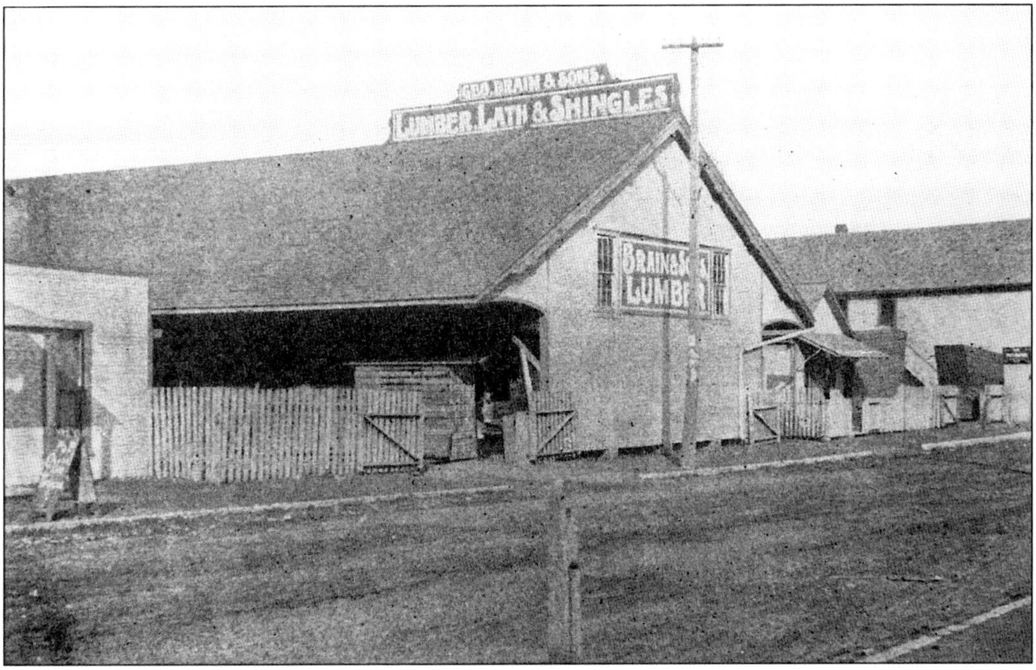

BRAIN LUMBER COMPANY, LOCATED AT 401 EAST STREET, EARLY 1900S.

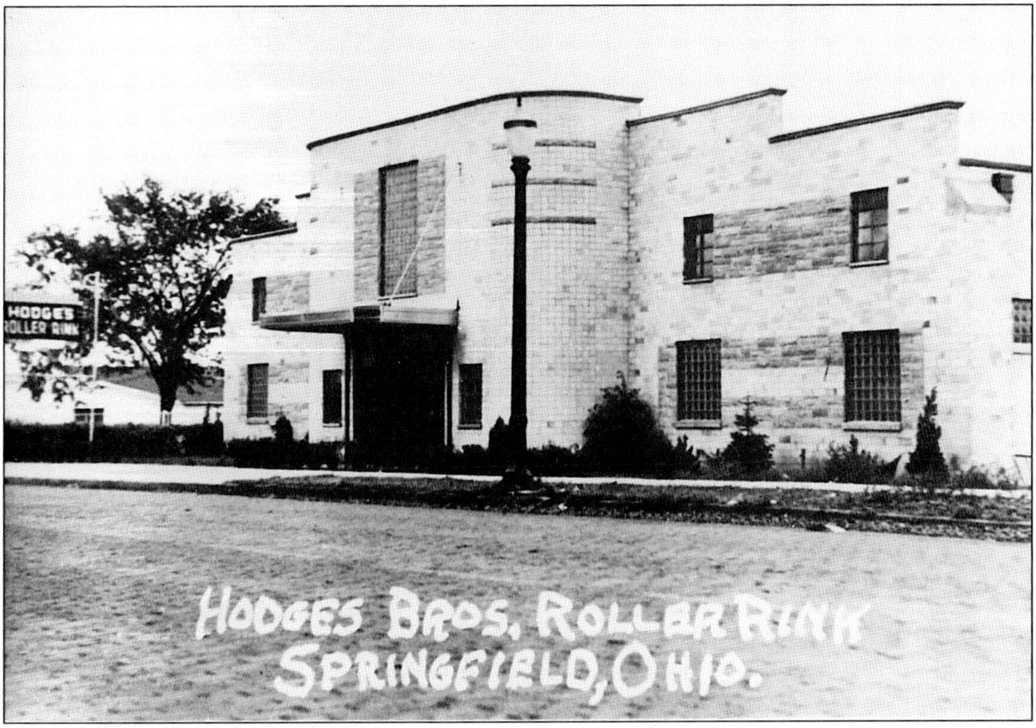

HODGES BROTHERS ROLLER SKATING RINK, LOCATED AT 1620 WEST MAIN STREET. This roller skating rink opened in 1948 and was a popular place amongst the people of Springfield. The W-W Electric Company bought the building in January 1964 and operated there until the current owners, All-Phase Electric Company, took over in September 1975.

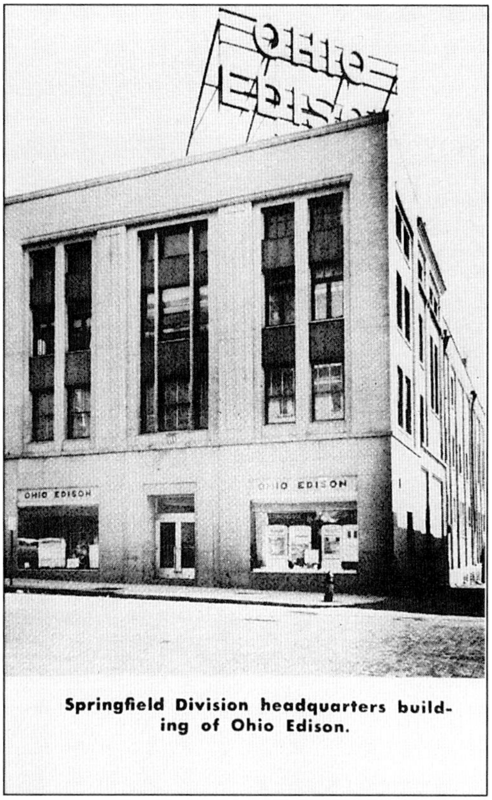

Springfield Division headquarters building of Ohio Edison.

Ohio Edison Company, Located at 125 East High Street, 1940s. The Ohio Edison Company supplied electricity to Springfield from this location until it was torn down in June 1992.

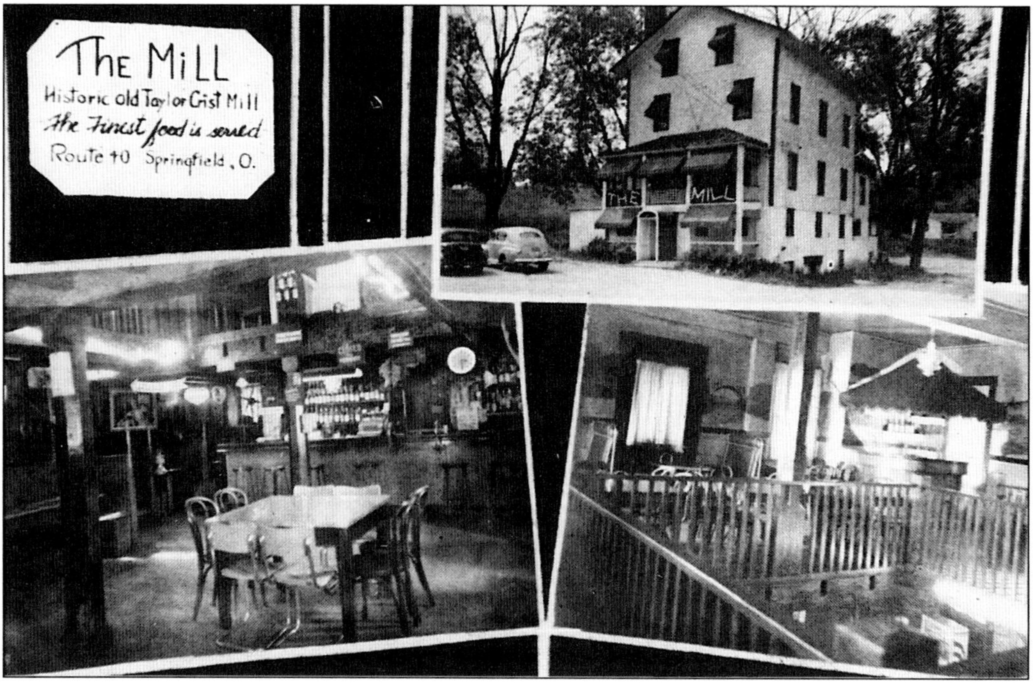

The Mill Restaurant (Formerly Taylor Grist Mill), Located at 3404 West National Road, 1940s.

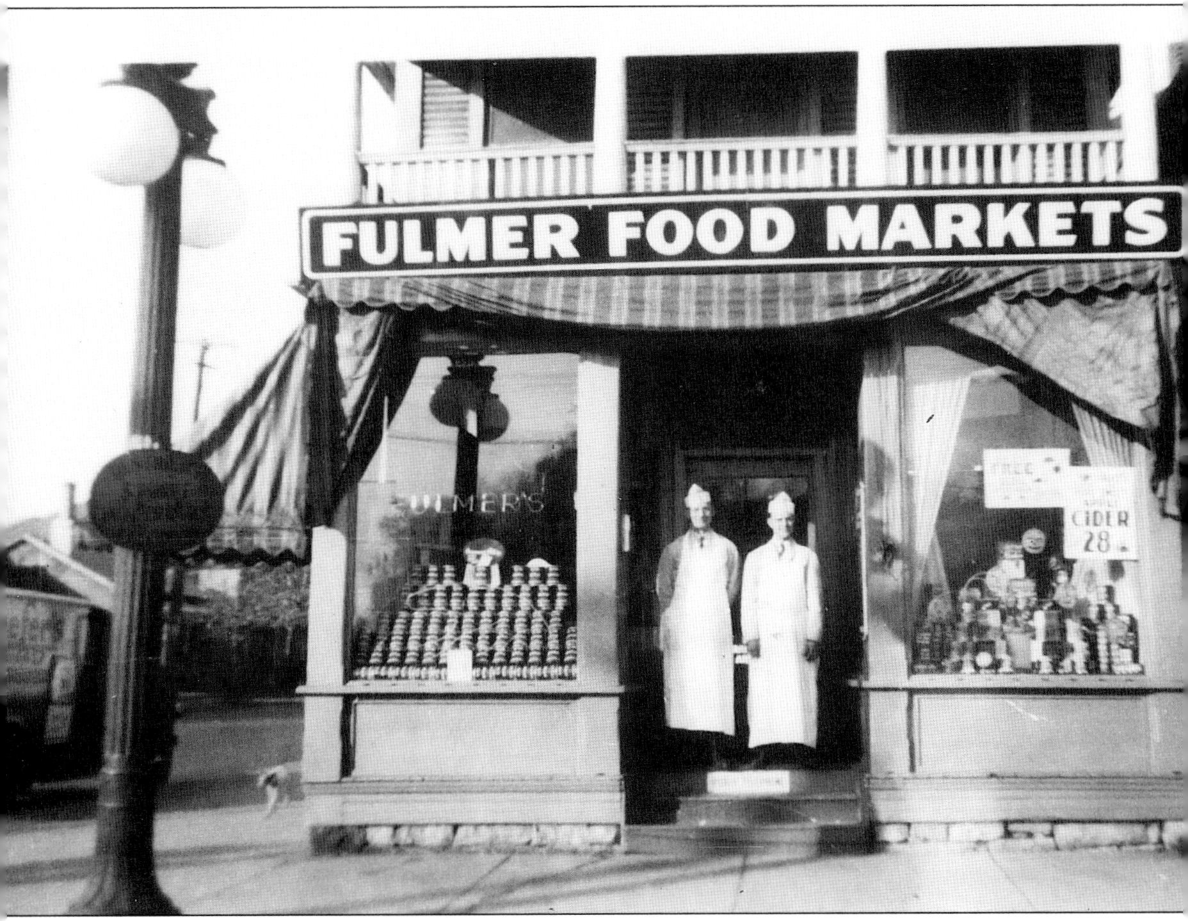

FULMER'S STORE, LOCATED AT THE NORTHEAST CORNER OF WEST HIGH STREET AND SOUTH YELLOW SPRINGS STREET, 1939. Carl Thomas is pictured on the right.

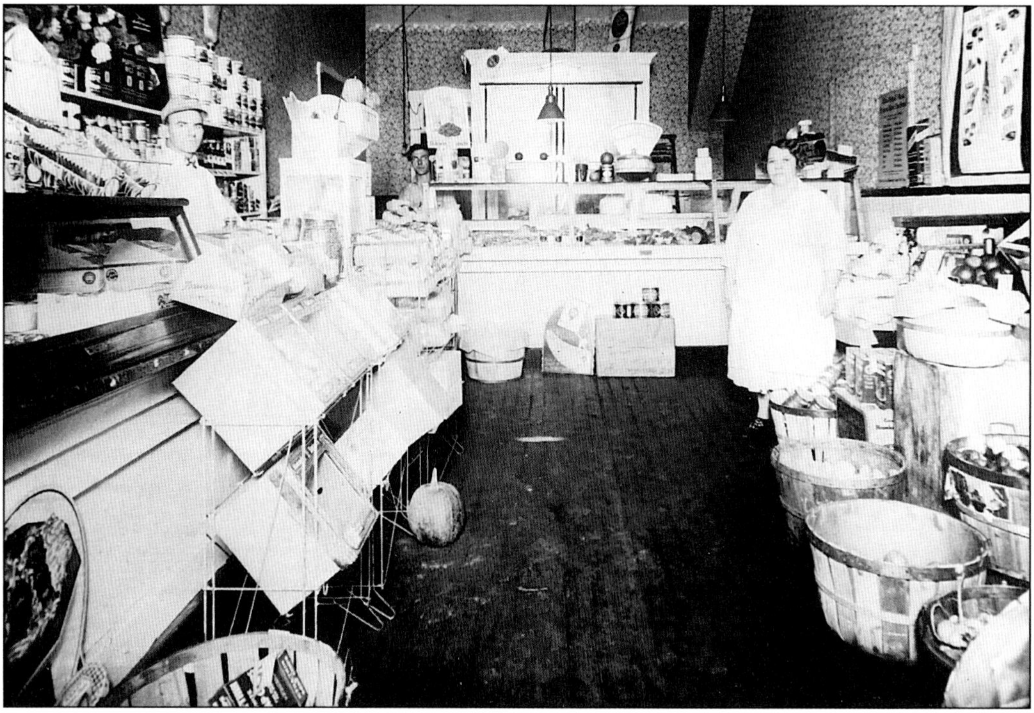

Martin's Market, Located at 538 West Main Street on the Northeast Corner of Race and West Main Street, 1930s. Homer Martin is in the back of the store and Ruth Martin is on the right.

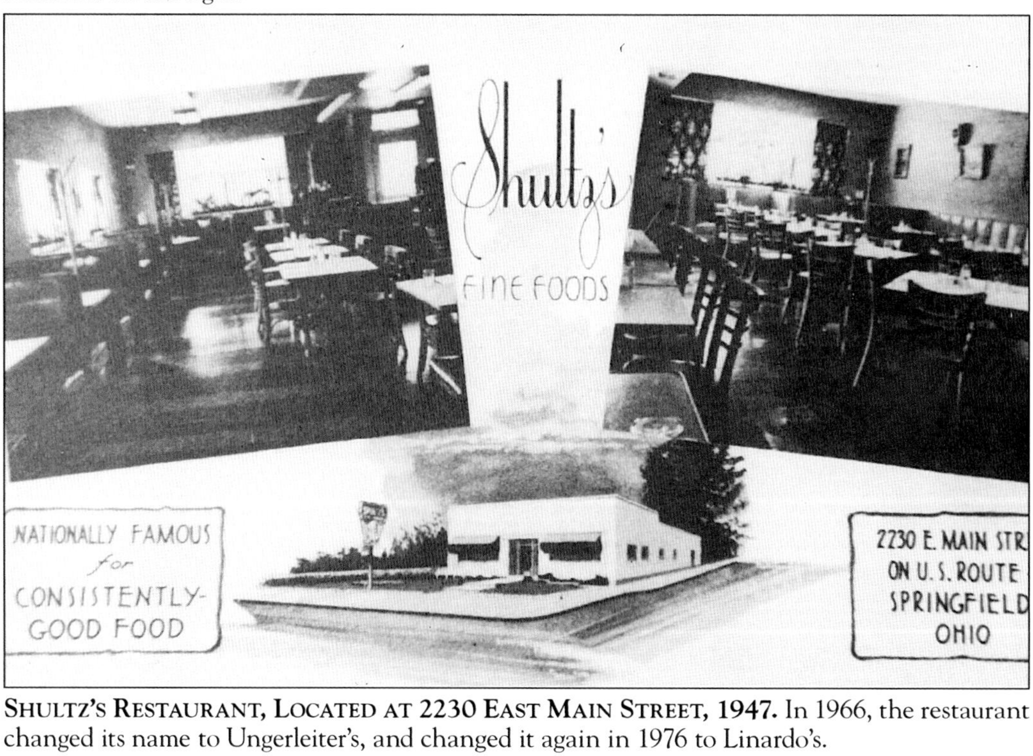

Shultz's Restaurant, Located at 2230 East Main Street, 1947. In 1966, the restaurant changed its name to Ungerleiter's, and changed it again in 1976 to Linardo's.

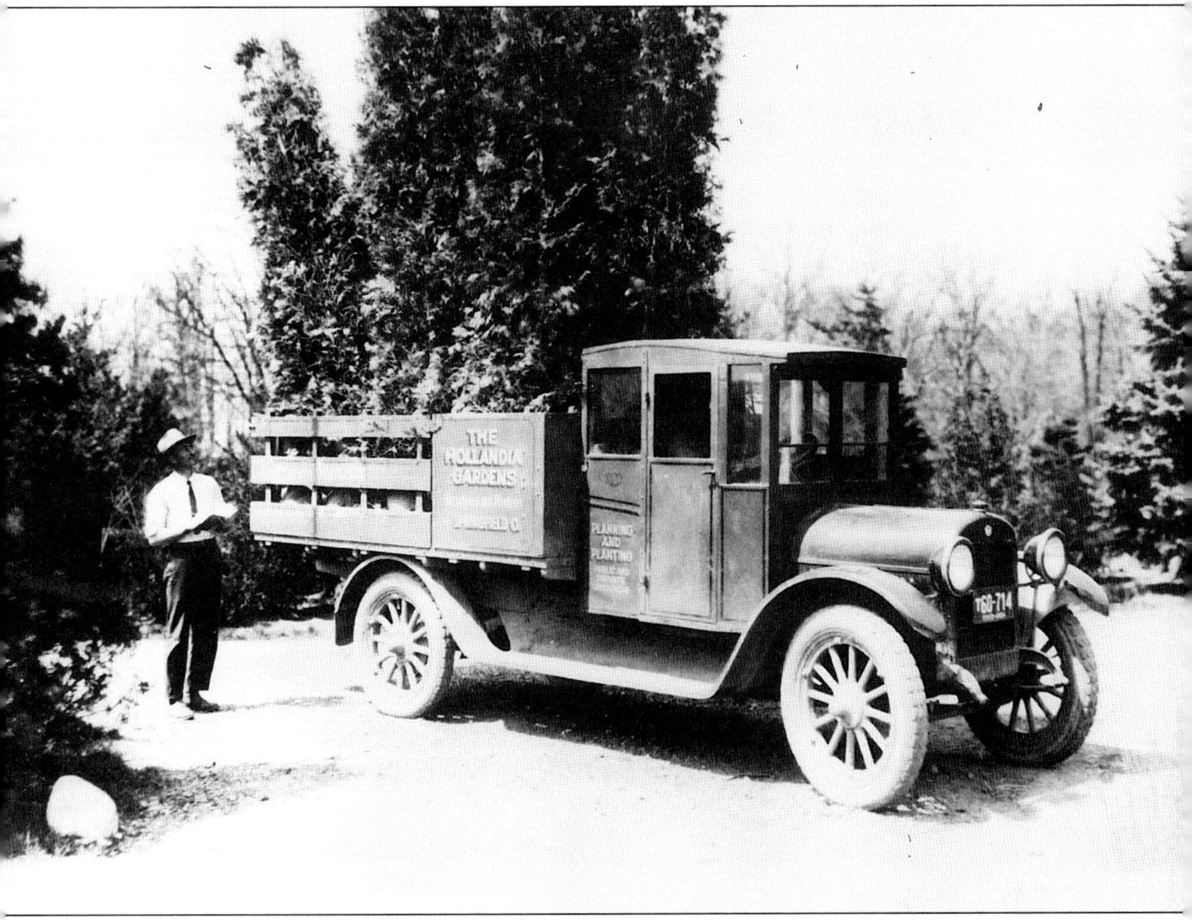

HOLLANDIA GARDENS, AT ITS NORTH LIMESTONE STREET LOCATION ON THE EAST SIDE, LATE 1920S. This photo was taken when the Gardens were located at this site about two blocks north of Home Road. The truck was a Reo and the salesman pictured was an employee of Hollandia.

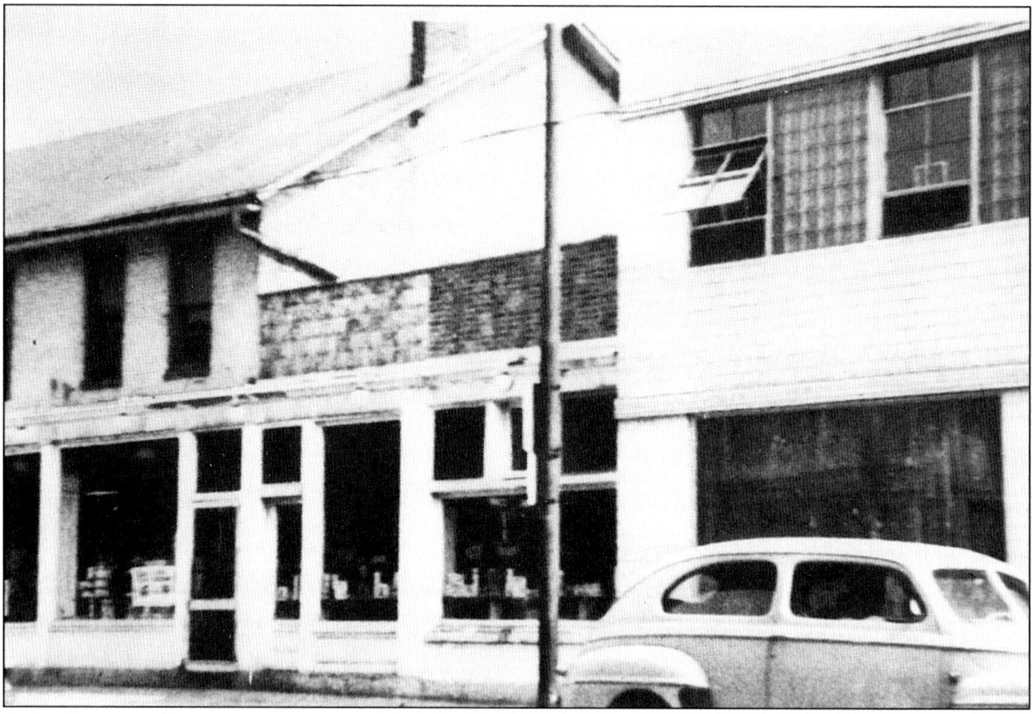

P.D. COSMOS COMPANY ON THE SOUTHWEST CORNER OF WEST MAIN AND PLUM STREET, 1930S. This was a popular dairy until it was taken over by Lawson Milk Company. Today it is the site of the Salvation Army.

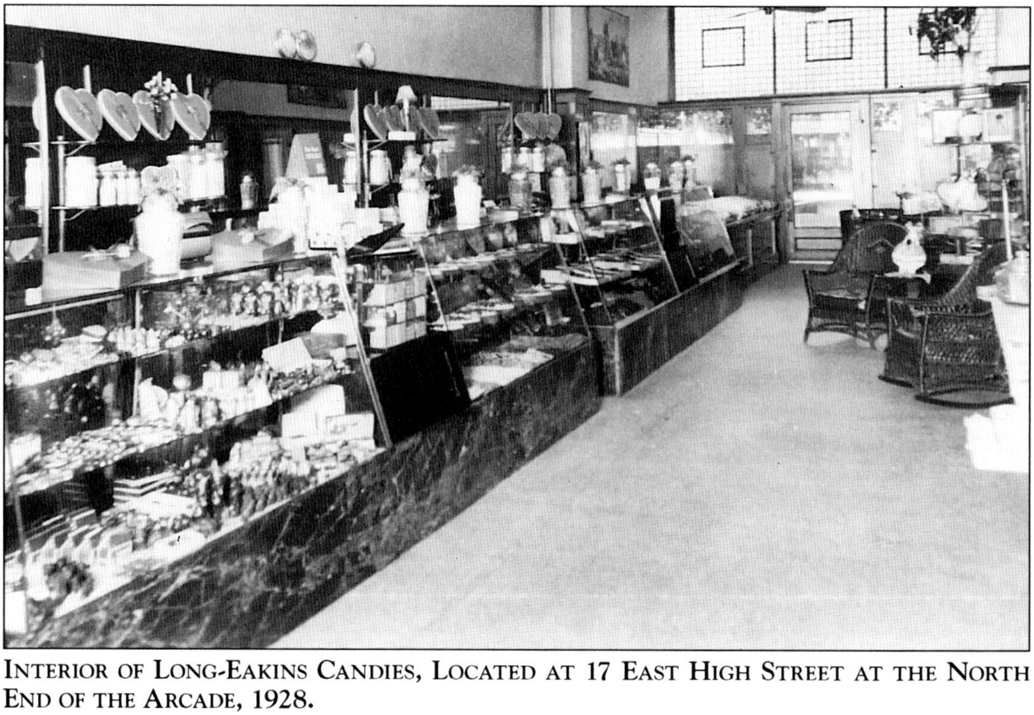

INTERIOR OF LONG-EAKINS CANDIES, LOCATED AT 17 EAST HIGH STREET AT THE NORTH END OF THE ARCADE, 1928.

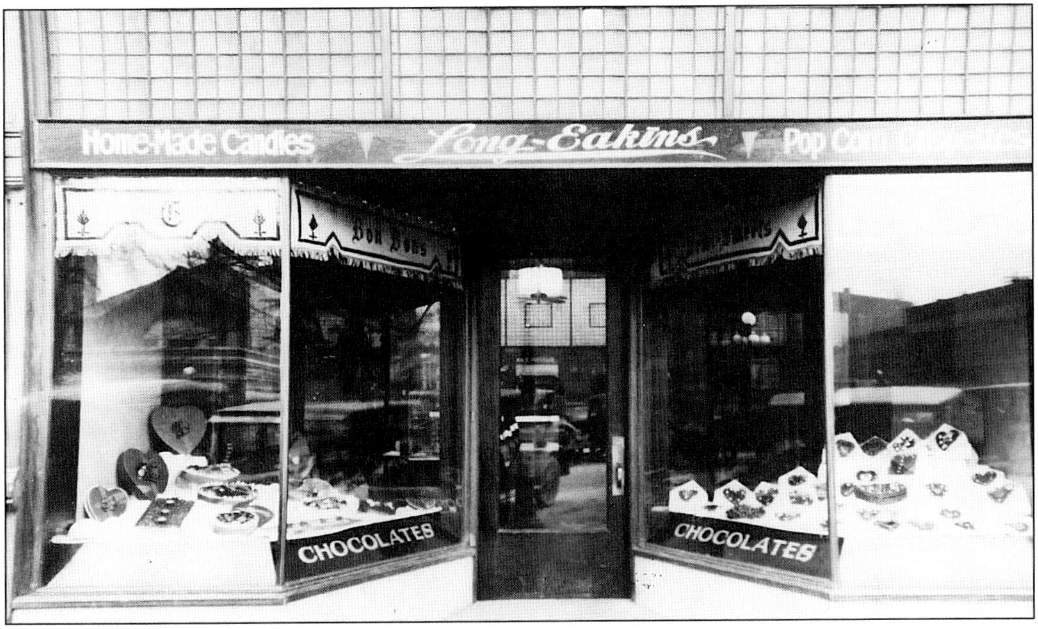

EXTERIOR OF LONG-EAKINS CANDIES, 1928.

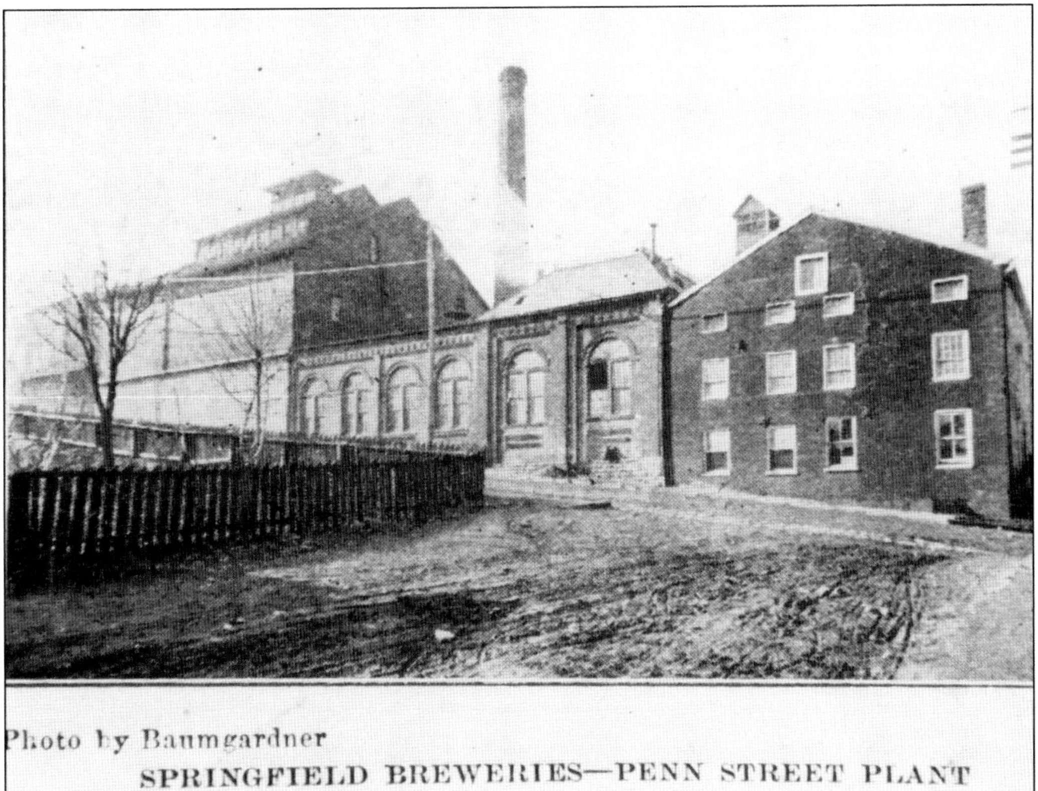

SPRINGFIELD BREWERIES, LOCATED ON PENN STREET BETWEEN EAST MAIN STREET AND EAST HIGH STREET BEHIND SCHULER'S BAKERY, c. 1915.

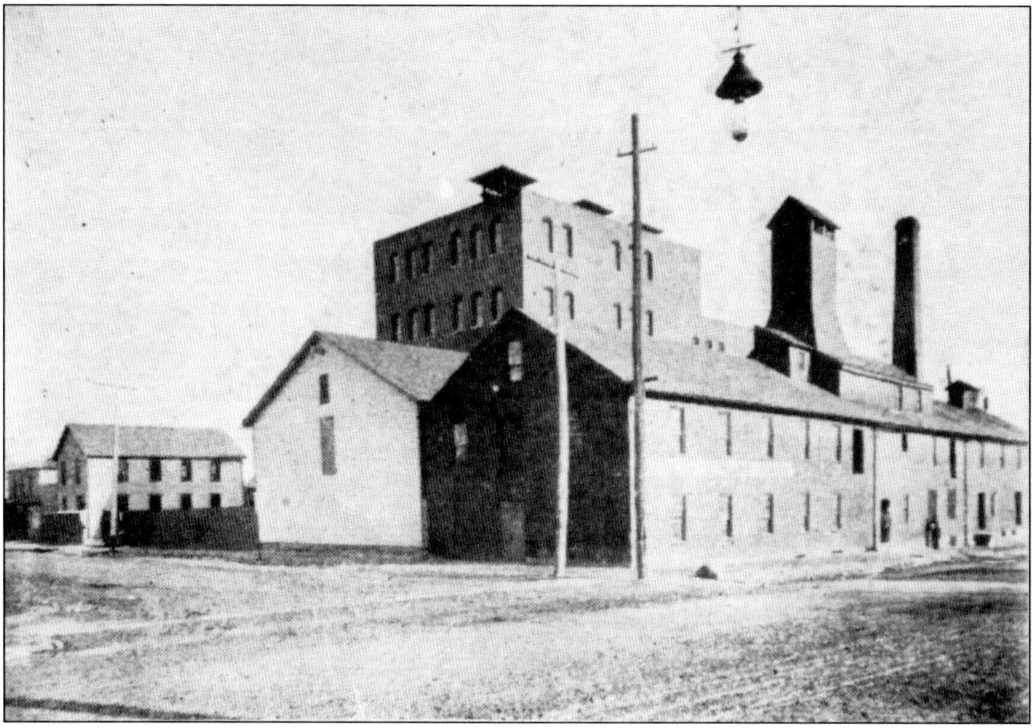

SPRINGFIELD BREWERIES, LOCATED ON THE EAST SIDE OF SPRING STREET BETWEEN NORTH STREET AND COLUMBIA STREET, C. 1915.

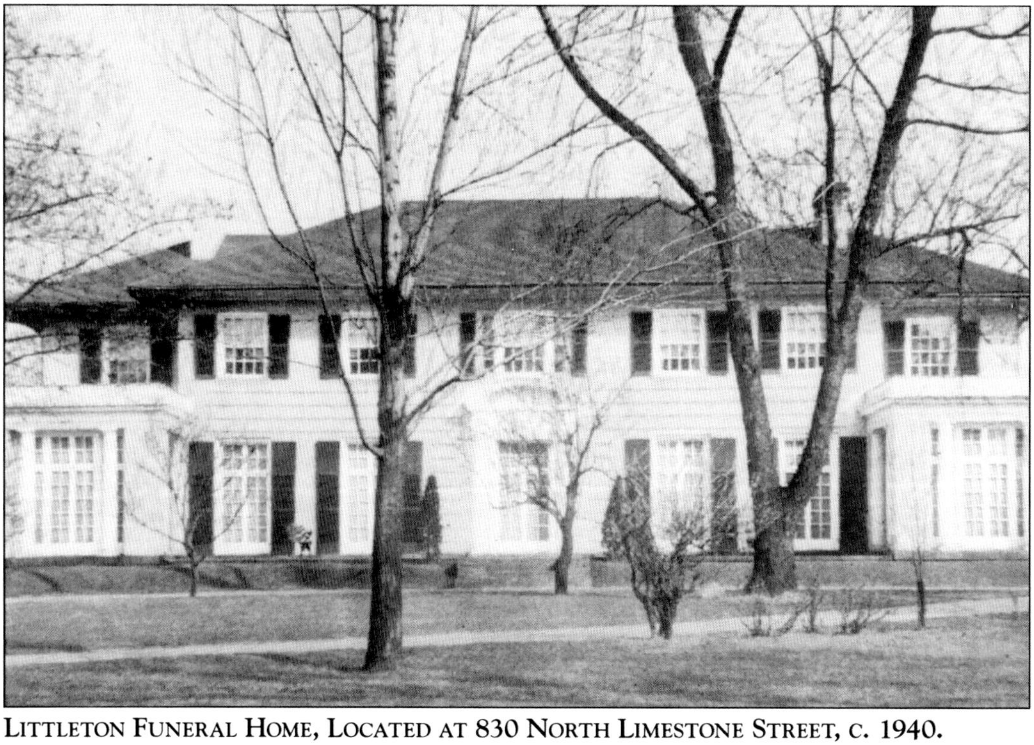

LITTLETON FUNERAL HOME, LOCATED AT 830 NORTH LIMESTONE STREET, C. 1940.

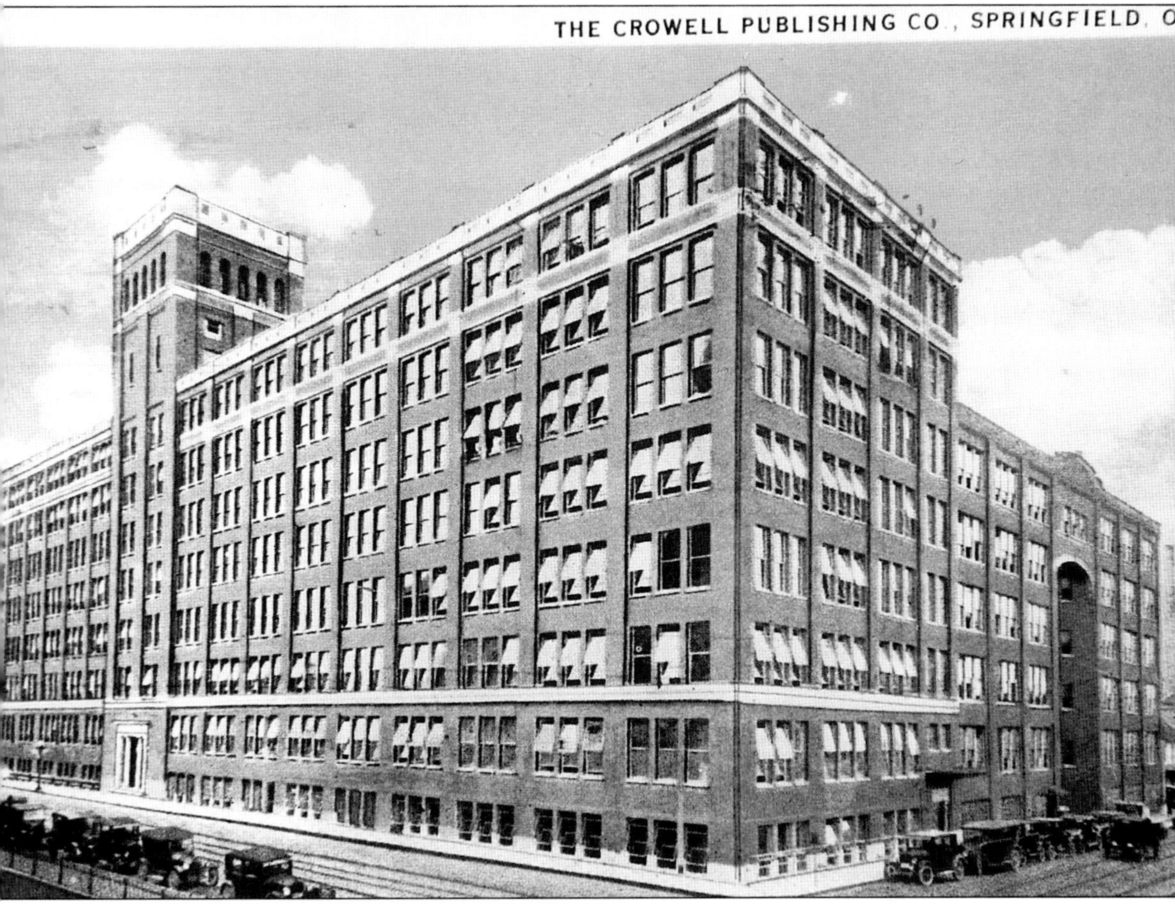

CROWELL COLLIER PUBLISHING COMPANY, LOCATED ON THE NORTHWEST CORNER OF WEST HIGH AND SOUTH WITTENBERG, 1920S. Crowell Collier published popular magazines such as *Colliers*, *American*, *Country Gentlemen*, and *Farm and Fireside*.

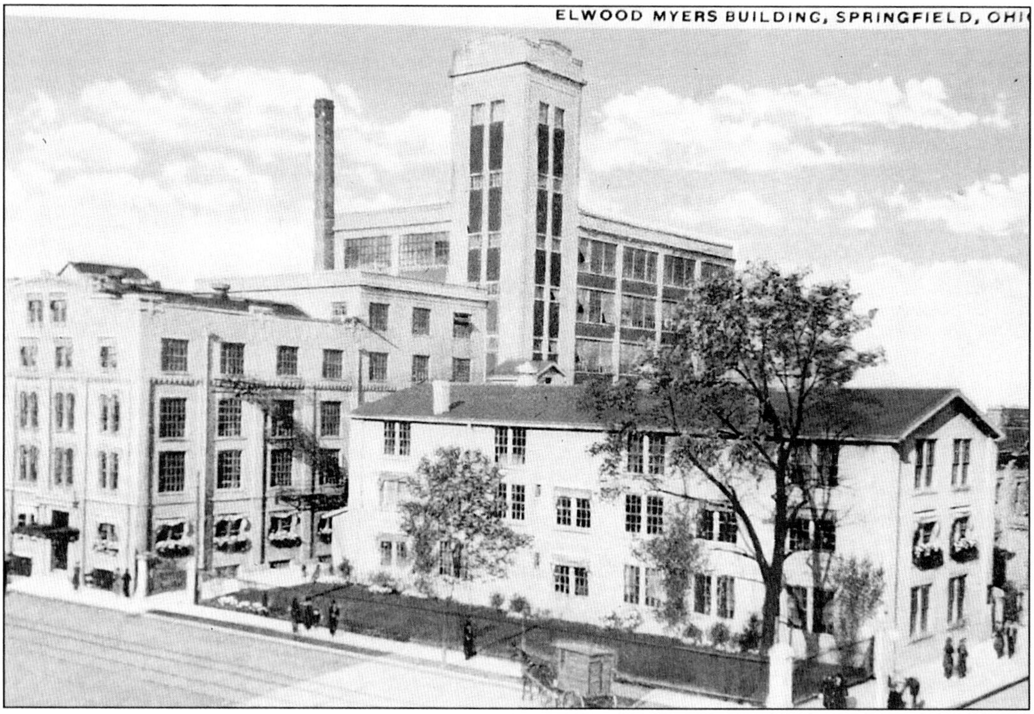

Elwood Myers Company, Leather Products Manufacturer, Located at 14 North Lowry Street, Early 1900s. Today this building is the Robertson Can Company.

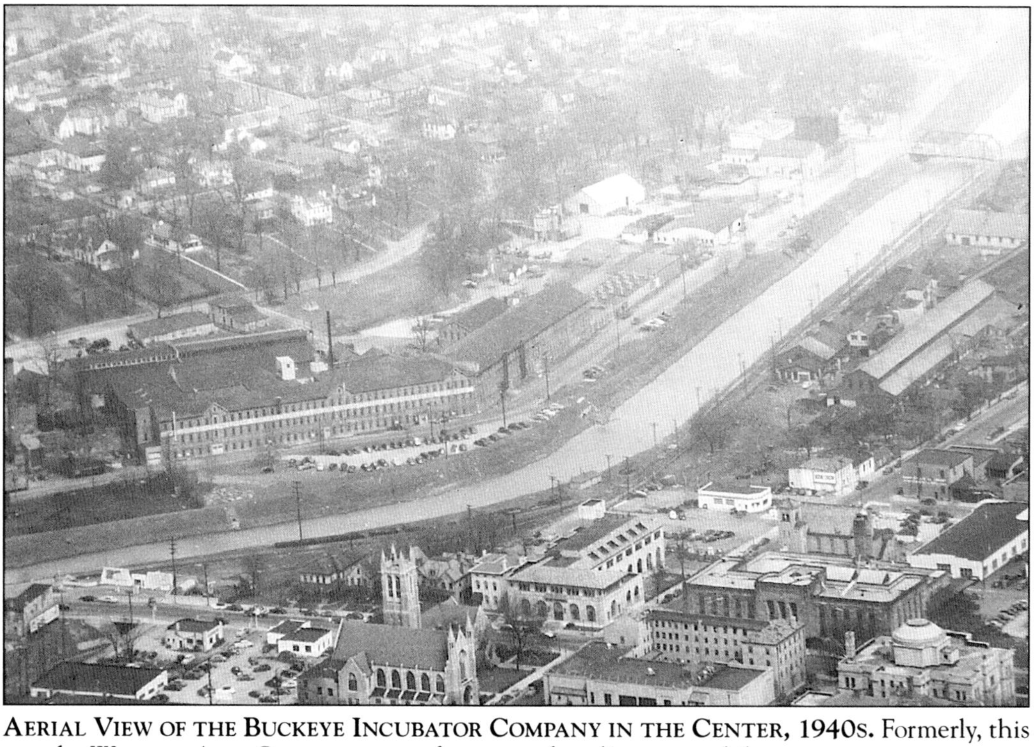

Aerial View of the Buckeye Incubator Company in the Center, 1940s. Formerly, this was the Westcott Auto Company, manufacturers of quality automobiles.

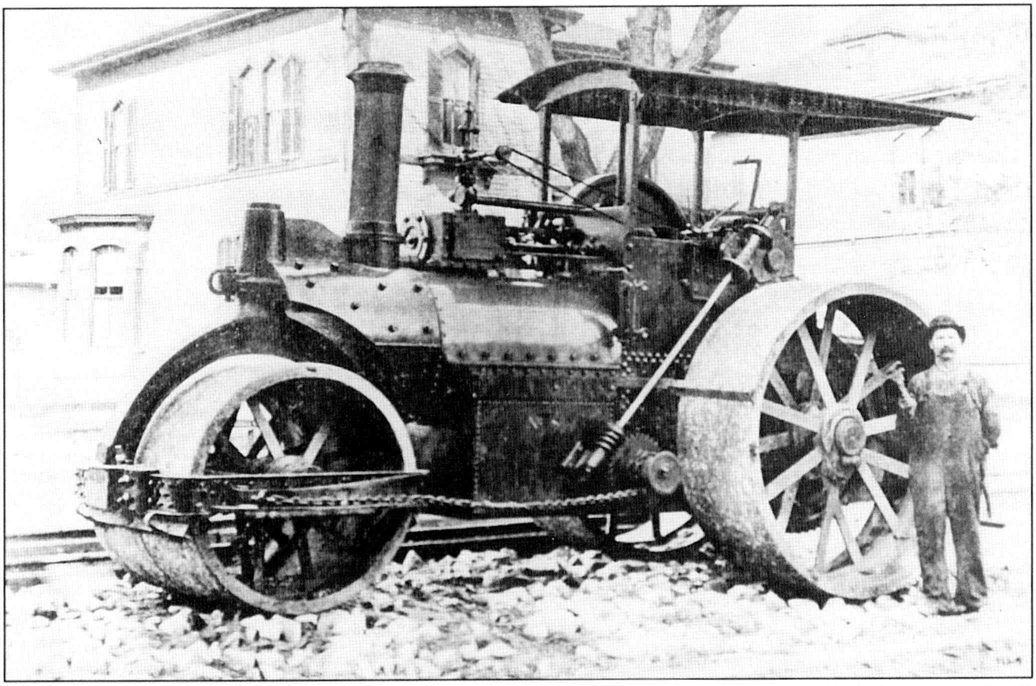

KELLY SPRINGFIELD ROAD ROLLER, 1890S. Later, Kelly Springfield became Buffalo-Springfield, until it finally settled on the name Bomag Manufacturing. Their offices were located on Kenton Street, although they are no longer in business today.

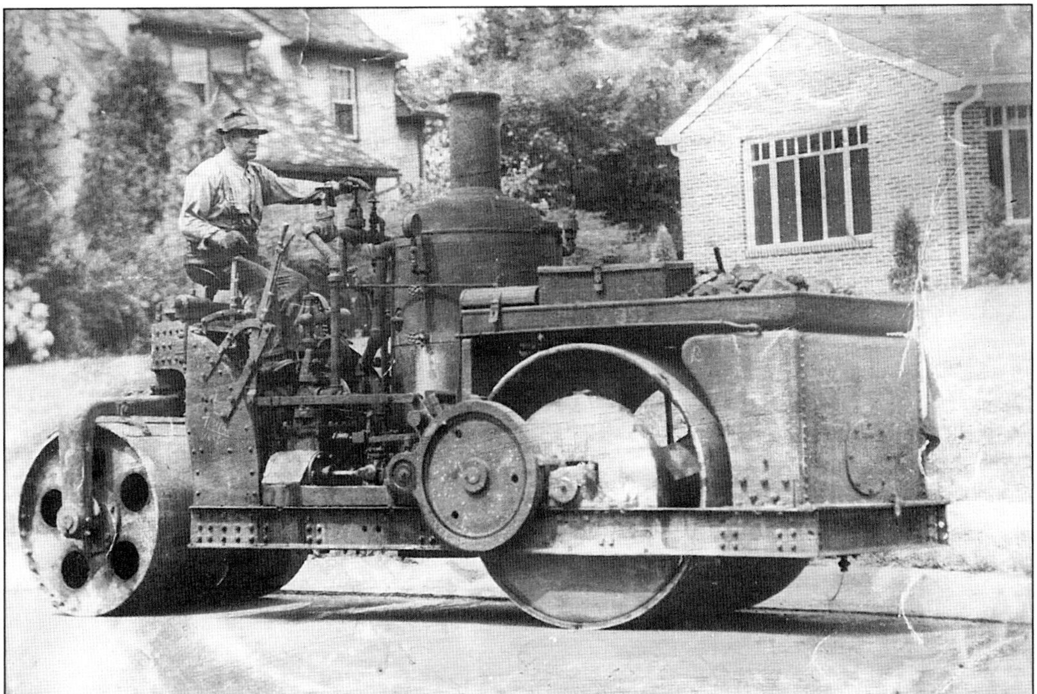

JOHN SCHRADER OPERATING A BUFFALO-SPRINGFIELD ROAD ROLLER, 1920S. Since this machine was powered by coal fire, it was possible to view the coal storage in the front.

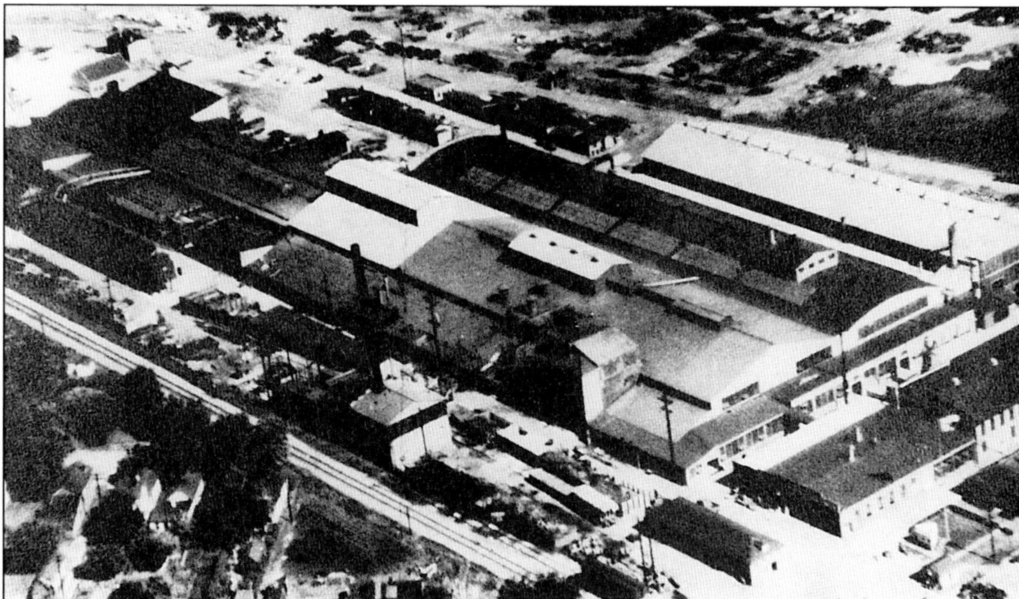

Ohio Steel Foundry Company's four electric furnaces produce about 750 tons of steel castings per month.

THE OHIO STEEL FOUNDRY, LOCATED AT 1075 JAMES STREET, 1940S. This company manufactured steel castings.

National Supply Company covers 17 acres and manufactures diesel and gas engines ranging from 250 to 2000 horsepower.

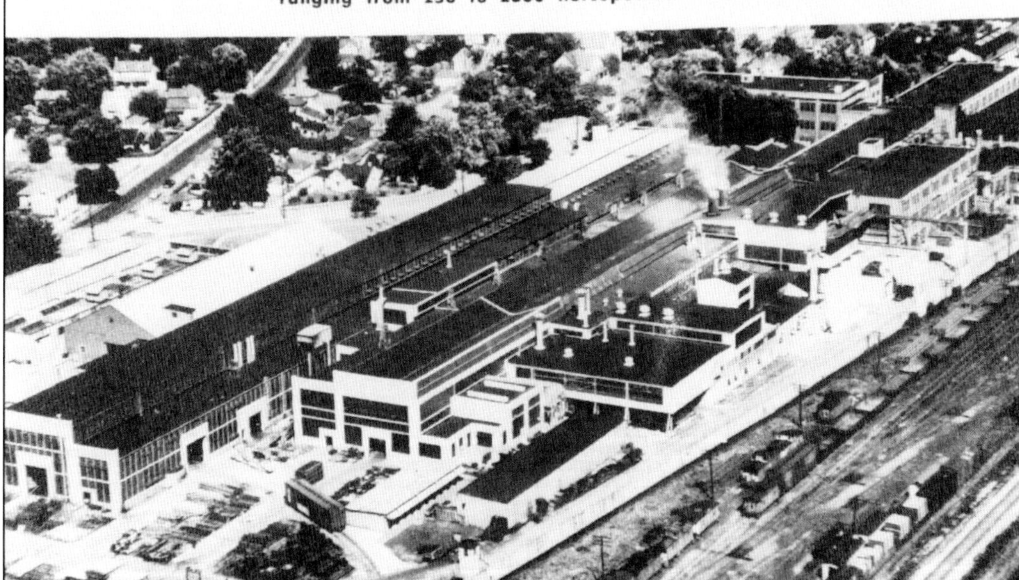

NATIONAL SUPPLY COMPANY, LOCATED AT 1401 SHERIDAN AVENUE, 1940S. The National Supply Company manufactured gas and diesel engines.

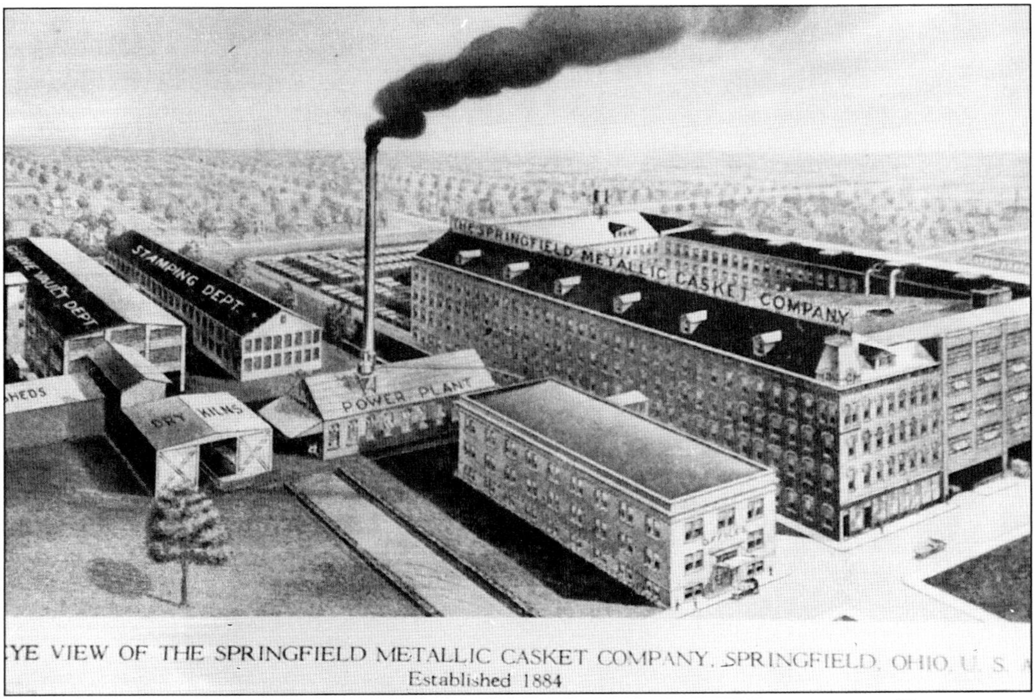

THE SPRINGFIELD METALLIC COMPANY, LOCATED ON THE NORTHWEST CORNER OF WEST COLUMBIA AND NORTH CENTER, C. 1915. This business manufactured burial vaults and caskets.

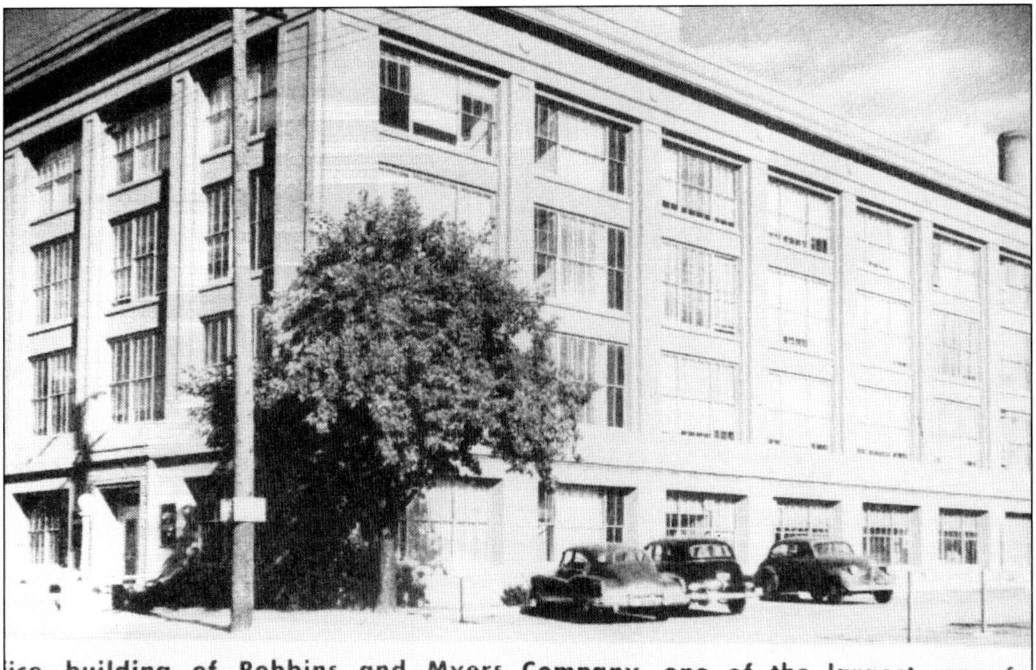

ROBBINS AND MYERS COMPANY, LOCATED AT 1345 LAGONDA AVENUE, 1940S. Robbins and Myers manufactured several items including fans, hoists, and electric heat.

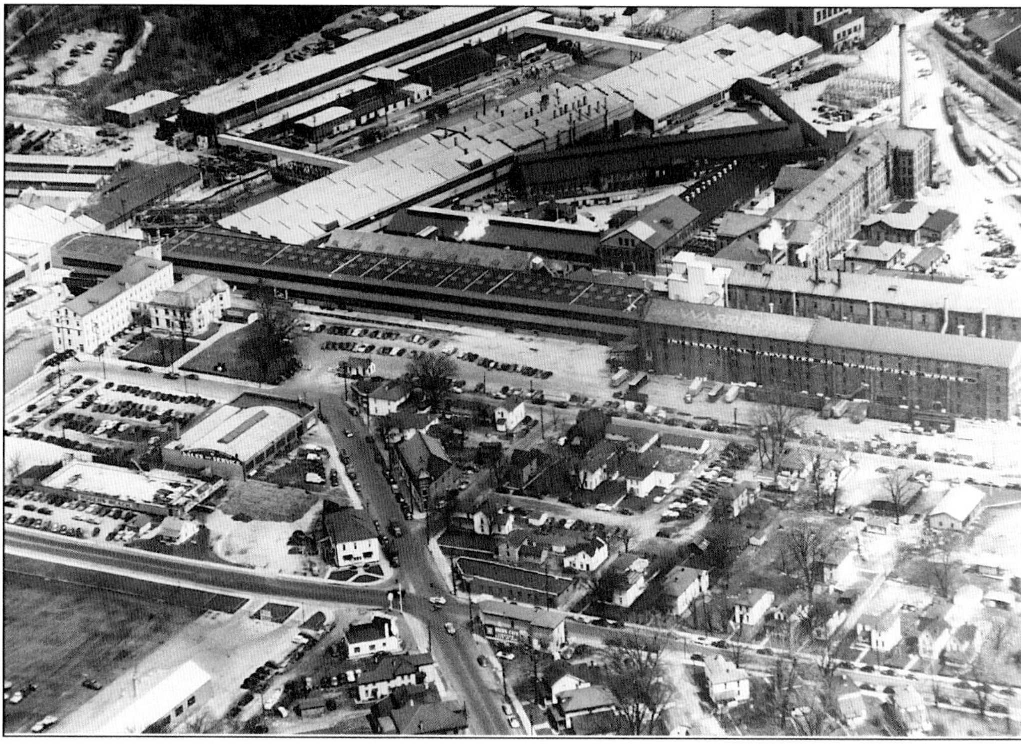

Aerial View of International Harvester Company Plant, 1930s. Notice the Rogers Beach swimming pool (formerly Marston's pool) at the left.

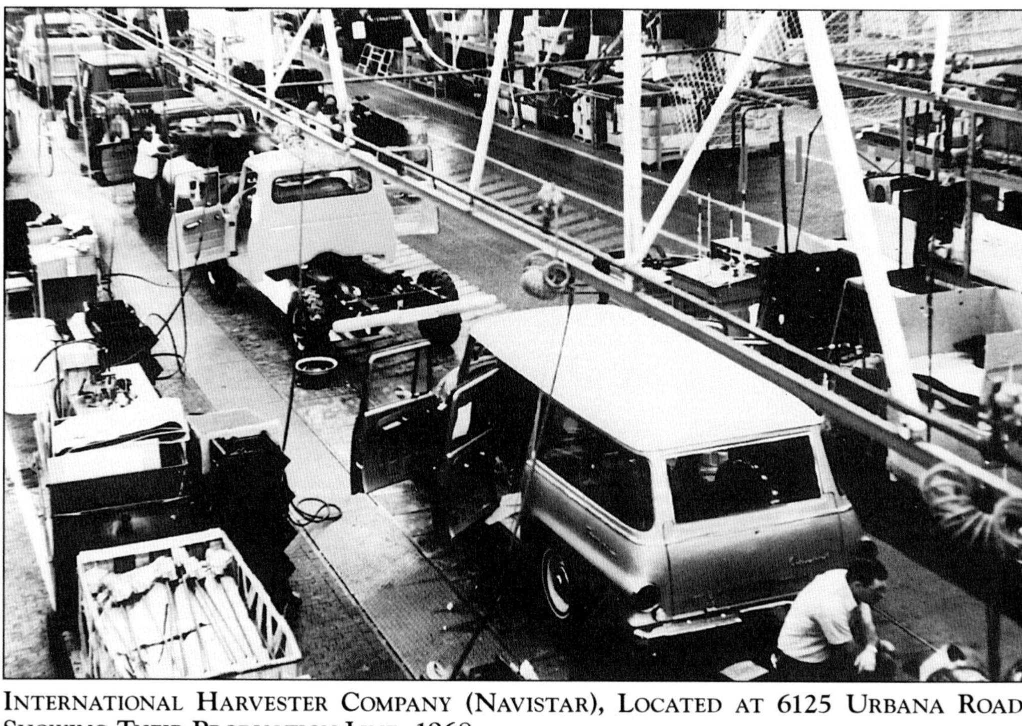

International Harvester Company (Navistar), Located at 6125 Urbana Road, Showing Their Production Line, 1968.

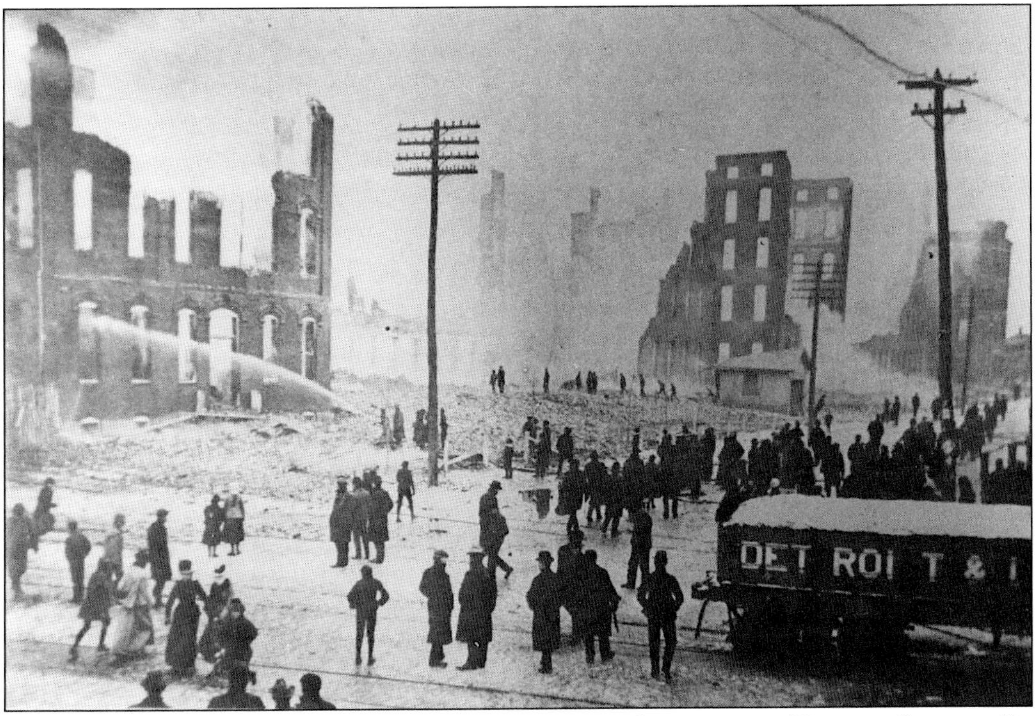

The East Street Shops on the Corner of East Street and Kenton Street. On February 10, 1902, these shops were the victims of a disastrous fire. Before the accident, they were the second largest industrial complex in the world, next to Krupp's in Germany.

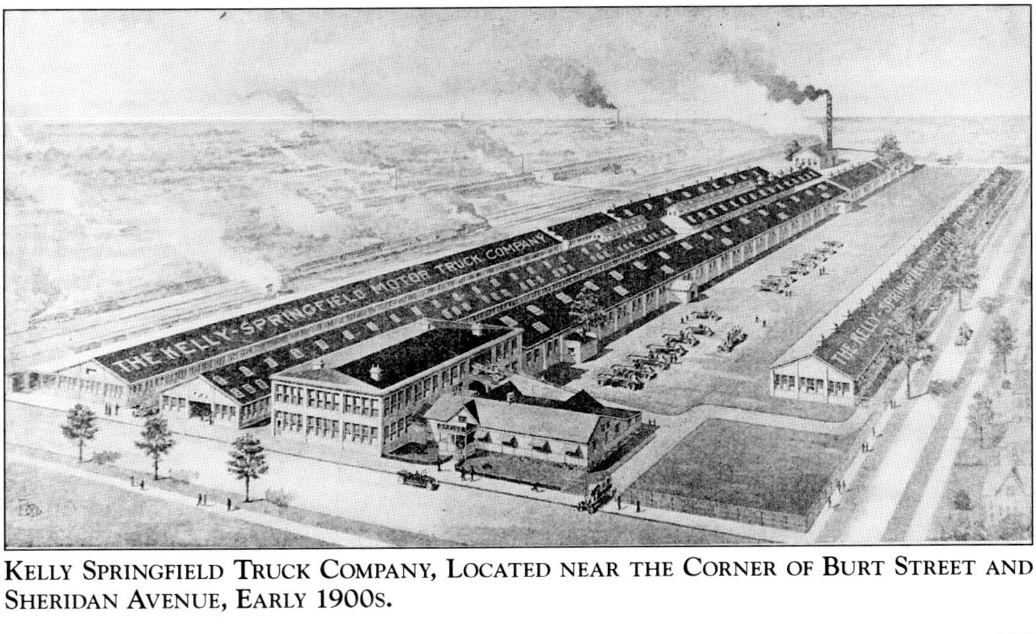

Kelly Springfield Truck Company, Located near the Corner of Burt Street and Sheridan Avenue, Early 1900s.

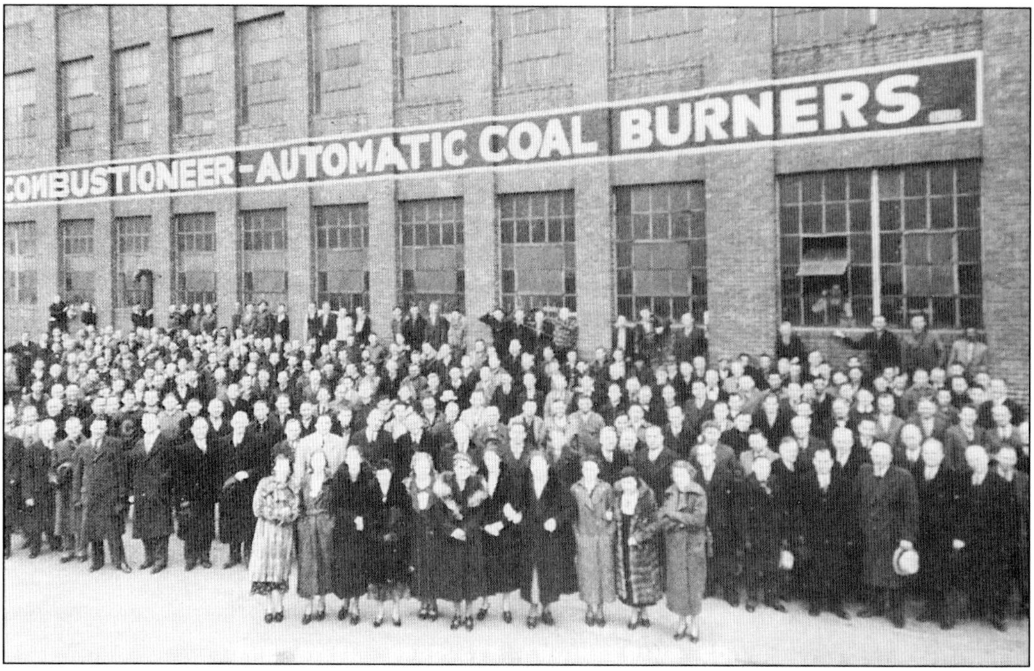

STEEL PRODUCTS ENGINEERING COMPANY (SPECO), LOCATED AT 1205 WEST COLUMBIA STREET, 1937. This company also made stokers, which were machines used to feed coal into furnaces.

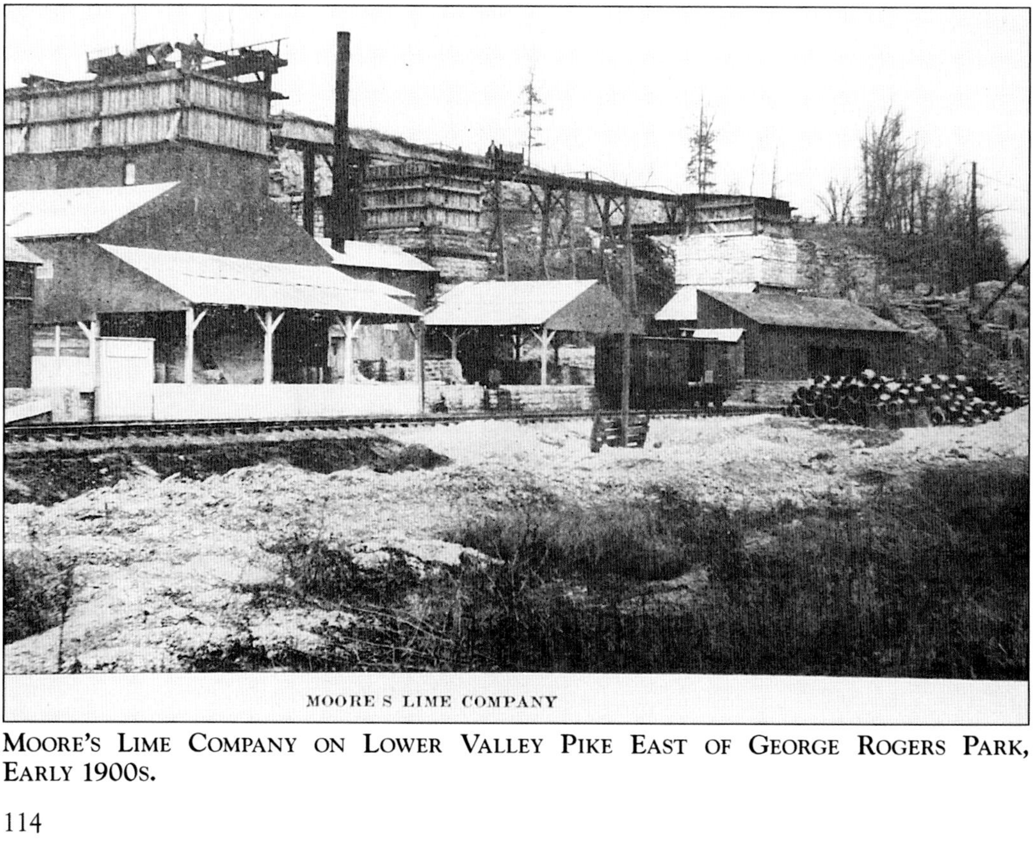

MOORE'S LIME COMPANY ON LOWER VALLEY PIKE EAST OF GEORGE ROGERS PARK, EARLY 1900S.

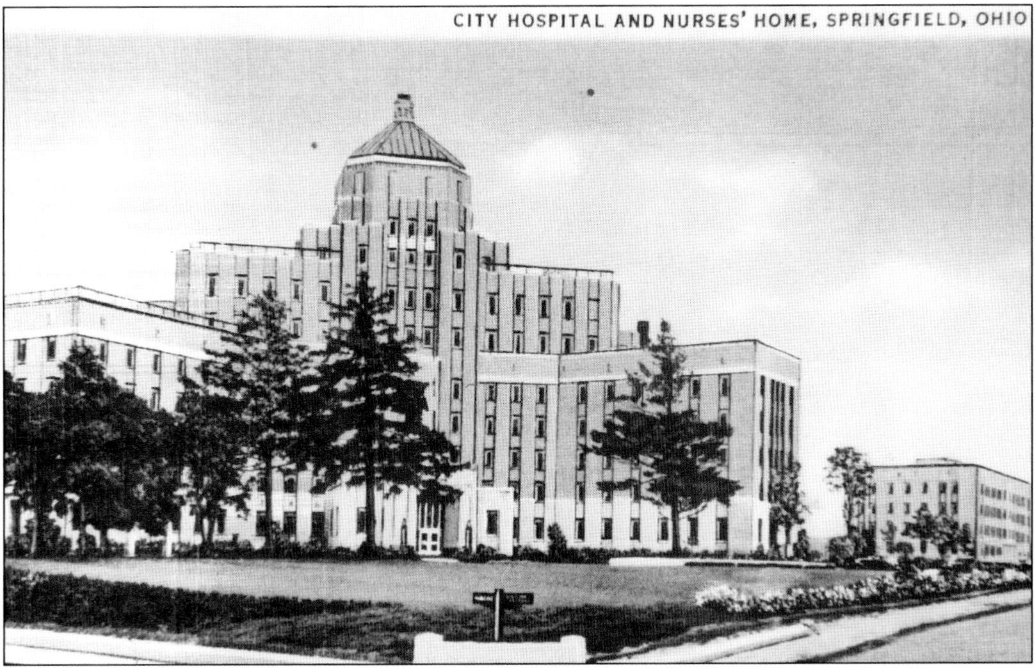

THE NEW CITY HOSPITAL (NOW CALLED COMMUNITY) ON THE SOUTHEAST CORNER OF EAST HIGH AND SOUTH BURNETT ROAD, SEPTEMBER 22, 1932.

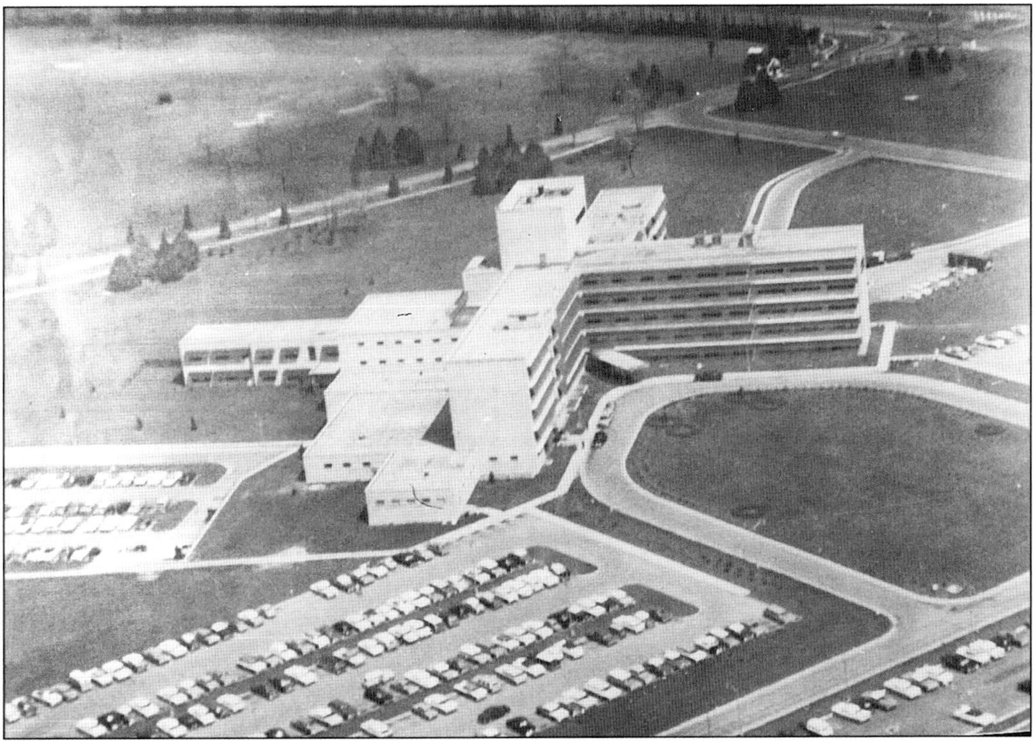

AERIAL VIEW OF MERCY HOSPITAL, LOCATED AT 1343 NORTH FOUNTAIN BOULEVARD, 1960S. This photo was taken before the many expansion programs.

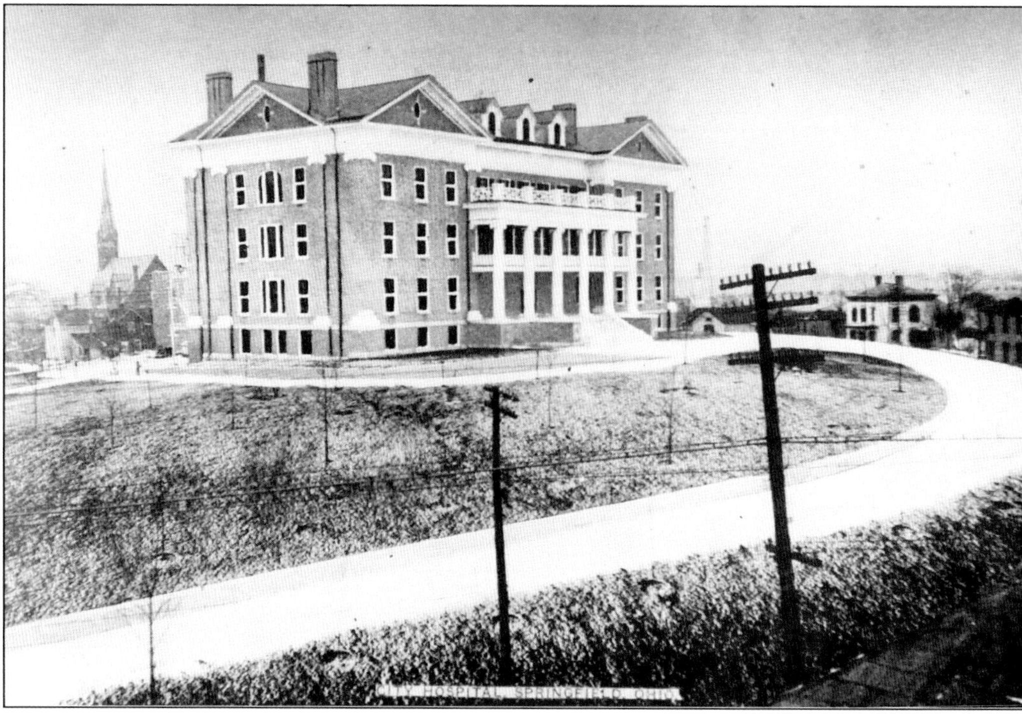

OLD CITY HOSPITAL ON THE CORNER OF SELMA ROAD (CLIFTON) AND EAST STREET, DECEMBER 19, 1904.

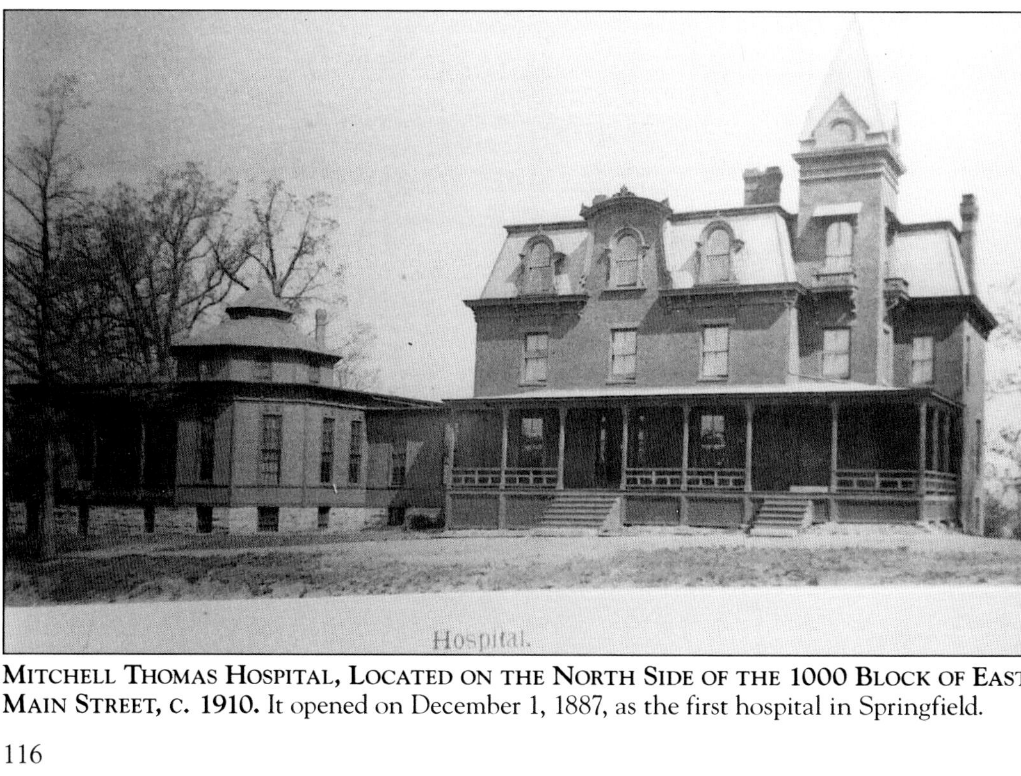

MITCHELL THOMAS HOSPITAL, LOCATED ON THE NORTH SIDE OF THE 1000 BLOCK OF EAST MAIN STREET, C. 1910. It opened on December 1, 1887, as the first hospital in Springfield.

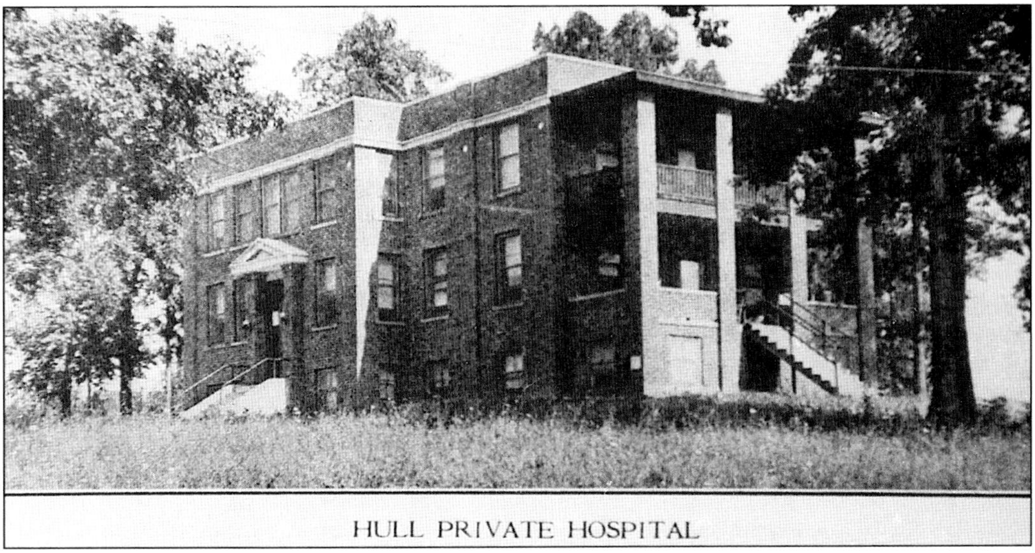

HULL PRIVATE HOSPITAL ON THE SOUTHEAST CORNER OF WEST PLEASANT STREET AND DAYTON ROAD, 1915.

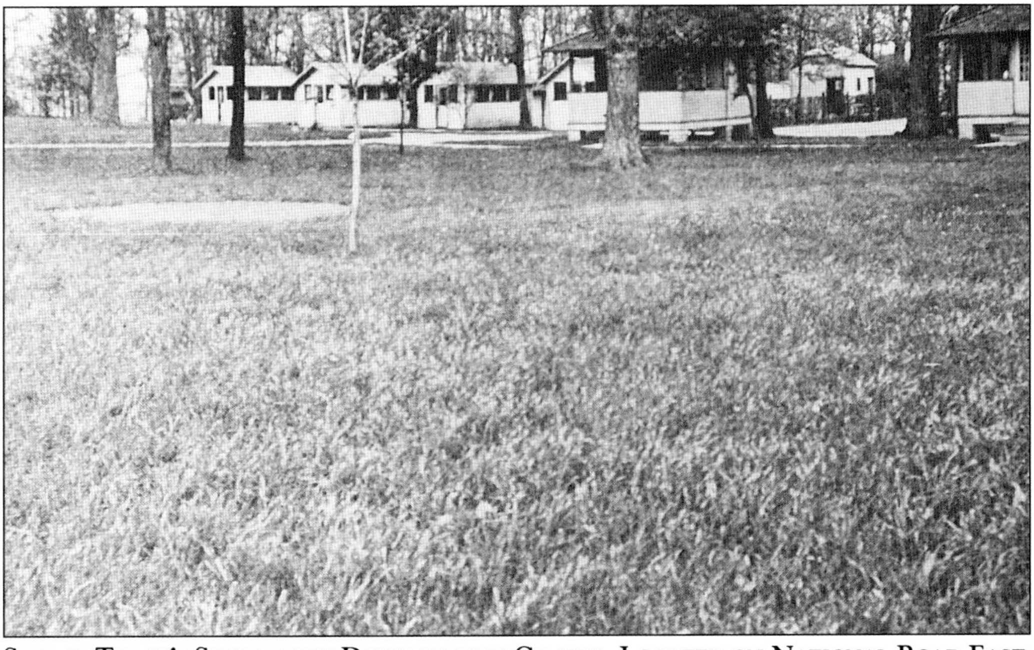

SITE OF TODAY'S SPRINGVIEW DEVELOPMENT CENTER, LOCATED ON NATIONAL ROAD EAST. Through the years, this building has had several different names. As shown in this photo from the 1920s, it was originally a district tuberculosis hospital.

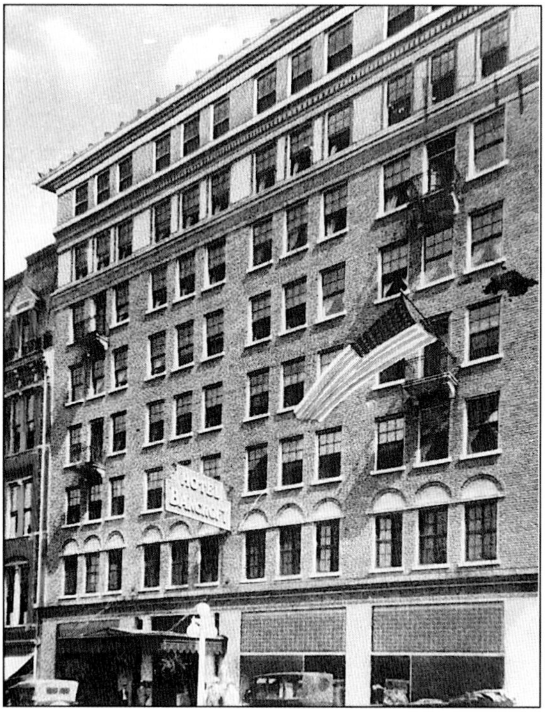

The Old Bancroft Hotel. Today it is the parking lot for Security Bank.

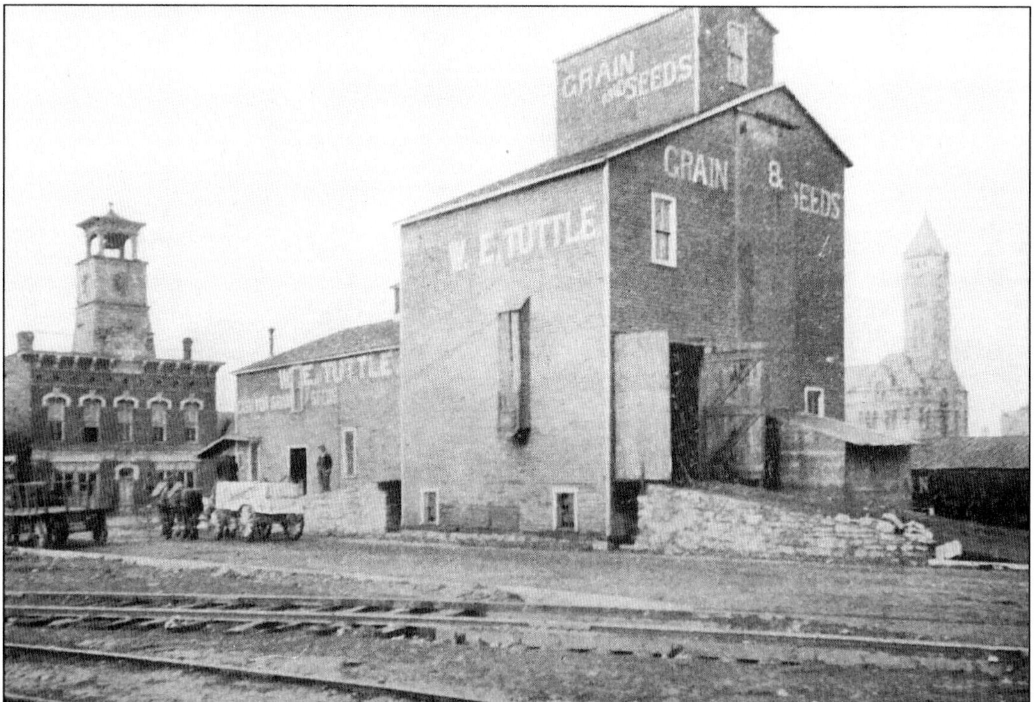

The Old W.E. Tuttle Grain and Seeds Elevator, Located on South Fountain Avenue, across from Fire Engine House #1. Later, the grain elevator was located on Monroe Street. Note the old City Hall visible in the background.

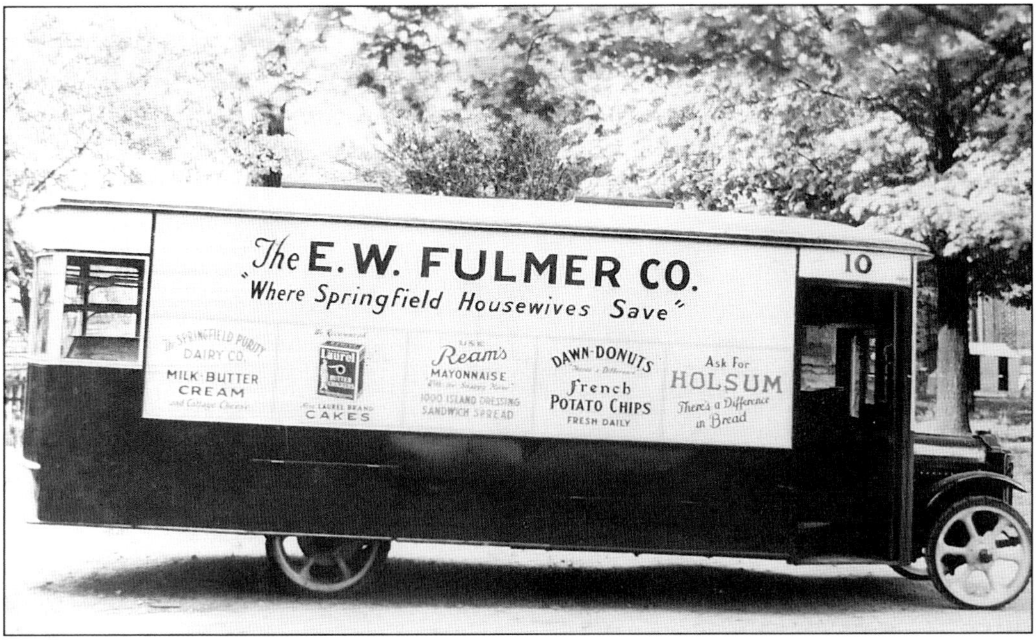

FULMER COMPANY TRUCK. About five trucks came to the neighborhoods to sell groceries on a regular basis.

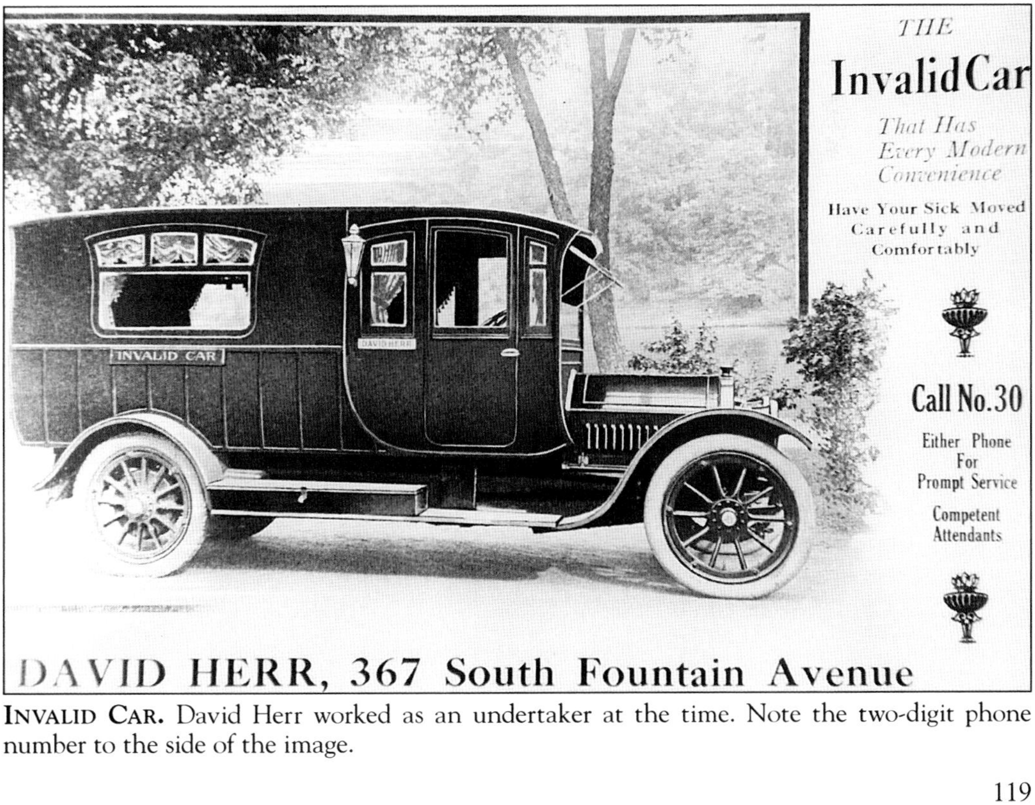

INVALID CAR. David Herr worked as an undertaker at the time. Note the two-digit phone number to the side of the image.

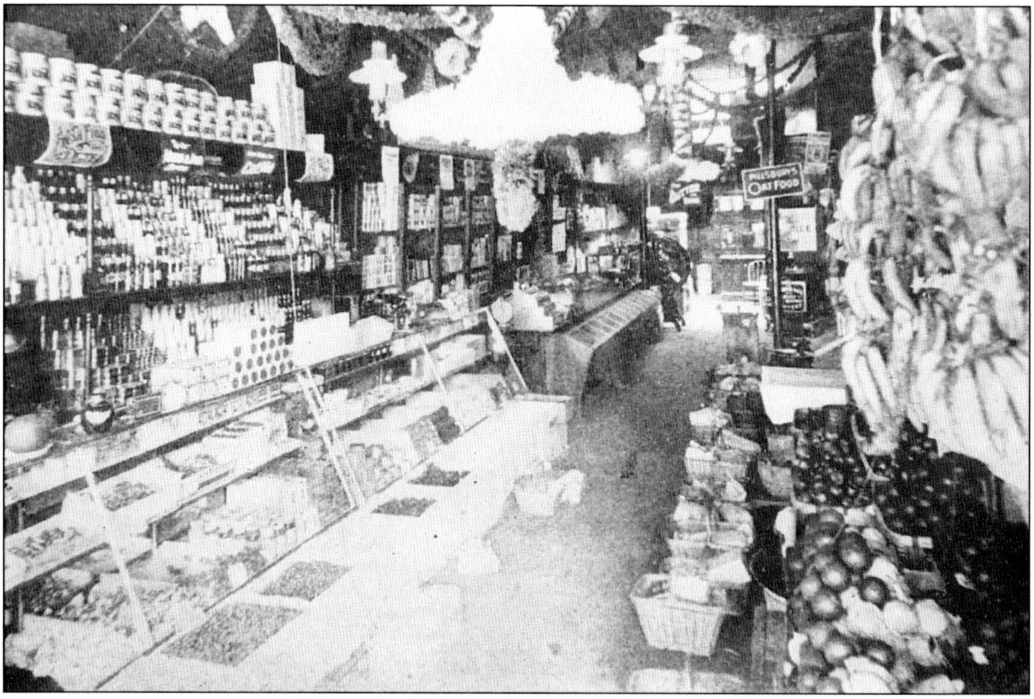

CHARLES VANANDA GROCERY, LOCATED AT 18 EAST HIGH STREET. In those days, the grocer personally waited on each of his customers.

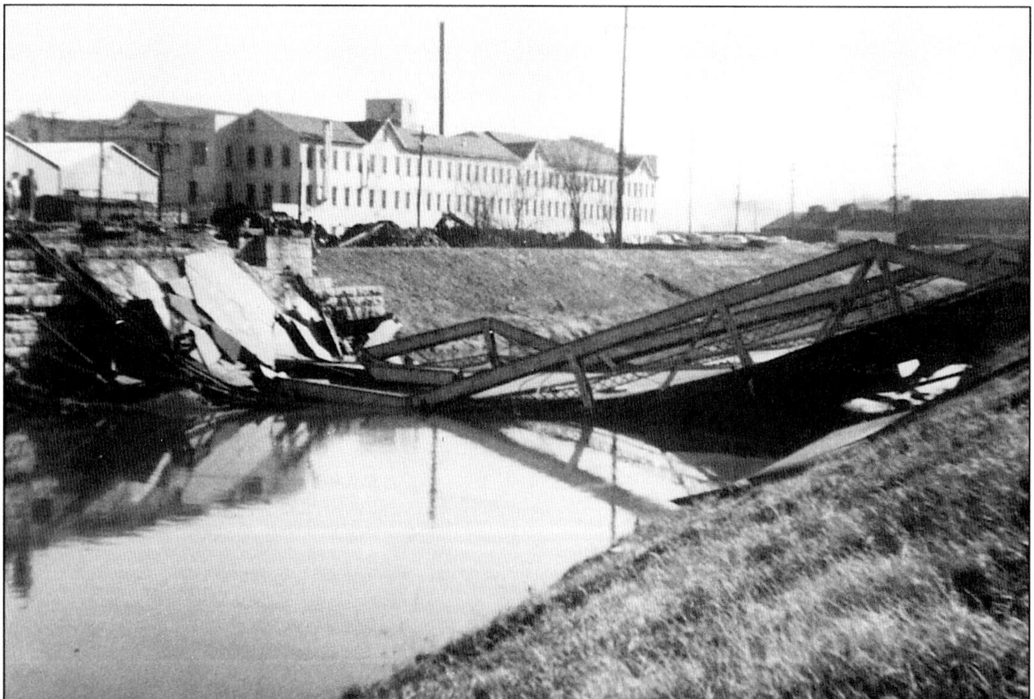

BUCK CREEK BRIDGE AFTER COLLAPSE, DECEMBER 1957. Fortunately, no one was hurt when this bridge collapsed on North Limestone Street.

Seven

Modern Springfield

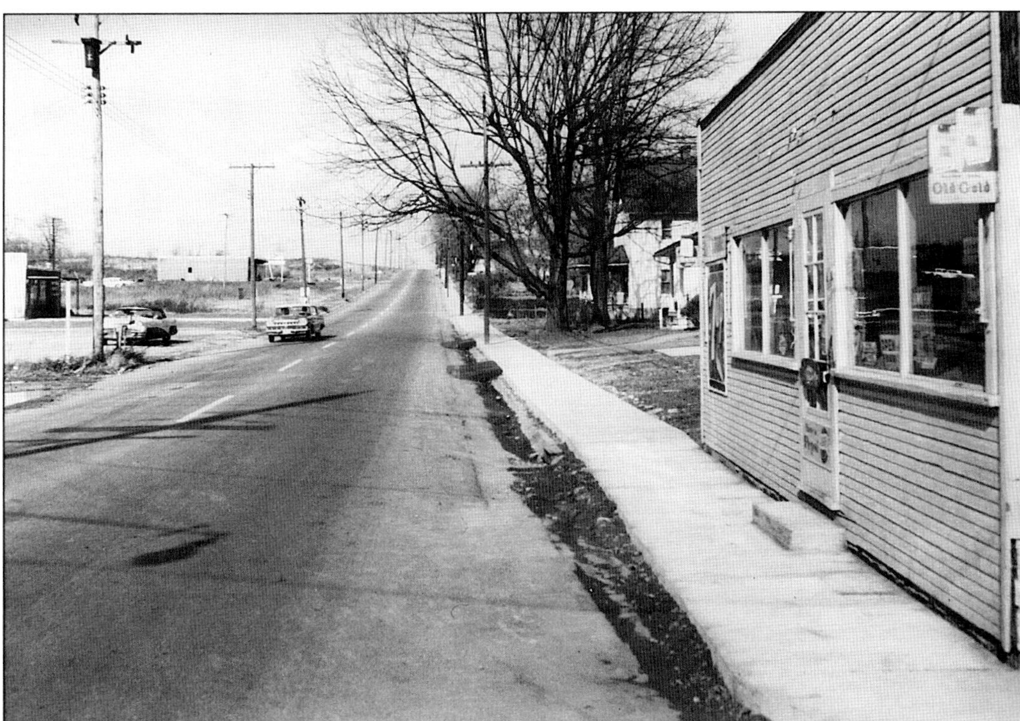

A Street View of Bechtle Avenue Taken from Perry Street at the Snyder Park Bridge, 1960. The AAA Club and Brockman Furnace Company are visible on the left.

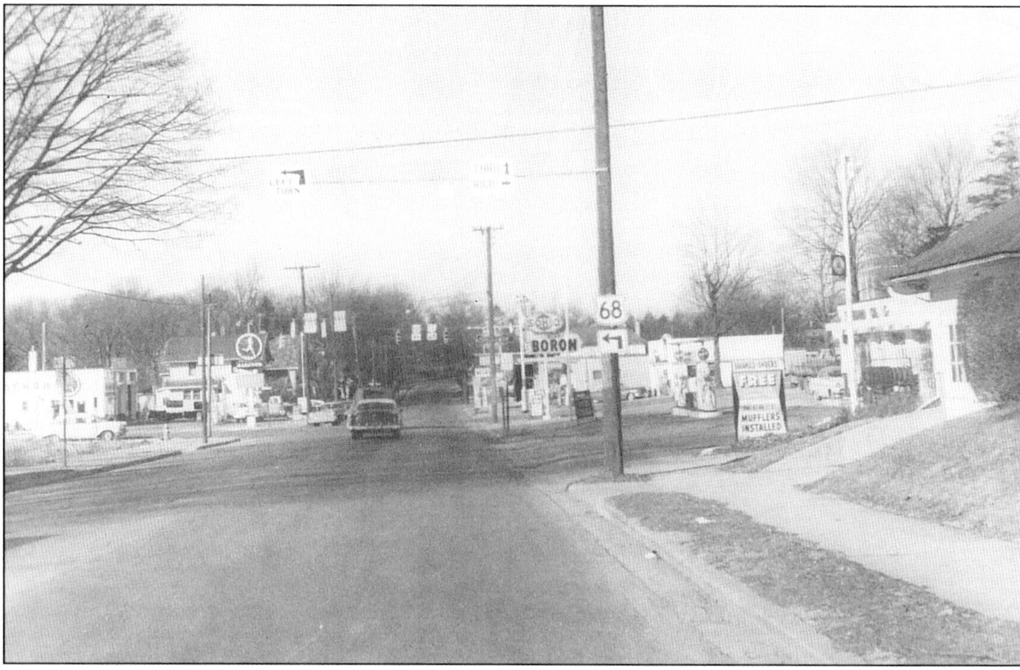

West McCreight Avenue Looking West to North Plum Street, 1960. To the right is a Sohio gas station, and on the left, a Marathon gas station. Today, these two gas stations have been replaced by Mike and Rosy's Deli and a Burger King, respectively.

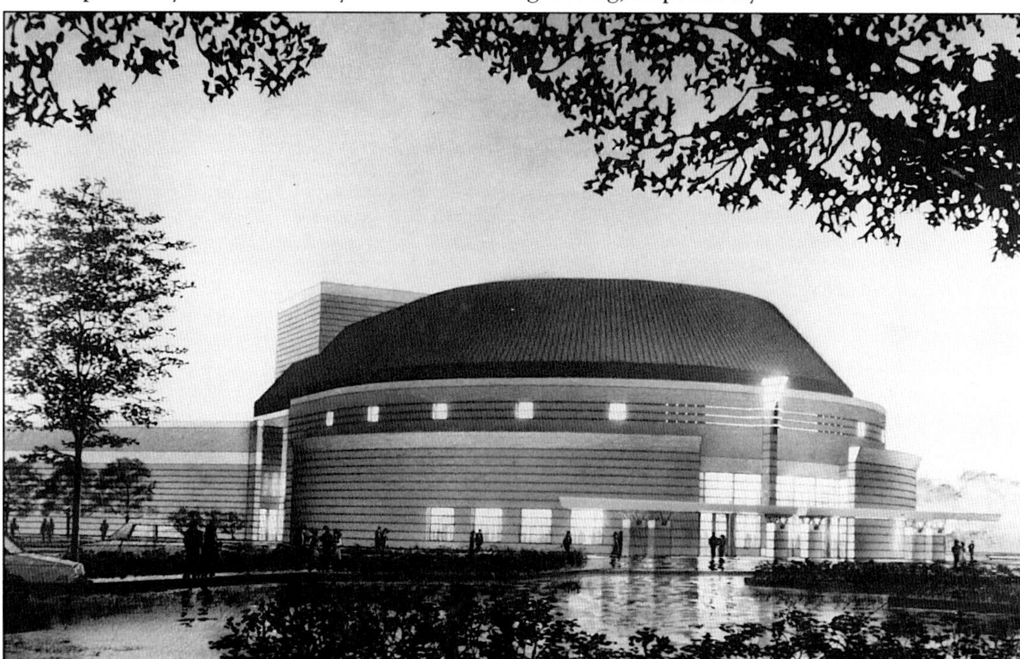

The New Clark State College Kuss Auditorium, Located South of the New Springfield Inn, between Washington and Monroe Street. Construction began in November 1991, and the structure was completed in 1993.

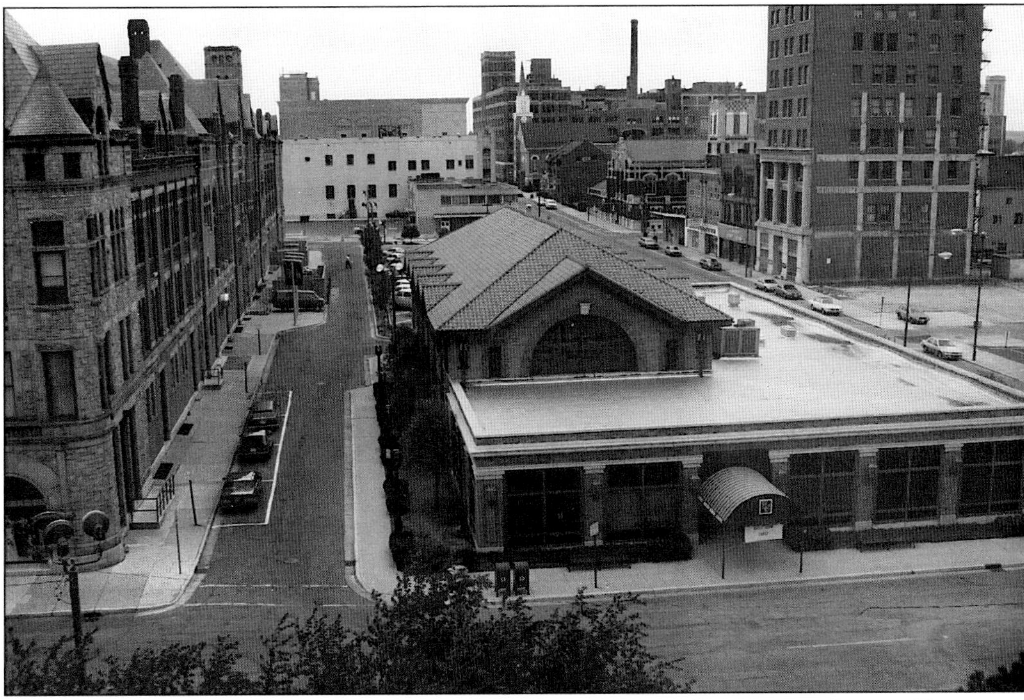

The Old Myers Market Building at the Southwest Corner of South Fountain Avenue and High Street, 1990. This is now the site of the Elderly United organization.

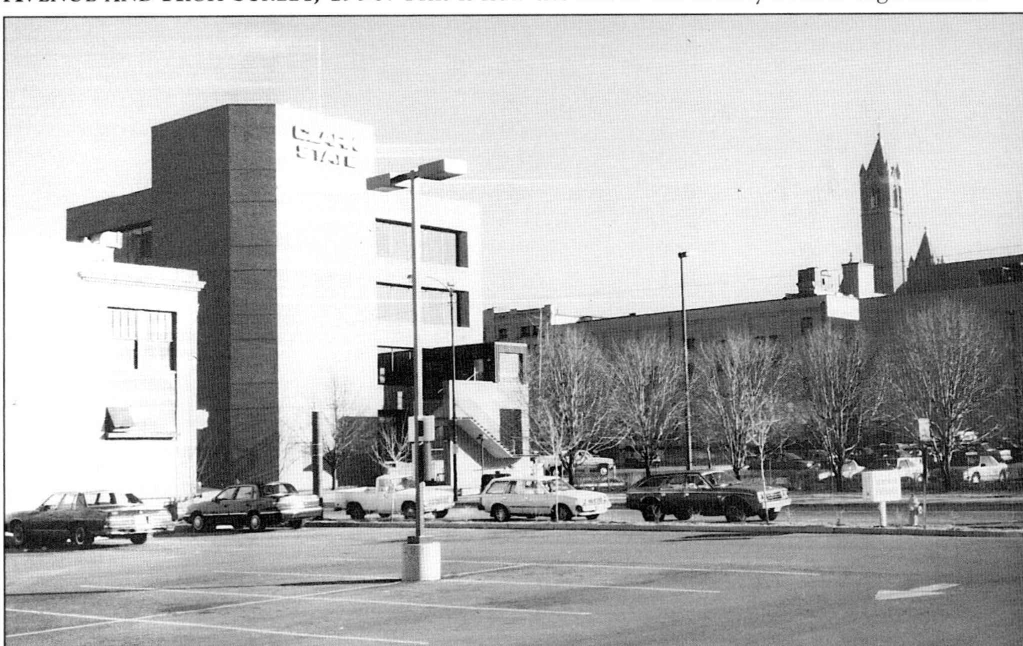

Clark State Community College, Located at the Southeast Corner of East High Street and South Limestone Street, 1990. This photo shows the back of the building as viewed from East Washington Street. Built in the 1970s, this building was originally the Credit Life Building.

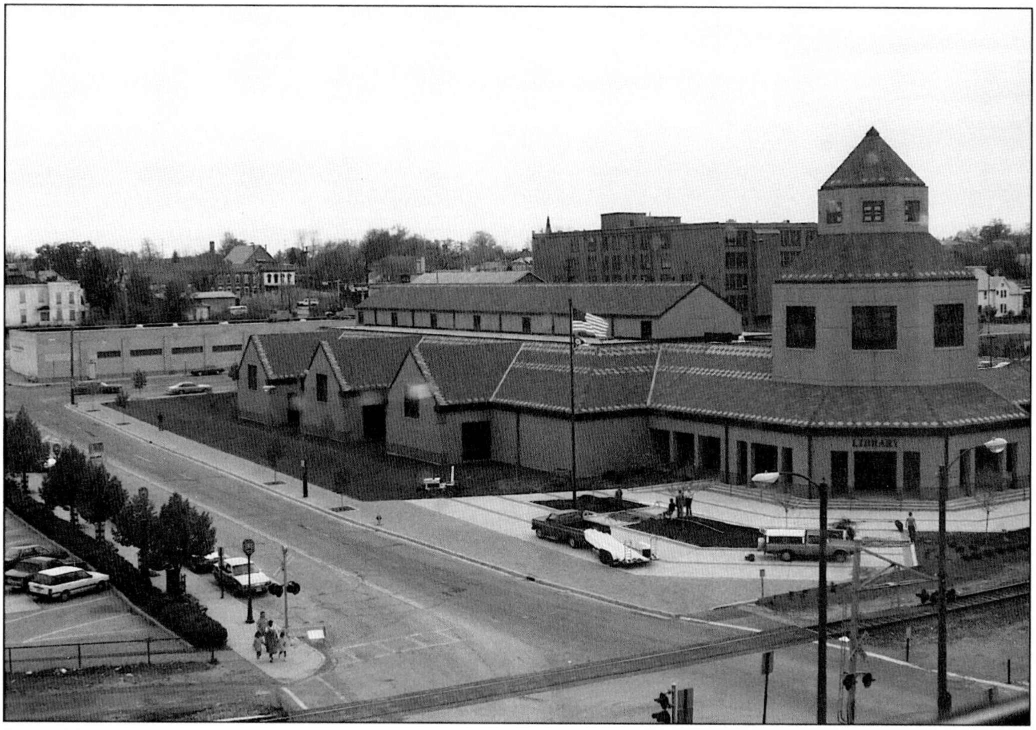

The New Clark County Library at the Southwest Corner of South Fountain Avenue and Washington Street, 1990. When it was finished in 1989, the library and its parking lot occupied an entire square city block.

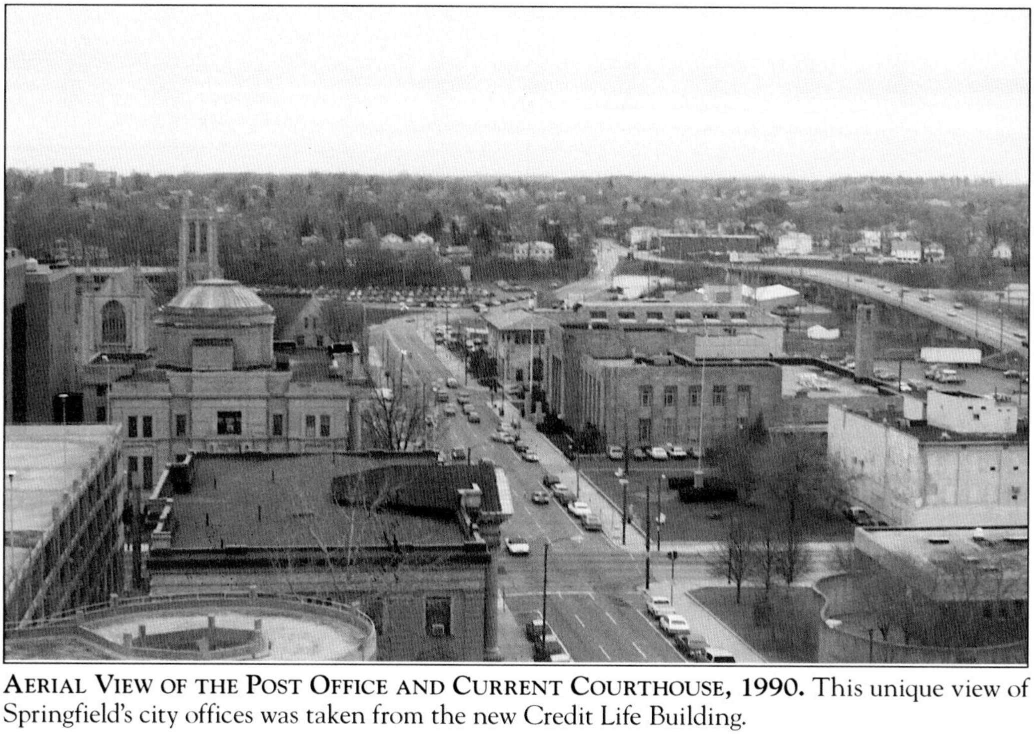

Aerial View of the Post Office and Current Courthouse, 1990. This unique view of Springfield's city offices was taken from the new Credit Life Building.

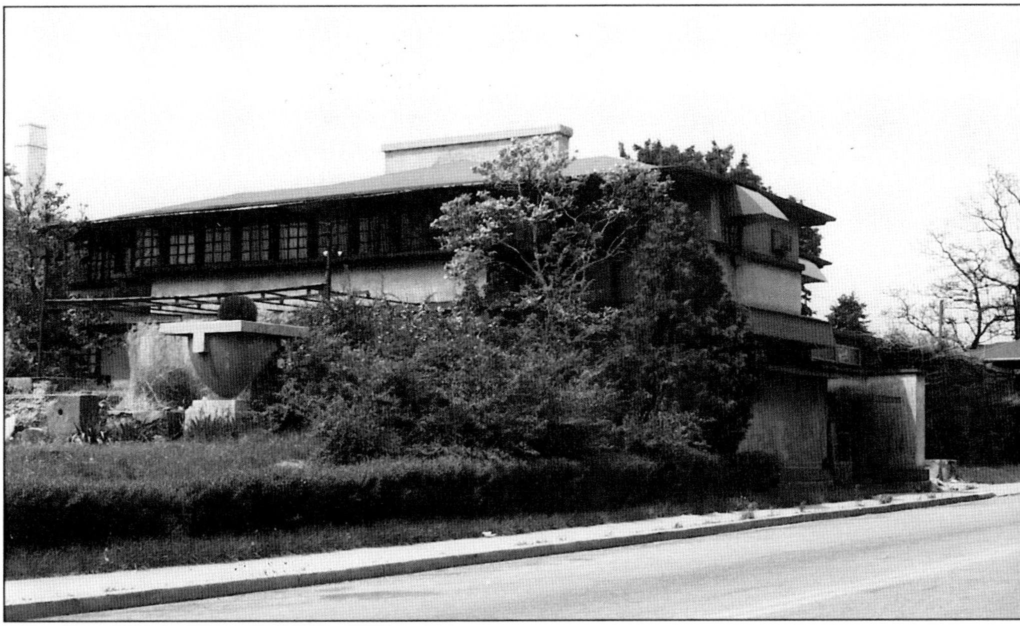

THE OLD WESTCOTT HOME ON THE NORTHWEST CORNER OF SOUTH GREENMOUNT AND EAST HIGH STREET, 1990. The architect Frank Lloyd Wright built the home in 1908.

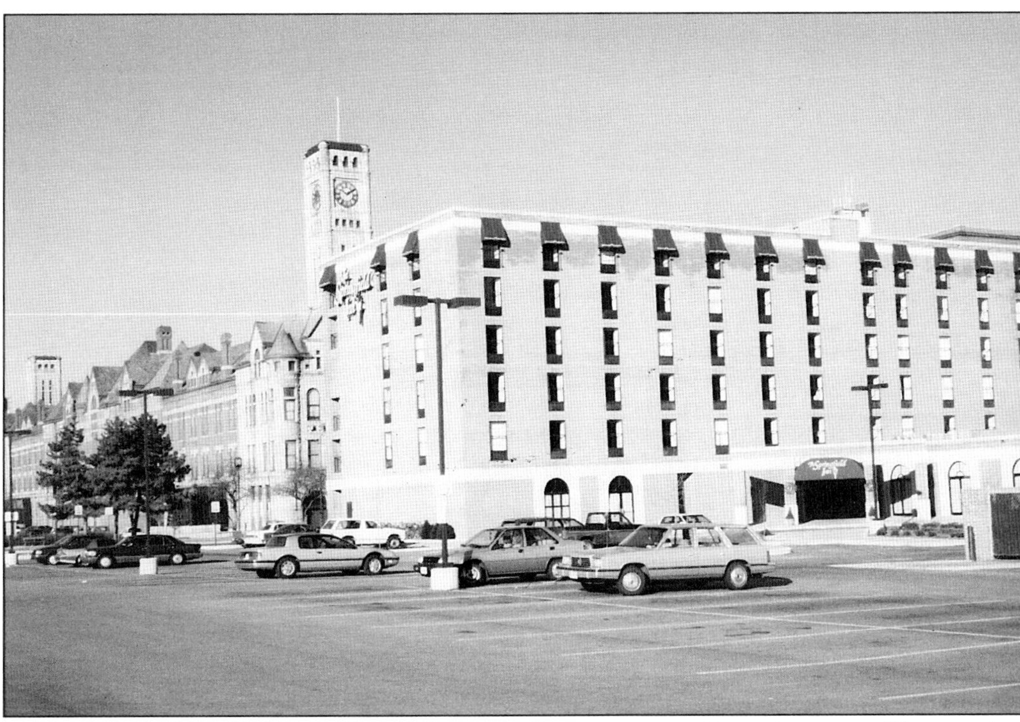

THE SPRINGFIELD INN, LOCATED ON THE SITE OF THE OLD ARCADE. This modern hotel, which opened in April 1990, has rooms for 124 guests. The old City Hall is visible in the background.

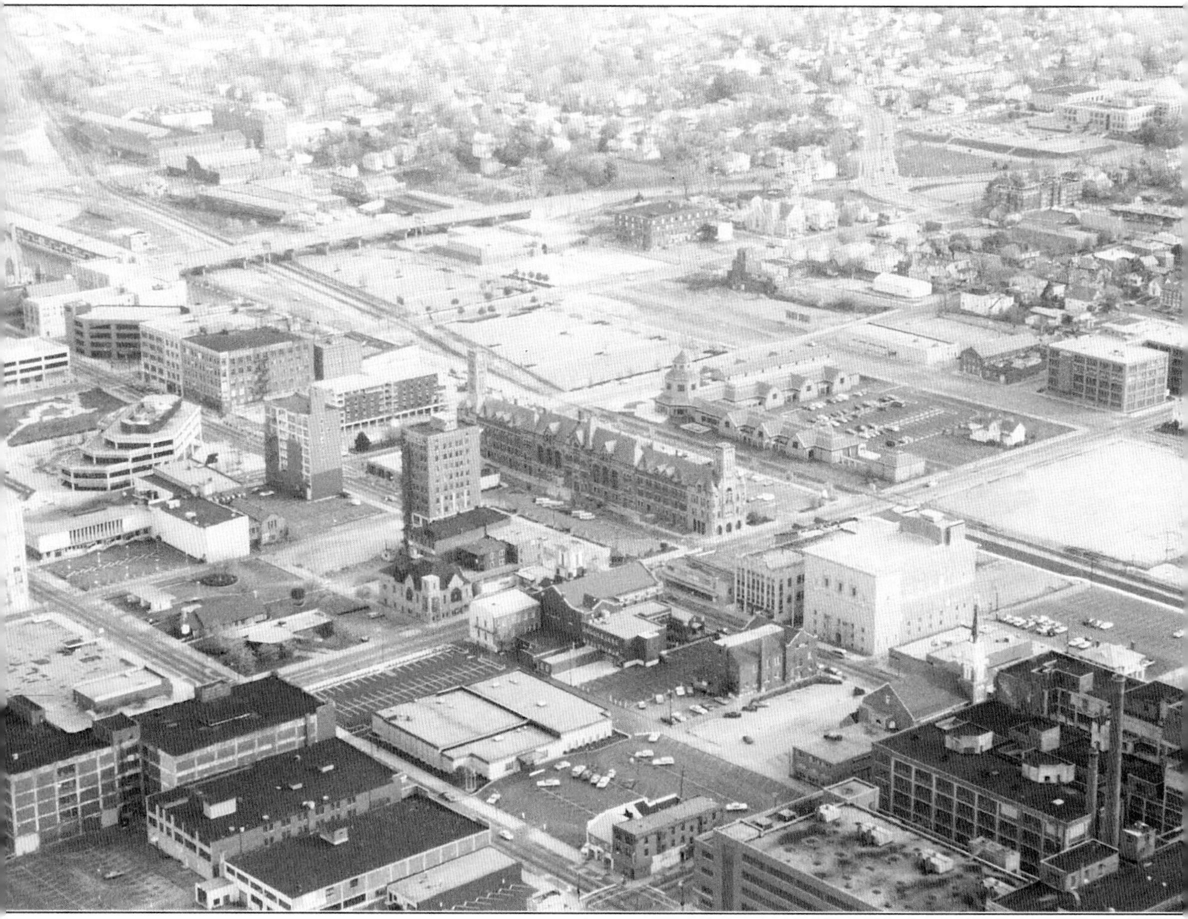

Aerial View of Downtown Springfield, 1989. The new City Hall is pictured on the left. Marketplace and the Clark County Library is in the center, and the Masonic Temple is on the right.

Facts about Springfield, Ohio

Compiled by The Springfield Commercial Club on August 8th, 1914

1. SPRINGFIELD was first settled in 1799.
2. SPRINGFIELD was named by the wife of its founder, Mrs. James Demint, in 1801.
3. SPRINGFIELD was incorporated as a village in 1834, and became a city in 1850.
4. SPRINGFIELD has the great honor and privilege of having as its city manager, Mr. Charles E. Ashburner, the first city manager in the United States, and the man who "invented" the commissioner-manager form of municipal government.
5. SPRINGFIELD is governed by a commission of five successful businessmen and has been conducted since January 1, 1914, as a strictly business corporation.
6. SPRINGFIELD has by actual test the purest drinking water in the state of Ohio.
7. SPRINGFIELD has over 300 industries and products of its great manufacturing plants encircle the globe.
8. SPRINGFIELD grows more roses under glass than any other city in the United States.
9. SPRINGFIELD makes more agricultural implements than any other city in the United States, except Chicago.
10. SPRINGFIELD ranks first in the United States in the production of metallic caskets and burglar-proof burial vaults.
11. SPRINGFIELD, for its size, employs more men in its factories more days per year than any other city in the United States.
12. SPRINGFIELD has three great State Fraternal Homes—Masonic, Knights of Pythias, and Odd Fellows. At the Grand Lodge of the Knights of Pythias held in Cincinnati in June (1914), funds were voted to establish another home in Springfield for aged members of the order.

Items of Interest in 1914

Springfield had the following:

- An elevation of 979 feet.
- Average rainfall, 40 inches.
- Birth rate, 20 per 1,000.
- Death rate, 12.57 per 1,000.
- Area, 7,490.3 acres, 11.7 square miles.
- Area in water, 9.7 acres, .02 square miles.
- Total area, 7,500 acres, 11.72 square miles.
- Parks, 250 acres.
- Area of residential district, 5,000 acres.
- Area of industry, 2,500 acres.
- 120 miles of paved streets.
- 40 miles of unimproved streets.
- 96 miles of storm and sanitary sewers.
- 134 miles of water mains.
- 1,000 fire hydrants.
- 320 cluster lights.
- 671 arc lights.
- 998 electric lights.
- Pumping station capacity per 24-hour day, 30,000,000 gallons.
- Average daily output, 10,000,000 gallons.
- Telephones in the city limits, 11,333.
- Automobiles, 12,000.
- 33 greenhouses, total square footage of glass, 1,500,000.
- 40 steam trains in and out of Springfield daily.
- 120 electric cars, in and out, daily.
- 120 buses, in and out, daily.
- Average of 3,000 freight cars in and out of city daily.
- 11,000,000 copies of magazines published monthly.
- 1,000,000 pounds of ink used annually in magazines.
- 10 motion picture and vaudeville houses —seating capacity, 6,925.
- Annual growth of 4,500,000 rose plants.

ACKNOWLEDGMENTS

Many people have contributed photos for this book and I am very thankful for the response. This volume is by no means a complete history of Springfield, but it may be a good start for the next person who undertakes a photographic-type history of our community. This city has been very good to me and I felt I owed the community something in return.

I would like to extend a special thanks to the following people who helped me in this project: Mr. and Mrs. Richard Brown; Ms. Fern Bauer; Mrs. Virginia Weygandt, curator of the CCHS; Mr. and Mrs. EM Shay; Mrs. Dorothy Shank (deceased); Mrs. Donna Detrick (deceased); Mr. and Mrs. John Bryan; Mr. W.E. (Curly) Martin; Mr. and Mrs. Harry Van Pelt; the Clark County Library; the *Springfield News Sun*; Mr. Michael Chakeres; Mr. Frank Ryan; Mrs. Vernon Hayes; Mr. and Mrs. Roger Devers; and Mr. Verne Theopolis.